2001: Building for Space Travel

2001: Building for Space Travel

John Zukowsky, editor

with contributions by Rachel Armstrong, David Brodherson, Rebecca Dalvesco, Thomas Foltz, Anne Collins Goodyear, Peter Bacon Hales, Theodore W. Hall, Roy F. Houchin II, Howard E. McCurdy, Frederick I. Ordway III, Scott W. Palmer, Dennis Parks, Leonard Rau, Johann N. Schmidt, Deane Simpson, and John Zukowsky

Harry N. Abrams, Inc., Publishers, in association with
The Art Institute of Chicago

For Harry N. Abrams, Inc.
Editor: Diana Murphy
Designer: Judith Hudson

For The Art Institute of Chicago
Editors: Robert V. Sharp, Lisa Meyerowitz
Photo Research: Karen Altschul

Library of Congress Cataloging-in-Publication Data
2001: building for space travel / John Zukowsky, editor.
     p.   cm.
Catalog of an exhibition sponsored by the Art
Institute of Chicago and the Museum of Flight in
Seattle. Includes bibliographical references and
index.
ISBN 0-8109-4490-1 (hardcover)
ISBN 0-86559-188-I (AIC pbk.)
1. Launch complexes (Astronautics)—Design and
construction—Exhibitions. 2. Architecture,
Postmodern—Exhibitions. 3. Space vehicles—
Design and construction—Exhibitions. 4. Space
vehicles in art—Exhibitions. 5. Astronautics—
Popular works—Exhibitions. 6. Astronautics in
literature—Exhibitions. 7. Science fiction—
Illustrations— Exhibitions. I. Title: Building for
space travel. II. Zukowsky, John. III. Art Institute of
Chicago. IV. Museum of Flight (Seattle, Wash.)

TL4015 .A15 2000
629.4'074'77311—dc21   00-058278

Exhibition Itinerary

The Art Institute of Chicago
March 24–October 21, 2001

Museum of Flight, Seattle
December 15, 2001–May 15, 2002

This is a publication of the Ernest R. Graham
Study Center for Architectural Drawings at
The Art Institute of Chicago.

The book is made possible with the support of
the Benefactors of Architecture at The Art
Institute of Chicago, a challenge grant from
the Graham Foundation for Advanced Studies
in the Fine Arts, and the Architecture and
Design Society of The Art Institute of Chicago.

This project is made possible in part by the
National Endowment for the Humanities,
expanding our understanding of the world.

Pages 2–3: B-52 mother-ship above an HL-10
lifting body of 1966–67 (see page 141)

Harry N. Abrams, Inc.
100 Fifth Avenue
New York, N.Y. 10011
www.abramsbooks.com

Contents

Foreword

When one thinks of the buildings and structures that have served the American aerospace industry, particularly that segment devoted to space exploration, what immediately comes to mind are the launch facilities at Cape Canaveral, the Mission Control rooms at the Johnson Space Center in Houston, and possibly the aerospace corporations and factories in Washington and California. Although the Midwest is not usually thought of as integral to this industry, it is important to recognize the many ways that this region has been actively involved with space exploration over the past century. Chicago's World's Columbian Exposition presented astronomical exhibitions to the Midwest in 1893 and was soon followed by construction of the University of Chicago's Yerkes Observatory in Williams Bay, Wisconsin, designed by Chicago architect Henry Ives Cobb in 1897. Chicago also houses the Adler Planetarium, founded in 1930 – the first planetarium in the western hemisphere and one of the landmark buildings related to our perception of the universe. More recently, the Mercury and Gemini capsules of the 1960s were produced by the McDonnell Aircraft Corporation in St. Louis. Furthermore, a number of architects and designers who have developed space-related structures, for science fiction or reality, either trained in the region or worked for Chicago firms before starting their current specialty. Prominent among this group are *Star Trek* production designer Herman Zimmerman, who studied at Northwestern University, and architects Max Urbahn and Charles Luckman, both trained at the University of Illinois, who went on to design structures at the Kennedy and Johnson space centers in Florida and Texas, respectively. Rod Jones of the Johnson Space Center and David Nixon of Altus Associates – both of whom design space habitations – spent part of their formative years in the Chicago offices of Lohan Associates and Skidmore, Owings and

Merrill, respectively. These two architectural firms have themselves created major structures related to space exploration: Myron Goldsmith of SOM designed the striking angular solar telescope at Kitt Peak National Observatory (1962), and Dirk Lohan produced the sensitive addition to the Adler Planetarium (1999). The work of these and other architects and designers on a variety of structures and space vehicles is, therefore, a provocative and timely subject for the Art Institute's Department of Architecture to explore.

The Department of Architecture, under the leadership of its curator John Zukowsky, produced the very successful exhibition and book *Building for Air Travel* in 1996. This project examined the contributions of architects and designers in the field of commercial aviation, from airports and airplane factories to aircraft interiors and airline corporate identity. The current show and publication are both a sequel to that innovative precursor and an important reminder to us all that visual arts professionals – artists, architects, set designers, and industrial and graphic designers – have played as important a role in shaping our notion of space travel as have scientists and aerospace engineers. Our partner in the creation of this project, the Museum of Flight in Seattle, confirms that museums dedicated to the history of art as well as to the history of science and technology can work together to provide new access to the general public to one of the most important accomplishments of the past century – space exploration. We appreciate all the work that John Zukowsky and his team of museum staff members in Chicago and Seattle, the book's essayists, and the exhibited architects, designers, and corporations have contributed to this project. We are also grateful to the agencies and corporations that have financially supported this endeavor to present a new perspective on the phenomenon of space travel.

James N. Wood
Director and President
The Art Institute of Chicago

Few things have influenced modern life as much as the technological developments in air travel and space exploration. From transport vehicles, which have shrunk our world and allowed us to venture into other worlds, to global positioning satellites, which enable us to know exactly where we are at any given moment, the scientific breakthroughs in air and space exploration set new standards and inform trends. Our desires to fly higher, faster, and farther not only satisfy a very basic craving in our human nature, but also push us to excel and discover new protocols in a host of fields as diverse as medicine and engineering. Architecture, art, literature, and music all reflect the depth of this profound movement, enunciating our fascination with and our devotion to the wonders associated with air and space exploration.

In its previous book *Building for Air Travel,* the Art Institute helped us understand the relationships between the forms and functions of airports and our dreams for a brave new world. *2001: Building for Space Travel* is the logical next step. It examines our structures and lifestyles as we push out into the universe. What we do is often deter-mined by how we view ourselves and how we master our environment. In space, we are on one hand the masters, and on the other hand very much the servants of forces far greater than humankind. Architectural structures protect us and facilitate our work. In the process of creating them, however, we hope that they elevate, not destroy, our spirits.

In *2001: Building for Space Travel,* we take a look back to the beginnings of spaceflight and consider what life will be like in the future. Our experience in the past hundred years of flight has increased our capacity to dream big dreams and hold on to radical visions. Now, as we venture out into the universe, we must think boldly both to survive and to thrive. As we look at space architecture, our challenge is not only to live, but also to match the quality of life with our achievements.

The Museum of Flight is proud to coorganize the exhibition *2001: Building for Space Travel* with The Art Institute of Chicago. We hope that it will elicit discussion and challenge our assumptions. The conquest of space is much more than an adventure. It continues to help define who we see ourselves to be.

Ralph A. Bufano
Executive Director
Museum of Flight, Seattle

Acknowledgments

Following the success of *Building for Air Travel* at The Art Institute of Chicago in 1996 and its opening at the Museum of Flight in Seattle in 1997, Joan Piper, then Director of Exhibitions and Programs at the Museum of Flight, Thomas Foltz, one of the members of her education staff, their former Exhibitions Coordinator John Summerford, and curator Dennis Parks all enthusiastically endorsed the idea of working with the Art Institute to create a comparable exhibition and book on architecture and design for space travel in science fiction as well as reality. James N. Wood and Ralph Bufano, the directors of The Art Institute of Chicago and the Museum of Flight, respectively, encouraged us to undertake this joint endeavor. With this foundation for cooperation established, we hosted, through the support of the Benefactors of Architecture at The Art Institute of Chicago, two major planning meetings in Chicago in November 1997 and March 1998. These meetings brought together the relevant staff of the two institutions as well as interested historians and designers. All of them enthusiastically contributed to shaping the final product and deserve our thanks: Dmitry Azrikan, Associate Professor of Design, Western Michigan University; Robert Bruegmann, Professor of Architectural and Art History, University of Illinois, Chicago; Larry Ciupik, Sky Show Production Manager, Adler Planetarium and Astronomy Museum; Vernard Foley, Professor of the History of Technology, Purdue University; John Frassanito, industrial designer and President, John Frassanito and Associates; Douglas Garofalo, architect; Peter Bacon Hales, Director, American Studies Institute, University of Illinois, Chicago; Neil Harris, Preston and Sterling Morton Professor of History, University of Chicago; Eva Maddox, architect; Victor Margolin, Professor of Design History, University of Illinois, Chicago; Scott Palmer, Assistant Professor of History, Western Illinois University; and Stanley Tigerman, architect. Additional smaller planning meetings were held in Chicago and Seattle in 1998, which resulted in the submission of a National Endowment for the Humanities grant request as well as corporate fundraising in 1999–2000. We are grateful to the NEH for their financial support of this project. A special thank you goes to Clay Lewis, NEH program officer, who provided us with substantive comments on our grant proposal. Additional support came from the Benefactors of Architecture funds at the Art Institute as well as the museum's exhibitions and programs account established by a challenge grant from the Graham Foundation for Advanced Studies in the Fine Arts and the Architecture and Design Society of The Art Institute of Chicago.

With this support, we were able to complete the extensive checklist, secure the loans to the exhibition, and complete this volume. The exhibition checklist, the basis for many of the illustrations and information found in the color plate section of this book, was compiled by a variety of people including myself as well as researchers, interns, and volunteers in the Department of Architecture: Lawrence Ebelle-Ebanda, Chelly Fahrbach, Janine Maegraith, Carole Merrill, Anna Minta, Emily Pugh, and Annemarie van Roessel. They deserve special thanks for all the effort they put into assembling this massive amount of material. We are grateful for the generous cooperation of the architects, designers, aerospace corporations, space agencies, libraries, and museums who are lenders to the exhibition or have contributed photographs and information to the book. A number of individuals who compiled information for publication and exhibition deserve our thanks: Nancy Senken, Anspach Grossman Enterprise; David A. Nixon, Altus Associates; Marie-Vincente Pasdeloup, former Director of Communications, Arianespace, Inc., her successor, Birgit Zacher, and especially retired Ariane-ESA executive Raymond Orye; Kirsten Tedesco, Collections Curator, Arizona Aerospace Foundation; Col. Charlie Simpson, Executive Director, Association of Air Force Missileers; Janet Sinnadurai, Office Manager, Astronauts Memorial Foundation; M. Joan Rattay, Corporate Communications Coordinator, The Austin Company; Larry P. Miller, Public Relations Department, Bechtel, Inc.; Judith Macor, Corporate Archives, Lucent; the late Harold E. Lucht, Lawrence D. Bell Museum; Mr. Ludwig,

Bildarchiv Preussischer Kulturbesitz; F. C. Durant III, Bonestell archives and estate; Jill Thomas and Donna Davidson, Project Development, BRC Imagination Arts; D. M. Ashford, Bristol Spaceplanes, Ltd.; Kaye M. Boggs, Marketing Coordinator, BRPH Architects and Engineers; Mike Lombardi and Tom Lubbesmeyer, Boeing Historical Archives in Seattle, and Larry Merritt, St. Louis division of Boeing's archives; Fritz Johnson, Senior Manager, Corporate Identity Program, Boeing; Mary E. Kane, Contracts Manager, Boeing; Brent Sherwood, Program Development Manager, Reusable Space Systems, Boeing; Terrance L. Scott, Communications Manager, Sea Launch (a Boeing operation), and Walter Costa of Kellor and Gannon, architects for Sea Launch's homeport in Long Beach, California; Keith Takahashi, Principal Public Relations Representative, Boeing at Huntington Beach, California; Mr. Boehm, Bundesarchiv-Militaerarchiv; Robert O'Brady, Canadian Space Agency; Monika Kock and Hans-Ulrich Willbold, Daimler-Chrysler Aerospace; Jeffrey C. Cannon, Leo A. Daly; Lysa R. Romain, Business Development, Deutsch Associates; Wolfgang Voigt, Deputy Director, and Inge Wolf, Archivist, Deutsches Architekturmuseum; Hans-Peter Reichmann, head of the collection, and Ursula Neeb, Deutsches Filmmuseum; Peter Mainz, Stiftung Deutsche Kinemathek; Margrit Prussat, Archive, Deutsches Museum; Susanne Tabbert, Registrar, Andrea von Hegel, Poster Collection, Claudia Kuechler, Photo Archive, and Vera Reise, all from the Deutsches Historisches Museum; Christiana Garda, Senior Marketing Director, Encounter 2001; Bob Sauls and Kathi Longaria, John Frassanito and Associates; Steve Featherstone, Garmin; Steffanie Mikel, Giffels Associates; Edwin C. Krupp, Director, and Tony Cook, Curator, Griffith Observatory; Robert R. Scagni, Marketing Department, Hamilton Standard; Ronnie Garson Heller, Visual Aids Coordinator, HLW International; Lori Moran, Hellmuth, Obata and Kassabaum; Tina Carroll, Holt Hinshaw Architects; Emery S. Wilson, Jr., Public Relations Manager, Hughes; David Parry and John Delaney, Photographic Archive, Imperial War Museum; David Penn, Keeper of Exhibits and Firearms, Martin Garnet, Aeronautica Curator, and Loans Officer Kim Gale, all from the Imperial War Museum; Philip M. Spampinato, Program Manager for Shuttle and Advanced Space Suits, ILC Dover; Paul Jackson, Commercial Marketing Manager, Johnson Engineering; Donna Eatinger, Kelly Space and Technology; Michele Pacleb, Kistler Aerospace; Bernd Evers, Director, Kunstbibliothek, Berlin; Ms. Baer, Landesbildstelle Berlin; Lance Bird, Principal Partner, La Cañada Design Group; David Redhill, Beth Floyd, and Rita Frumkin, all from Landor Associates; Mark Thomas, Vice President, Landmark Entertainment Group; Lockheed-Martin Personnel, including: Cary Dell, Manager of Communications, Akron branch; Michael Roundtree and Joe Stout, Tactical Aircraft Division, Ft. Worth; Larry Stone, Manager of Public Affairs, Princeton, New Jersey, facility; Ellen Bendell, Public Relations Representative, T. Cleon Lacefield, X-33 Program Manager, and Ron Williams, Sverdrup's X-33 Project Manager for construction, at Skunk Works; John Janulaw, Luckman Partnership; John E. Thoman, A. C. Martin Partners; Patrick Koridi, Matra Marconi Space; Minuteman, Titan, and air force missile experts Lt. Col. John W. Darr, Maj. Greg Ogletree, and David Stumpf; Dixie Dysart, Archivist, Air Force Historical Research Agency, and Diane Cline, Research Division, Army Institute of Heraldry, for their documentation on the Missileman's badge; Tim Parsey, Vice President and Director of Consumer Design, Motorola; Terry Geesken, Film Stills Archive, The Museum of Modern Art, New York; Ginney Beal, Outreach Coordinator, National Optical Astronomy Observatories; NASA personnel, including: Johnson Space Center staff architects Rod Jones and Kriss Kennedy, consultant Constance Adams, and human factors specialist Frances E. Mount, Laurel Lictenberger from the Kennedy Space Center, as well as Jack Schmid, Exhibits Coordinator, and Paula Cleggett-Haleim, Director, Public Services Division; Alex Panchenko for access to his collection of Soviet space memorabilia; Lori Valles, Manager of Corporate Relations, Parsons Corporation; Susan Strauss, Director of Research, Polshek Partnership; John M. Crump, Jr., Vice President, Reynolds, Smith and Hills; Ben Sarao for access to his space history collection and photographs; Judy McKee, Julius Shulman Photography; Isabelle Beson, SEP/SNECMA; Nobuo Isome, Shimizu Corporation, Space Design Division; Jim Costopulos, Space Access; Tiffany Clements, Manager of Public Relations, Spacehab; Ray Wagner, former Archivist, San Diego Aerospace Museum; Sara McFarland, Registrar, SAC Museum, Ashland, Nebraska; Betsy Slemmer, Registrar, San Bernardino County Museum; Debra B. Trace, Manager of Corporate Communications, STV Group; Peter Maenz, Stiftung Deutsche Kinemathek; William E. Brown, Jr., Archives and Special Collections, University of Miami; Martin and Rafael Stein, Urbahn Associates; Larry Procious, U.S. Space and Rocket Center, and his successor, Curator David W. Alberg; Richard Dreiser, University of Chicago Yerkes Observatory; Mark Tawara, Marketing Manager, Wimberley Allison Tong and Goo; and Gregg E. Maryniak, Executive Director, X Prize.

Film studios were also very helpful, and we are especially grateful for their generous cooperation with our illustration and object requests. In particular we would like to thank Paramount, especially *Star Trek* personnel Herman Zimmerman, Production Designer, and Michael Okuda, Scenic Art Supervisor, as well as Chuck Myers and Kay Erickson. Additionally, we would like to thank the following film and television studio people for their help with our research requests: Babylonian Productions design personnel, including John Iacovelli, Production Designer, Mark L. Waters, Art Director, and Jeffrey Willerth, Producer's Associate; John Copeland, Producer; Margarita Medina, Columbia Pictures; Jake Easton, Twentieth Century Fox; Cecilia Pierce, MGM; Margaret Adamic, Disney Publishing Group; and Judith Singer, Warner Brothers/Time Warner.

Finally, outside the Art Institute, a number of individuals should be thanked for helping to make this exhibition and book a reality. Architect Douglas Garofalo created a spectacular fabric and metal ribbed environment for the exhibition, which was constructed by

Chicago Scenic Studios under the supervision of Gary Heitz. Gene Young Effects, a lender of a number of the models on display, also fabricated or assembled most of the other models for the exhibition. The authors responsible for the thirteen essays in this book deserve our gratitude for their ideas and scholarly contributions, as does the endorsement of Harry N. Abrams, Inc., Publishers, Senior Editor Diana Murphy, and Senior Designer Judith Hudson.

Many Art Institute staff members should also be thanked for their participation in this project. First and foremost among them are Karin Victoria, Director of Government Relations, and her former assistant, Jennifer Harris. We also acknowledge Meredith Hayes, former Director of Corporate and Foundation Relations, her assistant, Lisa Key, and their chief, Edward Horner, Executive Vice President for Development and Public Affairs, for their corporate fundraising efforts on our behalf. These individuals were essential to raising sufficient funds to successfully implement this project. The staff of the Department of Architecture devoted numerous hours to this project, particularly Research Assistant Annemarie van Roessel and Secretary Linda Adelman. The museum's Publications Department, as it has with so many of our books, did a stellar job in editing the manuscript and helping to acquire and clear the publications rights to the illustrations. Robert V. Sharp, Associate Director of Publications, and his coeditor Lisa Meyerowitz are to be thanked for their diligence in this regard. They were assisted in their efforts by Karen Altschul, Photography Editor, and former assistant Laura Kozitka. Robert Sharp, along with Jane Clarke, Associate Director of Education, and Michelle Taufmann, Acting Director of Evaluation and Research, all shaped the final exhibition label and panel texts that I prepared.

Jane Clarke coordinated the development of an extensive series of public programs hosted in conjunction with the exhibition. Barbara Scharres, Director of the Film Center at The School of the Art Institute of Chicago, actively worked with us in preparing the challenging film series shown in tandem with our installation of this exhibition, and she generously opened her archives for the exhibition. Advice and assistance regarding the financial operations for the exhibition were provided by Robert E. Mars, Executive Vice President for Administrative Affairs, his assistant, Cheryl Povalla, Calvert W. Audrain, Assistant Vice President for Administrative Affairs-Operations, and Dorothy M. Schroeder, Assistant Director for Exhibitions and Budget. Executive Director of Registration Mary Solt, with the assistance of Darrell Green, Associate Registrar for loans and exhibitions, insured that the pieces on loan were appropriately recorded, and they organized the intricate shipping arrangements for the exhibited works. Craig Cox, Manager of Art Handling, and his crew installed the objects, working in conjunction with the staff of Chicago Scenic and William Caddick, Director of Physical Plant, and William Heye, Manager of Building Trades. Associate Director of Graphics Ann Wassman sensitively designed the exhibition graphics to complement Douglas Garofalo's striking installation. The Public Affairs Department, through the efforts of Executive Director Eileen Harakal and Associate Director John F. Hindman, promoted the exhibition to a large audience. In all, my colleagues throughout the Art Institute combined their efforts with those of lenders and outside supporters to shape the final product and bring this exhibition and book to completion. I am grateful for the cooperation of all who created this new and different way to look at the significant phenomenon of space travel.

John Zukowsky
Curator of Architecture
The Art Institute of Chicago

Architecture and Design for Space:

Vision and Reality

JOHN ZUKOWSKY

"Five, four, three, two, one, ignition – we have liftoff!" How many times have we heard these words on television and in film – words that preceded launches at Cape Canaveral, including the historic Mercury, Gemini, and Apollo flights of the 1960s and 1970s? Likewise, phrases such as "Beam me up, Scotty" and "Energize!" have become part of our everyday vocabulary thanks to the long-term influence of the *Star Trek* television shows and films produced since the 1960s. When we think of the design professionals who work on these movies and television programs we immediately think of set and costume designers. Perhaps this is because we are already used to hearing about these professions from watching broadcasts of the Academy Awards ceremonies. Despite our superficial familiarity with rocketry and space travel from the media, few of us think of architects, civil engineers, industrial designers, and graphic designers as actively involved in space exploration. The primary purpose of this volume is to remind us that these design professionals are as integral to the implementation of the dream of space travel as set and production designers are to the creation of the environment in which a movie is filmed. Beyond that initial goal, this book explores the various facets of architecture and design for space exploration as found within three thematic groupings that, in many ways, mirror human experiences on Earth:

1. images of the cosmos and space before and after the advent of space travel;
2. conflict and the conquest of space, whether military, political, or, especially after the cold war, commercial;
3. the exploration of space as parallel to our image of the exploration and inhabitation of the wilderness.

The essays that follow this introduction, as well as the color-plate sections of the book, present examples of architecture and design for space in reality and science fiction within these three groupings. In so doing, we recognize that design professionals have been a part of this subject as much as scientists and aerospace engineers,

and have offered a new way of looking at space travel beyond what has been displayed and published by aerospace, science, and history museums. Before we proceed on this journey, however, it might be wise to examine, in relation to our tripartite structure, the historic role of visual arts professionals, such as architects and designers who have worked on space-related projects, in addition to that performed by aerospace engineers and production designers.

The Cosmos: Perceptions of Space

Archaeo-astronomers have shown that humans have always built structures with some relationship to the cosmos and the meaning of life, even though we may not know the real meanings of every aspect of such structures. Stonehenge and other prehistoric monuments in Europe, as well as Mayan pyramids and their calendar sculptures, and even the thirteenth-century woodhenge at Cahokia, Illinois, all indicate some role in determining their respective culture's place within the seasons and, by extension, the cosmos, since all have some relationship to the summer or winter solstice. Medieval cathedrals, conceived as earthly embodiments of the "New Jerusalem" of the afterlife, are often oriented with their altars facing east to the rising sun, the emblematic source of life in Christianity. At the same time, their west fronts, oriented toward the setting sun, usually depict scenes from the end of the world and Last Judgment. Architects in our own time sometimes play on these historic traditions. For instance, Stanley Tigerman's Powerhouse Museum in Zion, Illinois (1992), is a basilical structure that serves as an energy museum for Commonwealth Edison, Chicago's electric company. Tigerman sited the building so that its east facade, behind which is an auditorium, faces the morning sun, the primal source of Earth's energy.

Although there are other instances throughout history of buildings that refer to their society's image of the cosmos, there are two interrelated building-types that directly correspond to modern-day exploration of the heavens – observatories and planetaria. The earliest

Fig. 1
J. C. Austin and Frederick Ashley,
architects. Griffith Observatory,
Los Angeles. 1935

Fig. 2
Skidmore, Owings and Merrill,
architects. McMath-Pierce Telescope,
Kitt Peak National Observatory,
Tucson, Arizona. 1962

modern observatories, architecturally at least, date to the sixteenth and seventeenth centuries: Uraniborg (1576–97) and Stjerneborg (1584–97), both in Denmark, and the Royal Observatory at Greenwich, England, founded in 1675 and designed by Sir Christopher Wren, are among the most famous. Others followed throughout the western world, the typology being distinguished by its globelike dome housing a powerful telescope. Examples are too numerous to cite, but some of the architecturally distinctive American ones include the Yerkes Observatory in Williams Bay, Wisconsin, from 1897, designed in the Gothic Revival style by architect Henry Ives Cobb (see Brodherson, fig. 2), and the Griffith Observatory and Planetarium in Los Angeles (1935), executed in Moderne style by J. C. Austin and Frederick Ashley (fig. 1). The latter is currently being restored and expanded by architects Hardy Holzman Pfeiffer Associates. Certain more recent examples depart from this formula, such as the angular McMath-Pierce telescope at the Kitt Peak National Observatory, Tucson, designed by Myron Goldsmith of Skidmore, Owings and Merrill in 1962 (fig. 2), and the polygonal, multifaceted buildings of the new Paranal Observatory in Chile. But most observatories continue to adhere to the dome formula (fig. 3). These even include personal observatories – some six feet in diameter – that can be attached to a private house, products of a commercial outfit known as Observa-Dome Laboratories, Inc., of Jackson, Mississippi.

Architecturally, planetaria are related to observatories in that they frequently share the same design formula of a dome atop rectangular or polygonal bases that are often ornamented with traditional, classicist details as if they were early Christian churches or baptisteries.

The two types of buildings function in similar ways except that observatories house large telescopes with which to view the stars and planets, whereas planetaria are three-dimensionalized projections or models of the solar system, often executed for educational purposes. Although planetaria in the form of smaller representations of the solar system date back to the seventeenth and eighteenth centuries, the modern planetarium as we know it – a separate public building as prominent as an observatory – dates from early in the twentieth century. The Adler Planetarium in Chicago (1930; see plate 4), designed by Ernest A. Grunsfeld, Jr., as part of the 1933 Century of Progress Exposition, was the first in the western hemisphere, the type having been developed by Zeiss in central Europe during the preceding decades. Its stripped classical form was decorated with zodiacal and planetary reliefs by sculptor Alfonso Ianelli. Soon afterward, in New York in 1935, the Hayden Planetarium was constructed, making Chicago, New York, and Los Angeles the birthplaces of this public architectural form. Many can be found throughout American museum complexes, such as St. Louis's curvilinear Science Center, designed by Hellmuth, Obata and Kassabaum in 1967, and the poured concrete Brutalist example of the Hudson River Museum in Yonkers, New York (1969), by Sherwood, Mills and Smith. Even though some of these more modern buildings, like St. Louis's Science Center, depart from the convention of the dome atop the cube, this stereotypical formula still projects a strong image of how an observatory or planetarium should appear. Witness the planetarium cum observatory in Gotham City depicted in the 1997 film *Batman and Robin,* a structure that is a comic-book classic temple held aloft by a giant colossus.

Fig. 3
Liberstudio, architects. Solar
Observatory, California State
University, Northridge. 1998

The building itself, as much as some of the leading characters, is the star of the show since it is the focal point of several scenes, including the cataclysmic finale. Its dome is suggestive of its function and of the cosmos itself, as were early religious domical structures, from the Pantheon in Rome to the Dome of the Rock in Jerusalem.

Even if that fantasy example is an exaggerated one, it does not compare with the reality of what is arguably the most famous observatory, at least in terms of its architecture – the Einstein Tower in Potsdam, Germany, outside Berlin (fig. 4). Designed in 1919–20 by Erich Mendelsohn, Germany's famed Expressionist architect, this tiny building (it is only some fifty-two feet high) sits within a complex of nineteenth-century observatories and other scientific structures. The Einstein Tower was named after Albert Einstein by the client, Erwin Finlay Freundlich. Recent literature links, at least in principle, the strong curvilinear forms of the tower as a monument intended to express Einstein's theory of relativity.[1] The building's dynamism is reminiscent of the energy and excitement in art and design that existed in post-World War I Berlin, as seen in German cinema of the Weimar era, particularly in such works as *Metropolis* (1927) and *Frau im Mond* (1929) by director Fritz Lang.

The United States and the Soviet Union produced numerous science fiction radio shows and serialized films about space travel, such as *Buck Rogers* (beginning in 1928) and *Flash Gordon* (beginning in 1936) in the U.S. or *Aelita: Queen of Mars* (1924; see Palmer, figs. 1, 2) in the U.S.S.R. Compared with the fantasylike stories, spaceships, and environments of these depictions, Germany's *Frau im Mond* (*The Woman in the Moon*) is one of the most influential of the great science-fiction films (see plates 2, 3). This is partly because it depicted, in a relatively realistic way, a trip to the Moon using a multistage rocket similar, in principle, to one that actually propelled astronauts there forty years later. By contrast, earlier French creations such as Georges Méliès's movie *Le Voyage dans la lune* (1902; see Schmidt, figs. 5, 6) or Jules Verne's novel *De la terre à la lune* (1865) portrayed

the Moon ship as a projectile shot from a giant cannon. Space pioneers Hermann Oberth and Willy Ley were the technical advisors on the sets and rocketship; they were responsible for bringing realism to Lang's film. With *Frau im Mond,* spaceflight became a real possibility and not some fantastic vision. Although one might quip that the lunar landscape in *Frau im Mond* looks more like the Bavarian Alps (see Schmidt, fig. 7), the reality of the special effects for its day impressed a number of younger rocket pioneers who were to become influential at the army facilities at Peenemünde, Germany, during World War II. One of them, Krafft A. Ehricke, who became a design consultant to the Convair Corporation after the war, saw the film twelve times when it first opened.[2] Even the elaborate decorations outside the theater, which showed the rocket emerging from a German Expressionist city, could not top the technical effects being projected within. When the first German V-2 missile was successfully launched from Peenemünde on October 3, 1942, the tail fin bore a drawing of the *Frau im Mond,* an obvious credit to the film that inspired Ehricke and other engineers there.

A similar instance of realism in post-World War II set design and science-fiction illustration can be found in the works of Chesley Bonestell. Though trained as an architect, Bonestell made his mark in illustrating space-travel books and articles by Arthur C. Clarke, Willy Ley, and Wernher von Braun from the 1950s through the 1980s. He was influenced by the striking paintings of astronomer and artist Lucien Rudaux in the book *Sur les autres mondes* (1936). Early in his career Bonestell consulted on the sets and content for films such as *Destination Moon* (1950) and *The Conquest of Space* (1955). His seemingly realistic paintings of spaceflight and planets other than Earth, created for and with the best technical consultants and scientists of the day, brought the dream of interplanetary exploration to the general public (see Schmidt, fig. 8; plate 7).

This tradition of making the dream into a realistic vision continues today in the works of a variety of artists. A few examples include

Fig. 4
Erich Mendelsohn, architect.
Einstein Tower, Potsdam. 1919–20

the supersize murals and sets of Robert McCall, including work done in conjunction with Stanley Kubrick's film *2001: A Space Odyssey* (1968; see plate 71); the remarkably realistic, computer-generated images of John Frassanito and Associates, which often depict advanced future missions to other planets for the National Aeronautics and Space Administration (NASA) (see plates 83–85); the almost naïve, humanistic paintings of Pat Rawlings that portray comparable missions; and the futuristic visions of sci-fi artist Michael Böhme, showing alien cities on distant planets (see plates 8, 9). All these artists owe a debt to the pioneering space paintings of Bonestell, who paved the way for their populist visions of other planets.

The spectacular photographs from NASA's own Hubble Space Telescope, an observatory stationed in Earth's orbit since April 25, 1990, provides further inspiration for the dreams of the potential for life – human or other – in remote environments and prompts further questions about a supreme deity's role in the universe.[3] Our society's dreams about our place within the greater cosmos are still strong enough to inspire sculptors such as Ary Perez and Denise Milan to create Stonehenge-like environments related to the solstices. They also prompt a company such as the Houston-based Celestis to provide a variety of space services, from launching one's ashes into space as did *Star Trek* creator Gene Roddenberry and drug-culture guru Timothy Leary, to sending DNA samples, radio transmissions, and written messages on a deep-space voyage intended to contact another civilization one day. While some might dismiss the latter effort, the Celestis company has lined up more than 50,000 participants, including futurist writer Arthur C. Clarke and even a prominent former official of NASA.

CONFLICT AND THE CONQUEST OF SPACE

The Rocket as Weapon

Historians have documented that medieval Chinese used rockets, as did the eighteenth-century Hindu armies in their war against Britain. The British themselves used the Congreve Rocket (named after its inventor, Sir William Congreve) in the Napoleonic Wars and our own War of 1812. We might recall that our "Star Spangled Banner" acknowledges "the rockets' red glare" during the firing on Fort McHenry. American troops were equipped with similar rocket brigades, using British Hale rockets (invented in the 1840s by William Hale) on both the Union and Confederate sides during the Civil War. These mid-nineteenth-century rockets were relatively small projectiles, often not as effective as larger artillery pieces in their payload and accuracy. Two examples of this type of small solid-fueled rocket, which were developed and used up through World War II, are the German "Nebelwerfer" rocket launchers, nicknamed "screaming meemies" by American GIs, and the truck-launched "Katyusha" rockets of the Soviet Red Army.

But it was the Wehrmacht or German army during World War II that developed the modern ballistic missile as we know it: the A-4 (Aggregate 4) or V-2 (Vengeance 2). The weapon itself was the brainchild of Artillery General Walter Dornberger and the young engineer Wernher von Braun. The V-2 was an amazing machine for its day, reaching speeds of some 3,500 miles per hour and an altitude of fifty-five miles, approaching the edge of the atmosphere. When it was first launched, Dornberger stated that "today the space ship is born." Approximately 5,000 of these rockets were completed by war's end in May 1945, with over 2,800 landing on targets in London, Antwerp, and elsewhere. The missile itself had a reliability launch rate of 80 percent. This invention, and the American use of the atom bomb on Hiroshima and Nagasaki in August 1945, would forever change the world. With Germany's capitulation, however, the V-2 – along with its various engineers and scientists – became the basis for the postwar rocket programs in Britain, France, and, especially, the United States and Soviet Union.

When the V-2 and other weapons such as the V-1 "buzz bomb" and the Me 163 Komet rocket plane (see plate 23) were in their concep-

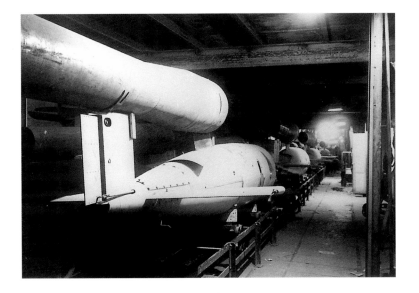

Fig. 5
V-1 assembly line at Mittelwerk II
after liberation in 1945

tual design stages in the mid to late 1930s, a joint Luftwaffe (air force) and army test base was created on the Baltic coast at Peenemünde, a small town out of sight from most of the population, and on the coastline, where falling rockets and debris would do no harm. Peenemünde's new facilities were designed and constructed by air force architects and Baugruppe Schlempp, headed by architect Walther Schlempp, and ultimately supervised by Hitler's chief architect and later armaments minister, Albert Speer. The entire town had new housing and other facilities for its workers, and a model production plant planned in 1937 that was only partly built (see plates 10–13). The works at Peenemünde were intended to be comparable to other showpiece modernist industrial complexes in the Third Reich, such as the Heinkel Aircraft factory at Oranienburg by architect Herbert Rimpl, begun in 1935.

Once Allied intelligence confirmed the rumors about these new wonder weapons, Peenemünde was a rather easy target, because it was isolated from other industrial and urban complexes. The Royal Air Force (RAF) staged its first raid, Operation Hydra, on August 17–18, 1943, followed by others carried out by the U.S. Army Air Force in summer 1944. Most of the damage in the RAF raid was inflicted on the workers' housing, with almost no hits to test facilities (see plates 11, 12), and production continued there until 1944, when Heinrich Himmler convinced Hitler that, for reasons of national security, V-2 assembly should be transferred to the infamous *Schutzstaffel,* or Protection Squad (SS), who would use slave laborers from their concentration camps to insure secrecy.

Assembly was thus moved to a bomb-proof underground factory within the Kohnstein Mountain near Niedersachswerfen; the new facility was called Mittelwerk Dora. Tunnels already existed within the Kohnstein Mountain, which had been excavated as early as 1917 for mining. The tunnel system was expanded by the SS and architects such as Rimpl to accommodate both V-1 and V-2 works and construction of Heinkel 162 jet fighters (fig. 5). Some other underground

assembly plants were designed for aircraft companies by architects Rimpl and Baugruppe Schlempp, but this project was directly under the SS control of architect and Major General or Brigadeführer Dr. Hans Kammler, infamous for being one of the planners of extermination camps at Auschwitz-Birkenau, Maidenek, and Belzec. Thousands of concentration camp inmates died, mostly from expanding Mittelwerk Dora's tunnels and partly while constructing more than 600 rockets a month from September 1944 to February 1945. It is a horror that will forever stain the records of the architects, engineers, and scientists, including Speer, Dornberger, von Braun, and others – all of whom knew of these atrocities. Those like Speer, who half-heartedly attempted to change the living and working conditions of the inmates, probably did so only so that production would be increased.[4]

The Cold War

With the war's end and division of the rocketry spoils and personnel among the Allies, a new regional contest between the East and West emerged – the cold war. The space race was as important a part of this conflict as was the Berlin Airlift of 1948 or the Cuban Missile Crisis of 1962. Propaganda of the era hailed Wernher von Braun as an American hero: his life and crucial work for the nation was popularized by *Life* and *Time* magazines, as well as by a feature film entitled *I Aim at the Stars* (1960), starring Curt Jurgens (fig. 6). Conversely, information paranoia within Soviet society prevented anyone but the inner circle from knowing about von Braun's counterpart in the Soviet space program, chief designer Sergei Korolev. Korolev, who designed the R-7 ballistic missile, the basis for most Soviet space launchers up through today's Soyuz (Union) rockets, including the Sputnik (Companion), Vostok (East), and Voshkod (Sunrise) spacecraft, would remain a state secret until after his death in 1966.[5]

This new type of war meant new work for architects and civil engineers as well as defense contractors.[6] Good examples of military work in the 1950s and 1960s, at the height of the cold war, range

from the Titan missile silos developed by architects Daniel Mann Johnson and Mendenhall and subsequent Minuteman missile silos by the Parsons Group, to the showpiece Convair Astronautics factory in San Diego, designed in 1955–58 by Charles Luckman and William Pereira (see plate 25). The Convair factory was constructed to assemble the Atlas missile, America's first intercontinental ballistic missile (ICBM) and launcher used for the Mercury manned orbital flights. Catalyzed by the successful launch of Korolev's famous *Sputnik I* on October 4, 1957, and subsequent Soviet successes in early manned spaceflight (for example, Yuri Gagarin's first orbital flight on April 12, 1961), the United States established the National Aeronautics and Space Administration (NASA) in 1958. Under Presidents John F. Kennedy and Lyndon Baines Johnson, America would again regain the lead, eventually landing a man on the Moon on July 20, 1969. As evidence of this resolve one need only recall Kennedy's stirring speech of May 25, 1961, in which he pledged a Moon landing within that decade, as well as Lyndon Johnson's earlier January 7, 1958, statement that "Control of space means control of the world."

Although the air force base at Cape Canaveral had built rocket testing and launch facilities soon after World War II, cold-war competition in the 1950s boosted construction. New gantries were built by the Noble construction company (see plate 19). Miami architect Maurice H. Connell designed launch and test facilities there as well, at roughly the same time that Soviet chief engineer Vladimir Barmin was laying out the first launch pads at the Baikonur Cosmodrome (in what is now central Kazakhstan) in 1955 for Korolev's R-7 ballistic missile.

Equally large construction projects resulted from the superpowers' subsequent race to the Moon in the 1960s. In the Soviet Union, Barmin's team expanded Baikonur for Korolev's new N-1 Moon rocket (fig. 7). Meanwhile, in the United States, architect Max O. Urbahn, with engineer Anton Tedesco and others in a consortium named URSAM, in addition to the architectural firm Giffels and

Rossetti, designed the new assembly and launch facilities on land adjacent to the earlier Cape Canaveral launchers of the 1950s. The new works were especially impressive, having the world's largest building in cubic volume – the VAB or Vertical Assembly Building, which was designed to house four of von Braun's massive Saturn launchers, each thirty-four stories high (see plates 29, 30). The new launch control complex featured metal louvers that would pivot to protect the large glass windows during a launch. New launch gantries 39A and 39B were serviced by a massive tracked-vehicle called the Crawler, which would take the assembled Saturn rocket and Apollo capsule to the gantries three miles away, at a speed of one mile per hour (see plate 31). By contrast, the Russians at Baikonur assembled their launchers and spacecraft in a horizontal position and took them out to the launch site via railroad, before pivoting them vertically there (fig. 8; see fig. 7).

Naturally, these new works of the 1950s and 1960s were not confined to government projects alone. They also included new corporate facilities for defense contractors to support the space race, including Boeing's Kent Space Center of 1962 by the Austin Company, and the McDonnell Space Center and Engineering Laboratories of 1958 in St. Louis by Harris Armstrong (see plate 27). The former division designed the Boeing Dyna-Soar, the prototypical space plane (see the essay by Roy F. Houchin II in this volume), and tested lunar satellites and Moon-landing equipment, whereas the latter site included the factory that produced America's Mercury and Gemini capsules.

Architects thus actively participated in the space race during the cold war. Like the architects and industrial designers who were actively creating new modernist airports and airline corporate identity for carriers as these entered the jet age of the late 1950s and early 1960s, architects who worked on space-related projects felt that they were participating in the same golden age. Martin Stein, who heads Urbahn's successor firm of Urbahn Associates, recalls the substantial construction budgets and wartime-like schedule in designing and

Fig. 7
Sergei Korolev, designer. N-1 Moon
rocket at Baikonur Cosmodrome.
February 21, 1969

building the Kennedy Space Center. Often these firms received the big commissions because of government and aerospace work they had done during World War II and soon after, and because of their engineering or master planning strengths. Hence, someone such as Luckman, after working on the very successful Convair complex for Atlas missile production in the fifties, was well positioned to become the chief design consultant for NASA's new Manned Spacecraft Center (now the Johnson Space Center) outside Houston in the early sixties.

Beyond the actual structures and buildings directly related to space vehicles and launchers, the world went space crazy at this time, and architects on both sides of the Iron Curtain drew upon the theme of the space race for their buildings. To illustrate this point one need only compare the futuristic Space Needle of the Century 21 Seattle World's Fair of 1962, by architect John Graham, with the Television Tower in East Berlin from 1965–69 by a team of architects using Hermann Henselmann's design concept (figs. 9, 10). Although the Space Needle and nearby Boeing Spacearium, within the Federal Pavilion by Minoru Yamasaki, touted American accomplishments and projections for the future of space, the Television Tower in East Berlin consciously referred to the triumph of Soviet socialism in space, its Sputnik-like globe part of the much larger design for a space monument, complete with a solar system fountain and pavement, and a Urania world clock executed at its base.[7] The tower in East Berlin, 1,186 feet high, visible from West Berlin as well, projected this image of technological supremacy to both the socialist and capitalist worlds.

This superpower space rivalry is expressed further in popular culture, even in science-fiction films. It has often been acknowledged that episodes of the *Star Trek* television series (beginning in 1966) intentionally projected Klingons as totalitarian communists. Earlier than that, the very character Ming the Merciless in *Flash Gordon* serials of the 1940s and 1950s reminded us of totalitarian cultures in Asia, particularly the Japanese empire of World War II and the Red Chinese of the Korean War. The East German and Polish film *Der*

Schweigende Stern (1959), released in English as *The First Spaceship on Venus* (1962), depicts an international team of cosmonauts led by Russians, some of whom arrive to the spaceport in their Russian-built Mig-15 jet bearing East German emblems. The team departs Earth in the *Cosmostrator* (in the German version, *Kosmokrator,* or "Ruler of the Cosmos"), a spaceship with a main observation screen whose design reminds one of the nose blisters on Tupolev airliners of the day (fig. 11). The woman broadcaster who reports on the launch works for Intervision, a parallel to one of the Socialist service corporations founded through East Germany, along with Interflug, East Germany's airline, and Intershop, the hard-currency chain of stores in the German Democratic Republic. When the *Cosmostrator's* astronauts arrive on Venus they encounter Sputnik-like insects, their round forms and trailing legs clearly reminiscent of the first satellite's shape. Similarly, it has been observed that in the *Star Wars* trilogy (1977–83), the costumes of Darth Vader and his storm troopers are derived from totalitarian uniforms such as those of Nazi Germany.[8] Yet the Imperial officers aboard the *Death Star* wear brown uniforms and caps that arguably relate more closely to those of the Imperial Japanese army of the 1930s and even the Red Army. Writer Vivian Sobchack has observed that our attitudes toward aliens in science-fiction films have changed with the social shift toward individualism in the late 1960s and early 1970s, from a negative to a positive view.[9] She cites Steven Spielberg's *E.T. The Extra-Terrestrial* (1982) as a primary example of this change. Yet many science-fiction films and television shows still portray aliens in an antagonistic way, even to the point of dehumanizing and demonizing them, as in the *Alien* trilogy (1979–99) and *Independence Day* (1996), and television shows such as *Space: Above and Beyond* (1995). Pejorative portrayals are especially evident in the film *Starship Troopers* (1997), where, as in the stereotypical war movie, the enemy embodies the ultimate demonization and dehumanization as giant insects (see plate 44). Thus, we initially and sometimes still tend to think of an alien being as

the enemy because of our fear of the unfamiliar. As a result, America's historic enemies during World War II, the Korean War, and the cold war are commonly typecast as extraterrestrials. These extraterrestrial beings, and their spacecraft and habitats, are often depicted in a sinister, organically mechanistic way in keeping with our negative images of the alien.

Commercial Space in a Post-Cold War World

With the fall of the Berlin Wall on November 9, 1989, the world entered a new era. Foes became business partners in order to keep their factories operable in an age of defense cuts on both sides of the former Iron Curtain. Perhaps one of the most creative efforts in this regard is Sea Launch, an ocean-going satellite launch system that gives clients the maximum flexibility to launch their satellites into orbit from different latitudes (see plates 56, 57). Even before the post-cold-war boom in this arena in the late 1980s, companies such as Arianespace were set up to provide commercial access to space services, particularly for European clients, exceeding what the American launch companies could provide. Their first facilities in Kourou, French Guyana, have been expanded to accommodate increased business from the late 1980s through today, the latest being Launch Facility No. 3 for Ariane 5 rockets, executed in 1989–95 by Christain Tinturier and Rainer Turk (see plate 55). In the past decade, other new launch structures range from the work that large firms such as Bechtel and BRPH have done for facilities at Vandenberg and Cape Canaveral, respectively, to the assembly and launch complex at Mojave Airport (fig. 12) designed for startup company Rotary Rocket by the small firm of Altus Associates. Some of the very latest constructions include a new Delta rocket factory in Decatur, Alabama, by the Austin Company for Boeing; a new satellite-manufacturing plant in El Segundo, California, by Steven Wooley and Associates for Hughes; and Sverdrup's design and construction of a prototype spaceport for the Lockheed Martin X-33 at Edwards Air Force Base, California.

Along with corporate expansion and the creation of new launch facilities in this commercial age of space comes a new emphasis on corporate imagery that reflects many of the mergers and acquisitions that have taken place in recent years, particularly in the defense industry. Two of the major players – Lockheed Martin and Boeing – hired design consultants Anspach Grossman and Rick Eiber, respectively, to redesign their logos in 1996–97. Telecommunications and Internet companies consistently hire Landor Associates in San Francisco, an established design firm that dates back to Walter Landor's packaging firm of the 1940s, to reshape their identities as commercial use of outer space expands (see plate 60). New companies such as Motorola's Iridium and Loral's Globalstar have introduced satellite telephone systems; airliners today (as well as NATO bombers) are guided by Global Positioning System (GPS) satellites; and services such as DIRECTV bring satellite television programs into our homes. Boeing is beginning to expand this emphasis on space one step further with Teledesic, their satellite Internet access company. And the Cadillac division of General Motors, which already has a GPS guidance system called "On Star" and an infrared Heads Up Display (HUD) like that used in military aircraft called "Night Vision," has introduced a satellite Internet and e-mail system in its latest cars. They previewed this idea in their 1999 concept car "Evoq."

In all, the world has come a long way in commercial space since *Telstar*, the world's first communications satellite, was launched by Bell Laboratories on July 10, 1962. Films such as the James Bond thrillers *You Only Live Twice* (1967) and *Moonraker* (1979) have often incorporated space themes within their plots (see plates 38, 47). But two of the more recent ones, *Golden Eye* (1996) and *Tomorrow Never Dies* (1997), remind us that satellites for telecommunications and navigation can have a sinister side and clear military uses, in disrupting communications and targeting enemy installations. Newspapers in the summer of 1999 were filled with stories about Chinese nuclear espionage and how American companies aided their ballistic missile

Fig. 9
John Graham, architect. Space
Needle, Seattle. 1962

development. Incidents such as this one prompted the U.S. Congress on March 15, 1999, to reclassify satellites as weapons. Yet these recent news stories remind us that space still has as many military and political uses, as it did in the past. The U.S. Air Force's research laboratory, aware of the historic importance of space for military superiority, is spearheading a new initiative in what is now a half-century-old issue related to President Johnson's cold war-era admonition about the control of space.[10]

Exploration and Inhabitation of the Wilderness

"Space, the final frontier. To boldly go where no one has gone before!" These are the words of Captain Jean-Luc Picard of the *Enterprise* as each *Star Trek: The Next Generation* (1987) television show opens. They repeat essentially the same words used by Captain James T. Kirk in the first *Star Trek* series. As Howard McCurdy has pointed out, the new frontier is one of our most prevalent images of space.[11] As with the American West, space is wide open for us to explore, conquer, and colonize. We have an image in our minds of the architectural environment of the American West through representations of it in paintings, old photographs, films, and television shows. Likewise, the media have conditioned our image of architecture and design for space exploration, above and beyond the limits of reality. Sometimes one may well influence the other in creating space in outer space.

Images of spaceships and space architecture in the film media began with the streamlined Art Deco ships from *Flash Gordon* and *Buck Rogers* and continued through their even more aerodynamic cousins in *Destination Moon* (1950) and *When Worlds Collide* (1951). These early 1950s examples were clearly influenced by the shape of the V-2, which was still the most advanced design of its day. Even Oldsmobile advertisements from the late 1940s and early 1950s that promoted their Rocket 88 engines and cars often included streamlined V-2s of the type tested by the army in White Sands, New Mexico (fig. 13). 1960s sci-fi spacecraft became more realistic in design, their interiors incor-

porating features of the molded panels used in airliners of the day. However, there are exceptions to this rule, for instance, the submarine-like staircase and levels of the East German *Cosmostrator,* cited above, as well as the shag-carpeted conversation pit of the spaceship in Roger Vadim's *Barbarella* (1968). By contrast, *Star Trek* and films such as *2001: A Space Odyssey* projected the image of a modularized, molded-panel interior resembling designs by Walter Dorwin Teague for Boeing jetliners in the late 1950s through 1960s, which culminated in the wide-body look of 747s in 1968. The interior architecture in *2001* (see plates 72, 73) took on a particular importance for von Braun, who encouraged his engineers, as well as designers with other contractors, to see this film for design inspiration. Similarly, *Star Trek* federation spacecraft interiors, designed under the supervision of production designer Herman Zimmerman, continue to this day the modular panelized look to convey the professionalism of Star Fleet.[12]

Unfortunately, this modular airliner look had little impact on the reality of actual spacecraft designed in the 1950s and early 1960s. One might say that the Russian spacecraft aesthetic differs from that expressed in American spacecraft of this early era, although only aerospace engineers (as opposed to industrial designers and architects) designed the capsules. Chief designer Sergei Korolev's preference for spherical craft, from Sputnik to Vostok, Voshkod, and even Soyuz, seems to bear this out, as does his famous comment about Sputnik that "this ball will one day be in a museum." But more practical reasons could well be behind this form since American spacecraft such as the Mercury capsule, designed by engineer Max Faget, who was an aerodynamics designer on the X-15 nose (see Houchin, fig. 3), and the successor Gemini and Apollo capsules are all essentially conical in shape, their broad base serving as a heat shield for reentry into the atmosphere (a maneuver the Americans controlled more accurately than the Soviets by guidance and retro rockets). In both Soviet and American spacecraft of this early era, however, the cramped interiors left much to be desired in terms of human space and amenities, and

Fig. 10
Hermann Henselmann and
Joerg Stretparth, design concept;
executed by Fritz Dieter and
Guenther Franke, architects.
Television Tower, East Berlin.
1965–69

could well have benefited from interior architecture consultation. This did not happen until 1967, when NASA hired noted industrial designer Raymond Loewy to help plan America's first space station, Skylab (see the essay by Rebecca Dalvesco in this volume). (The Soviet Union's 1971 Salyut – a salute to Gagarin's first flight ten years before – beat Skylab into space by two years.) And even though Loewy did not completely control all aspects of the design, his influence could be felt in interior design details.

The 1970s witnessed a major departure from the traditional launch-and-recovery systems of spacecraft. Both Soviet and American space capsules were launched atop a rocket, returning to Earth via parachute after the craft burned its way through Earth's atmosphere, the American capsules landing in the ocean and the Russian ones on land. With American development of the Space Shuttle or STS (Space Transportation System) in the 1970s, the launch took place in the same way, but reentry to Earth was made in an unpowered glide to an airstrip at the Kennedy Space Center (see plate 32). Aside from the rocket-powered X-15 of the 1950s, which soared over 354,000 feet high to the edge of space, the shuttle was the world's first spaceplane. Even before its first orbital flight in 1981, it became famous as the villain Hugo Drax's spacecraft in *Moonraker.*

Since the shuttle's inception, there has been only one disastrous accident (the explosion of the *Challenger* on January 28, 1986) out of more than one hundred successful orbital flights, principally by the current fleet, which comprises *Atlantis, Challenger, Columbia, Discovery,* and *Endeavor.* This is an amazing record. The shuttle's utility has made it something of an equivalent of a cargo plane, its size comparable to a smaller jet airliner, such as a DC9 or a Boeing 717 or 737. Although it looks a bit more aerodynamic than previous space vehicles, it still appears to have been designed by an engineering committee. Indeed, it is the result of many changes from concept to realization, all with the team approach to design. It is being

continuously upgraded so that it can fly well into the next century, when it is hoped it will be replaced by another reusable launch vehicle (RLV) such as the Lockheed Martin VentureStar (see plate 79). The Russians created a look-alike shuttle called Buran (Snowstorm), under the design leadership of Valentin Glushko in the late 1970s through construction in 1984; however, this vehicle flew orbitally only once – and unmanned – in 1988 before the program was finally scrapped at the end of the cold war. With the regularity, albeit an expensive one, of shuttle flights since the plane's inception, this program clearly approaches what von Braun had hoped for in terms of everyday access to space. But, as critics contend, the shuttle still resembles a truck with a race car price tag, especially as concerns launch support and maintenance. We are still some years away from the day when we will be taking the equivalent of airliners into space.

Nonetheless, repeated flights of the shuttle are important as a next step toward the goal of having humans living in space. In 1986, the Russians initiated the *Mir* (Peace) space station (see McCurdy, fig. 8). In so doing, they became experts in long-term living in space, terminating their experiment only in 1999, when *Mir* was abandoned. In the mid 1980s, the cold war was still alive and well, with proposals for a "Star Wars" laser ray initiative to defeat Russian nuclear missiles launched at the U.S. as well as Russian satellites, and plans by Boeing and architects at Sverdrup to build mobile ICBM's launched from railroad cars or highway vehicles.

Unlike the Russians, NASA did not have a permanent presence in space. It is the space station's image of permanence – that it should last ten to fifteen years, if not more – that I believe led NASA to hire a team of trained architects to work on their staff in order to develop Space Station Freedom through its current iteration as the International Space Station (ISS). The station has gone through numerous changes and redesigns since its first proposals in 1985, and NASA architects and human-factors specialists Rod Jones, Frances E. Mount,

Fig. 11
Alfred Hirschmeier, co-production
designer. Interior study for the
Cosmostrator, in *The First Spaceship
on Venus* (*Der Schweigende Stern*).
1959

Kriss Kennedy, and William Langdoc have worked together with outside contractors such as industrial designers Teague Associates for Boeing, John Frassanito (one of Loewy's team in 1968 on Skylab), and, more recently, architect Constance Adams. Frassanito has recounted the story of how, in one of those 1985 NASA meetings, he showed them The Museum of Modern Art's design catalogue *Italy: The New Domestic Landscape* (1972), convincing the team that a modular approach should be used in designing the station's interiors as well as its exterior components and nodes. This idea made sense because station components had to be fabricated on Earth with finished units capable of fitting within the cargo bay of the shuttle, to be assembled or connected in space by astronauts. In contrast with the dreams that von Braun and others have had for actually building a circular space station on orbit (see plates 67–70), NASA's design for the ISS was a more economical and practical way of constructing a space station, though the total costs are estimated to be approximately $50 billion. When finished sometime between 2002 and 2004, it will be some 290 by 356 feet, or more than three times the size of *Mir* (see plates 86–88).[13]

The space stations in John Iacovelli's *Babylon 5* (1994) and Zimmerman's *Star Trek: Deep Space Nine (DS9)* (1993) (see plates 92, 93) had modular elements to their design that related to the ISS, especially so within the *DS9* sets. As were other *Star Trek* sets, the *DS9* sets were constructed within the large studios of Paramount. Though the *DS9* station was supposedly designed by aliens (the militaristic Cardassians) and had a somewhat organic, nonrectilinear appearance, the window units were modularized fiberglass casts, and, as with all *Star Trek* sets, the large set had a highly finished quality. Even the graphics used by Star Fleet ships, developed by graphic designer Michael Okuda and called "Okudagrams" by the trekkies, were almost detailed enough to be read on the screen. The sets for *Babylon 5,* on the other hand, were the more traditional backlot

constructions of plywood and medium density fiberboard. They were intentionally not as finished as the *DS9* sets because their production designer consciously wanted to refer to the industrial appearance of living in space as demonstrated in the *Mir* space station. But even the *Babylon 5* set had a massive circulation corridor that was modularized in design, with repeating bays. Both of these science-fiction marvels demonstrate that our reality of living in space differs dramatically from the dream of inhabiting these massive structures that are almost planetary in scale compared with the ISS. Gravity and weightlessness are problems that both of these gigantic rotating constructions have solved by following the tradition of von Braun's proposals.

Surveys have shown that thousands of people would pay up to $100,000 for a trip in space. The X Prize was established in 1996 with a $10 million award for the first spacecraft to successfully launch three people on a suborbital flight of sixty-two miles high, two times in two weeks. Several teams are competing for this prize, and other private companies are looking for investors to help them make the dream of economic spaceflight a reality for a general public that is already greatly interested in the subject.[14] The Kennedy Space Center attracts some four million visitors a year, while the Smithsonian's National Air and Space Museum has approximately ten million visitors annually. Architects such as BRC Imagination Arts in Burbank, California, Architectura in Vancouver, British Columbia, and the Landmark Entertainment Group of Los Angeles all design museum displays and science-fiction theme parks that are visited by tens of millions of people each year (see plates 33, 75). In some ways, this activity harkens back to the days when Ley and von Braun consulted on the TWA Rocket to the Moon exhibit at Disneyland in 1955 (see plate 74), or when Pan Am was flooded with thousands of reservations for a lunar trip after people had seen the Pan Am spaceliner in the film *2001.*

Reality may one day catch up with the fantasy if Shimizu, a

Fig. 12
Altus Associates, architects.
Rotary Rocket Company Facilities,
Mojave Airport, Mojave,
California. 1998–99

Japanese design-build company, successfully completes its proposed orbiting Space Hotel. The renderings for this project (see plate 88) show it being visited by RLV's such as Kawasaki's proposed Kankoh-maru, the tourist spaceship it intends to launch from the new Kansai, Japan, airport.

Currently, NASA and Lockheed Martin are developing the prototype X-33, designed from the initial concepts of engineer Dave Urie (see plate 80). This experimental vehicle may lead to the development of the larger-scale Venture Star, a space plane that will lower the cost of satellite launches to $1,000 per pound, compared with the present $8,000–$10,000 per pound. In addition, NASA is planning missions for planetary exploration in the not too distant future that, with new propulsion systems, will halve the time of space travel, permitting manned missions to Mars and unmanned probes to more distant planets.

Designer Frassanito, working with the NASA teams to visualize these missions, has proposed inflatable fabric structures of Kevlar composite material for architectural structures (see plates 84, 85). Architects Kennedy and Adams are also working on such inflatable buildings for NASA missions to Mars, the Moon, and even for lightweight additions to the modules of the ISS. The growing popularity of these inflatable solutions to living-space problems in outer space reflects recent interest in fabric architecture (witness the great fabric roof of the new Denver International Airport by Fentress and Bradburn, 1989–95, the panels in the roof of Helmut Jahn's Munich Airport Center of 1999, or the roof of the Millennium Dome near

Greenwich, England, by Richard Rogers), along with increasing architectural interest in flexible structures derived from the structural principles found in plants and insects.[15] But it also recalls early architectural images of nineteenth-century settlers erecting simple, quickly built wooden balloon-frame buildings as they settled America's plains and prairies. Exploring and inhabiting the extraterrestrial wilderness will have as much to do with design precedents developed on Earth as with solving specific problems beyond Earth's atmosphere.

Thus, we have come full circle in our survey of architects and designers who have worked in helping to bring the dream and reality of space travel to the public over the past century. They have planned observatories and planetaria on Earth, participated in the design and construction of launch or assembly facilities, designed space habitations, created corporate logos, and brought the drama of future space travel to the public through renderings of future space mission as well as set designs, aerospace museums, and theme parks. This book recognizes their contributions to a field normally associated solely with engineers and scientists. The essays and plate sections that follow help illuminate the contributions of visual arts professionals to space exploration. Together, these architects and designers, along with scientists and engineers, develop design concepts from an idea into a visual expression of it, through either a sketch, a drawing, or a computer-generated projection. Their stories of the symbiotic relationship between art and science date back to the fourteenth-century master mason Jean Mignot, who presciently observed, "Ars sine scientia nihil est," or "Art without science is nothing."

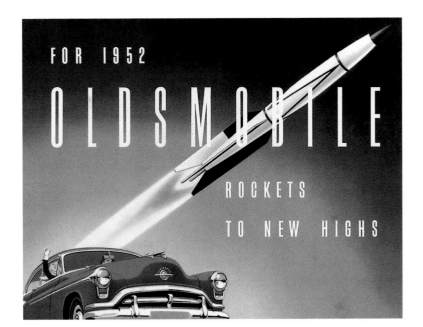

Fig. 13
Oldsmobile brochure. 1952

1. Kathleen James, "Expressionism, Relativity, and the Einstein Tower," *Journal of the Society of Architectural Historians,* 53: 4 (Dec. 1994), pp. 392–413.

2. John L. Chapman, *Atlas: The Story of a Missile* (New York, 1960), p. 169, among numerous pages about Krafft A. Ehricke.

3. Steve Kloehn, "God's Place in the Universe a Vexing Issue for Scientists," *Chicago Tribune* (Apr. 18, 1999), pp. 1, 14.

4. Of the many books on the V-1, V-2, and architectural facilities for constructing them, these are several of the most important: Yves Béon, *Planet Dora: A Memoir of the Holocaust and the Birth of the Space Age,* ed. Michael J. Neufeld (Boulder, Col., 1997); Manfred Bornemann, *Geheimprojekt Mittelbau* (Bonn, 1994), esp. p. 88 (architect list); Martin Middlebrook, *The Peenemünde Raid* (London, 1988); Michael J. Neufeld, *The Rocket and the Reich: Peenemünde and the Coming of the Ballistic Missile Era* (Cambridge, Mass., 1995); Dieter Hölsken, *V-Missiles of the Third Reich: The V-1 and V-2* (Sturbridge, Mass., 1994); Frederick I. Ordway III and Mitchell R. Sharpe, *The Rocket Team* (Cambridge, Mass., 1982) and Ernst Stuhlinger and Frederick I. Ordway III, *Wernher von Braun: Crusader for Space* (Melbourne, Fla., 1996).

5. Jamie Duran and Piers Bizony, *Starman: The Truth Behind the Legend of Yuri Gagarin* (London, 1998) and James Harford, *Korolev* (New York, 1997) are two of the more recent publications that discuss the anonymous Soviet chief designer in relation to the celebrity of the cosmonauts and westerners such as von Braun.

6. One of the very few architectural articles that survey this work is David B. Carlson, "Building for the Space Age," *Architectural Forum* (Sept. 1960), pp. 116–19, 202.

7. Peter Müller, *Symbol mit Aussicht: Die Geschichte des Berliner Fernsehturms* (Berlin, 1999), esp. pp. 54–58.

8. Mary Henderson, ed., *Star Wars: The Magic of Myth* (New York, 1997), pp. 144–46.

9. Vivian Sobchack, *Screening Space: The American Science Fiction Film,* 2d ed. (New Brunswick, N.J., 1997), pp. 292ff.

10. See, for example, Theodore R. Simpson, "Using Space to Win Wars," *Aerospace America* (Feb. 2000), pp. 28–31; the nine short essays by Craig Covault, William B. Scott, and Bruce D. Nordwall in *Aviation Week and Space Technology* (Apr. 5, 1999), pp. 46–60; and William E. Burrows, "Securing the High Ground," *Air and Space* (Dec. 1993/Jan. 1994), pp. 64–69.

11. Howard McCurdy, *Space and the American Imagination* (Washington, D.C., 1997), esp. ch. 6, "The Extraterrestrial Frontier."

12. On the spaceship in art, literature, and film, see: Frederick I. Ordway III and Randy Liebermann, eds., *Blueprint for Space: Science Fiction to Science Fact* (Washington, D.C., 1992); Ron Miller, *The Dream Machines: A Pictorial History of the Spaceship in Art, Science and Literature* (Malabar, Fla., 1993); and Dennis Meredith, "Planet of Origin: Hollywood. 'Engineering, what do you make of that vessel?'" *Air and Space* (Apr./May 1989), pp. 81–85.

13. For *Mir* in relation to the International Space Station, see Bryan Burrough, *Dragonfly: NASA and the Crisis Aboard Mir* (New York, 1998) and John Zukowsky, "Space Architecture," *The Work of John Frassanito and Associates for NASA* (Stuttgart, 1999), esp. pp. 12–13, 15, 23.

14. Patrick Collins, "We Have Liftoff," *Passenger Terminal World* (Jan. 1999), pp. 21–22, 25, and Paula Szuchman, "You Could Be Here," *Condé Nast Traveler* (Sept. 1999), pp. 47–50.

15. Steven Vogel, *Cat's Paws and Catapults: Mechanical Worlds of Nature and People* (New York, 1998).

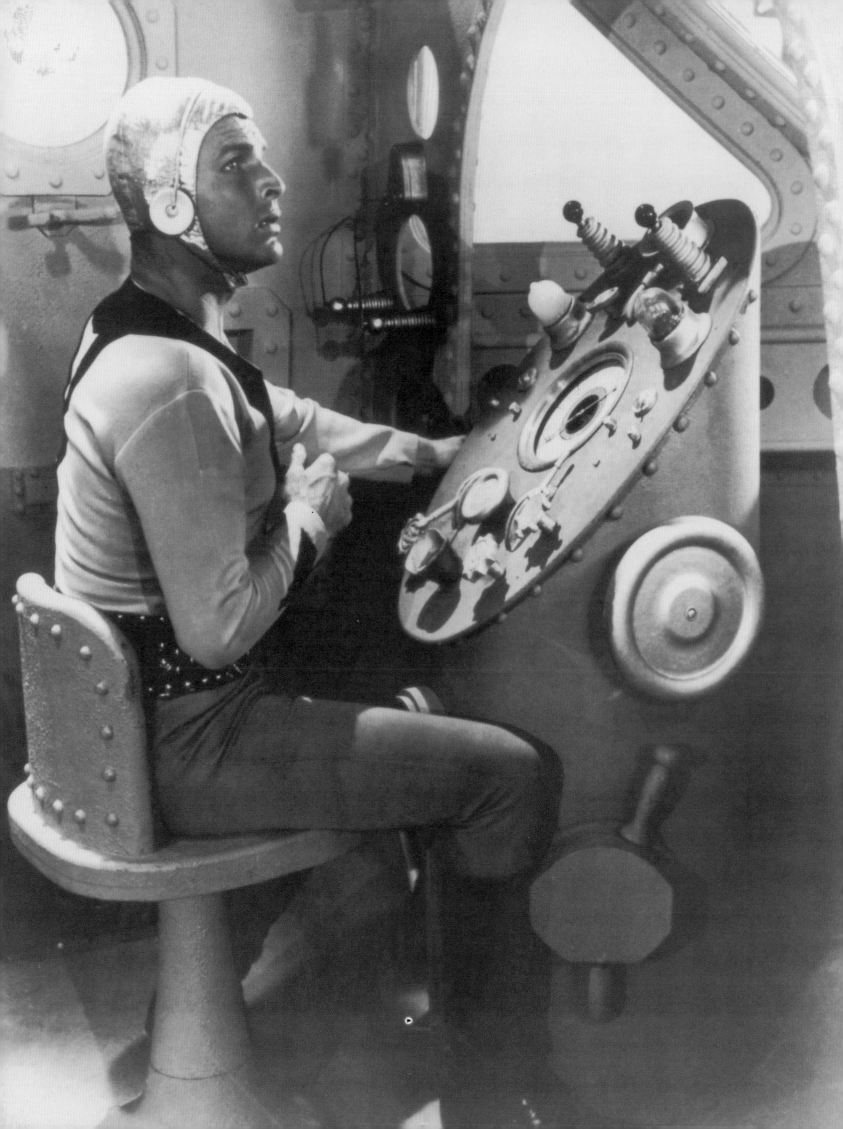

The Cosmos

Perceptions of Space

1
Buster Crabbe as Buck Rogers in his
spacecraft. 1940

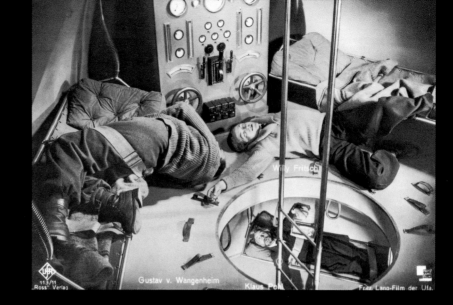

Americans were so familiar with Buck Rogers's exploits in comic strips and radio programs in the 1920s and 1930s that the 1934 Century of Progress Exposition in Chicago even included a Buck Rogers pavilion on the Enchanted Island. But Weimar Germany was also a nation that demonstrated popular interest in high-tech subjects such as aviation and aerospace. So it is no surprise that director Fritz Lang hired rocket pioneer Hermann Oberth and space writer Willy Ley to consult on the design of the spaceship and launch structures for his famous film *Frau im Mond* (*The Woman in the Moon*). The film caused a sensation in Berlin. Its realistic space-launch scenes and multiple-stage spacecraft design inspired the next generation of rocket scientists, who developed the A-4 or V-2 missile during World War II. The interior design vocabulary in these early film spaceships draws upon the nautical imagery of submarine interiors, much as terms for space and air transportation drew upon familiar nautical terminology, for example, in words such as port and starboard, captain and first officer.

2, 3
Fritz Lang, director. *Frau im Mond*
(*The Woman in the Moon*). 1929.
Production stills

4
Ernest A. Grunsfeld, Jr. Adler
Planetarium, Chicago. 1930, with
East Wing by Lohan Associates,
1999

The Adler Planetarium in Chicago was designed by Ernest A. Grunsfeld, Jr., in 1930 in conjunction with the 1933 Century of Progress Exposition. It was the first such public facility in the western hemisphere. The Lohan firm's recent addition, the East Wing, is a dynamic steel and glass building that encircles the historic structure, preserving its striking masonry form and sculptures and providing an unencumbered view of the original entry facade. The East Wing provides expanded exhibition space as well as a state-of-the-art theater.

By contrast, the Polshek Partnership has created a striking new structure to replace the famed but spatially inadequate Hayden Planetarium of 1935 in New York. The Rose Center for Earth and Space, designed in the mid to late 1990s and opened in 2000, has at its core an illuminated sphere that is approximately ten stories in diameter placed within a steel and glass box. The sphere, intended to evoke the design and function of the perisphere from the 1939 World's Fair in New York, contains a new planetarium as well as a "Big Bang" theater, which houses a program that describes the origins of the universe. The complex also has new exhibitions designed by Ralph Applebaum Associates.

5, 6
The Polshek Partnership. Rose Center for Earth and Space, American Museum of Natural History, New York. 2000. Computer-generated perspective from the north and east-west cross-section

THE EXPLORATION OF MARS

WILLY LEY & WERNHER VON BRAUN

PAINTINGS BY CHESLEY BONESTELL

7
Dust jacket from Willy Ley and
Wernher von Braun's *The Exploration
of Mars,* with illustrations by
Chesley Bonestell. 1956

Chesley Bonestell was one of the leading painters of
space scenes of the 1950s and 1960s; his numerous
published illustrations inspired a host of followers to
develop their own visions of space travel to other
planets. In the tradition of Bonestell's work, many of
these artists and illustrators collaborate with aerospace engineers and scientists to visualize the reality
of space travel. By contrast, others, such as Michael
Böhme (b. 1943), present us with their powerful, fantastic visions of space travel and alien civilizations.
Böhme, an attorney by training and a public prosecu-
tor in Konstanz, Germany, studied painting in his spare
time with Professor Hasso Bruse of the Art Academy
in Stuttgart and Böhme's wife, Angelika, who taught
painting in Konstanz. In the 1980s, Böhme became
best known for his surrealistic environmental paintings,
which critique our society's misuse of Earth's resources.
He has since expanded his oeuvre and become one
of the leading painters of science-fiction and fantasy
scenes.

8
Michael Böhme. *Foreign Civilization*. 1986. Acrylic on canvas, 23⅜ x 19¾ in. 1986. Planetarium Stuttgart, courtesy Michael Böhme

9
Michael Böhme. *Ark in Space*. 1997. Acrylic on canvas, 19¾ x 23⅜ in. 1997. Planetarium Stuttgart, courtesy Michael Böhme

Fly Me to the Moon

JOHANN N. SCHMIDT

Lunar Voyages in Literature and Film

Lunar voyages occupied the popular imagination long before they became possible. A visit to the Moon presupposed the existence of a planet similar to Earth. In ancient times, however, the Moon was regarded as mere never-never-land, ethereal and translucent and utterly immutable. Only a few Greek philosophers such as Thales, whom Aristotle considered to be the first cosmologist, ventured to speculate about the composition of the Moon and its relationship to our own planet. Pythagoras, who made important discoveries in mathematics, music, and astronomy, supposed that the Moon might be spherical. Philolaus, who was the first to describe Earth as a planet, took the view that the surface of the Moon was occupied by beings fifteen times larger than those on Earth. Plutarch, a remarkably prolific writer and biographer, came astonishingly close to the discoveries of Galileo Galilei by suggesting that "'tis probable that the Moon also lies open, and is cleft with many deep Caves and Ruptures, in which there is Water, or very obscure Air, to the bottom of which the Sun cannot reach or penetrate."[1]

If in Antiquity the notion of a plurality of worlds was believed possible, Christian faith downright rejected the notion of another habitable world set apart from the Earth. It assumed that all other planets reflected divine perfection in their permanence and inaccessibility, placing Earth at the center of the cosmos (fig. 1). Even the spots on the Moon were explained as mirrorlike reflections of the Earth's surface. Galileo later contradicted Aristotle's cosmology and advocated the Copernican heliocentric system (fig. 2). Galileo's announcement of his telescopic discoveries – that the Moon's surface was rough and uneven like Earth's – was published in 1610 in *Sidereus Nuncius* (*The Starry Messenger*); they led to the development of modern scientific method (generally known as "new science"). His discoveries also had far-reaching implications for man defining himself as an active participant in the universe. If the world was dispersed and the Moon was just another part of it, it could be mapped and finally visited. No wonder, then, that in the seventeenth century, the jour-

ney to the Moon developed into an archetypal theme of speculative fiction, inspiring tales of fantasy as well as pseudo-scientific treatises.

For a long time, Moon travel seemed to have become a paradigm for any cosmic voyage. It was, after all, a planet close enough to be observed, especially when the telescope brought it before the eye, and yet unattainable with any known means of transport. The Moon exerted perceptible influences upon Earthly forces (such as tides), but it was also part of an alien interplanetary system far beyond the frontiers of human experience. It was the geographical discoveries of Christopher Columbus, Vasco da Gama, Ferdinand Magellan, and others that inspired exploring and possibly colonizing strange new lands not only on Earth, but also in the sky. As literary critic Marjorie Hope Nicolson has explained: "The strange, the mysterious, the distant, the ultimately inaccessible – small wonder that the discovery of a new world remote in the ether should have roused again an imagination which had been lying dormant since geographers and explorers had proved the whole world discovered."[2] This "new frontier" and the pioneering effort to conquer virgin territories foreshadowed President Kennedy's famous speech launching the Apollo program in 1961.

Perceptions of the Moon's "strange" and "mysterious" attributes can be traced back to ancient myth and poetry in almost any society. The Moon, which cyclically waxes and wanes, has symbolized growth *and* decay, fulfillment *and* loss. In East Asian Buddhism it stands for complete knowledge and even for the deity himself. Its ever-changing form, however, also indicates a certain instability, fickleness, and melancholy moodiness. (The German word *Laune,* meaning "mood," is in fact derived from the Latin *luna*.) The Moon can be the consoling friend of poets and lovers who seek a companion to light their way at night. But folklore also held that it causes epileptic fits and makes the blood boil, and that it confuses the mind to the point of "lunacy." In fact, quite a few murderers in the past put the blame for their misdeeds on the full Moon – an inescapable source of evil.

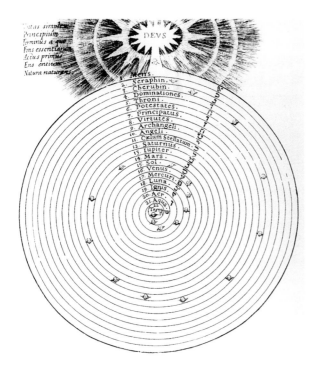

Fig. 1
Albertus Magnus. Aristotelian
and Christian conception of the
cosmos. 13th century

For poets, even the color of the Moon is ambiguous. For some it radiates a soft, seductive light of golden rays that can warm up to a red glow. For others it sends out a silvery coolness that borders upon icy indifference and cruelty. Gender associations further define the Moon's double nature. The Moon has been identified with Artemis, Diana, and Persephone, in addition to Selene, Greek goddess of the Moon, after whom the inhabitants of the Moon bear the name of "selenites." Even more compelling is the almost exact synchronism of lunar months and the menstrual cycle ("menses" also referring to counting months in terms of "Moons"). By contrast, female fertility – symbolized by growth, fullness, and warmth – yields to phallic aggressiveness in old illustrations presenting bulls whose sickle-shaped horns resemble the crescent of the waning Moon.

If, according to Dr. Van Helsing in Tod Browning's classic 1931 film *Dracula* (based on Bram Stoker's 1897 novel), "the superstitions of yesterday can become the scientific reality of today," it is small wonder that man wanted to throw light on the darkness that surrounded the Moon. Curiosity was kindled by two insurmountable problems: how to reach the Moon, and what to expect after the landing. Some texts pay only little attention to how man could physically make the voyage; it was enough simply to land and then explore foreign regions. Others were more interested in the theme of flight, and how to overcome the limits of gravity and the vicissitudes of the climate. Moon travelers of the first category were helped out by spirits, angels, and flying horses, or claimed to have fallen into deep sleep in the crucial moment of lifting from Earth. But there were also some remarkable forerunners in the history of aviation and aeronautics. The dream of using artificial wings may still have prevailed in the seventeenth century, but gradually the idea of flights

by "machines" gained ground in the thinking of philosophers and scientists alike. Whether with kites, balloons, iron engines operated by magnetism, or with "fiery speers" (that is, rockets as they had been brought into usage by the Chinese two thousand years ago), man's imagination knew no limits in how he might overcome the enormous distance between the Earth and the Moon. One of the outstanding pioneers, the Italian scientist Francesco Lana, published his *Prodromo* (1670), in which he described an "aerial ship" or "flying ship" that was to be rowed against the resistance of the winds. Four hollow copper spheres were attached by ropes to lift it into the air and hold it there. In hindsight, the idea of a spaceship launched into the universe by means of a rocket seems like the ultimate realization of thoughts that date back as far as the seventeenth century.

Paradoxically, the discovery by seventeenth-century scientists that the Moon, just like the Earth, was subject to corruption and alteration kindled the idea of an inhabited world. Despite Galileo's denial, at least some of his successors believed in the existence of lunar rivers and atmospheric conditions that met the breathing requirements for "lunarians." There remained the persistent question of whether the "plurality of worlds" was a creation in which man played the central role, or whether man was no more than just one species among many in the vast universe. Subsequently, the idea of colonizing the Moon and sending missionaries to its heathen inhabitants went hand in hand with the colonial ambition to be the first nation to raise its flag there. Thus the prestigious space race that ensued between the United States and the Soviet Union in the mid twentieth century had its precursors in an age when a sense of the magical and the burlesque superseded any realistic hope of ever reaching the Moon.

One of the functions of science fiction has been to present analogical worlds with imaginary landscapes in order to expose the existing conditions of contemporary society. Lunar voyages by Cyrano de Bergerac, Jonathan Swift, and H. G. Wells offered an

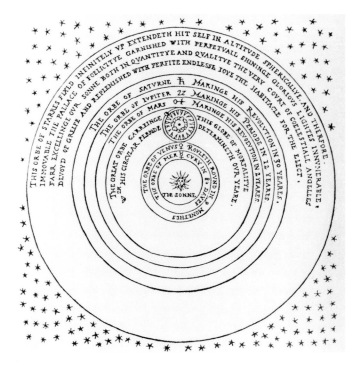

Fig. 2
Copernicus's heliocentric system,
from an English translation
of *De Revolutionibus Orbium
Coelestium (On the revolutions
of the celestial spheres).* 1543

opportunity to make satirical comments on humanity and the pride of individuals who believed themselves the perfection of nature. Especially in the Age of Enlightenment, mock societies on faraway planets served as a quasi-utopian foil against which the deficiencies of life on Earth became even more apparent.

Early science fiction in the seventeenth and eighteenth centuries attempted to reconcile man with the unknown, combining extrapolative or speculative science with transcendental elements. Technical hypotheses, however fantastic, cropped up in tales based on Daniel Defoe's *Robinson Crusoe* (1719), in utopian literature, and in the alternative worlds of satire and didactic tracts. Most science fiction and imaginary voyages promise the crossing of a frontier that opens up a vista of unknown or fabulous circumstances and events. Most stories share a common formal structure that comprises four different stages: the preparation of a journey, the trip itself, the arrival at a destination, and the return to the starting point. This structure not only resembles phases of a pilgrimage (to find the Holy Grail or to some sacred locus), but also mixes the authentic with the miraculous, giving the romance genre a trace of probability. Even if the travel tale was not true, it could happen in the foreseeable future.

If the findings of the "new science" prepared the ground for considering the possibility of cosmic voyages, it was the first English translation of Lucian of Samosata's second-century *True History* in 1634 that helped to make it a literary subject, influencing Cyrano, Swift, and Defoe. Lucian stresses the fictional character of his tale right from the beginning – "I am not telling a word of truth" – thus allowing him to pursue philosophic and satirical aims. Lucian/Ulysses

travels to the Moon by mere accident when his ship reaches the seas beyond the Pillars of Hercules, "a whirlwind suddenly arose, spun the boat about, raised her into the air about three hundred furlongs and did not let her down into the sea again." While still aloft, Lucian and his crew come upon "a great country . . . resembling an island, bright and round and shining with a great light." It becomes clear to the voyagers that the big island hanging in midair must be the Moon. The fantasy that follows describes an encounter with scurrilous types and fairy-tale star wars. The selenites are not dependent on food, men become pregnant and carry the babes in their calves, and when they grow old they do not die but just vanish into thin air. One of the most striking passages, however, deals with spotting another country far below, with cities and rivers and seas and forests and mountains: "This we inferred to be our own world."[3]

Within little more than a decade of the English translation of Lucian's *True History,* literary voyages to the Moon gained considerable popularity. Johannes Kepler's *Somnium, sive de Astronomia Lunaris* (posthumously published in 1634) used the old scheme of the Moon traveler being lifted "by rapture in sleep or in a dream."[4] Duracotus, Kepler's persona as narrator, is carried by demons above the "attractive power" of the Earth, in an early hint of weightlessness. Kepler's description of the Moon transforms Galileo's discoveries into somber images of an antediluvian world full of swamps, caves, and porous rocks. Since the climate shows "bitter change of fierce extremes," life is restricted to strange creatures of a serpentine nature and short-lived vegetation. Although it is obvious that Kepler was still ignorant of Sir Isaac Newton's discoveries, he delineates the lunar landscape with dispassionate interest in scientific detail.

Bishop Francis Godwin's *The Man in the Moone; or, A Discourse of a Voyage thither, by Domingo Gonsales* (1638) declared itself an "ingenious fancy." It bears all the characteristics of a prose romance, welding the fantastic with the realistic to an early sample of science fiction. Domingo Gonsales, the imagined author and hero of the

Fig. 3
Bishop Francis Godwin. *The Man in the Moone; or, A Discourse of a Voyage thither, by Domingo Gonsales.* 1638

tale, tries to harness a flock of wild swans to a "flying chariot" (fig. 3). Quite unexpectedly, they carry him away to the Moon, where, according to an old belief, they fly in order to hibernate. After they have overcome the "attractions" of the Earth and the "sphere of gravity," Gonsales is amazed at the "swiftness of Motion, such as did almost seem to stop my breath" while ascending rapidly to the ever-approaching Moon. If *The Man in the Moone* reflects contemporary scientific ideas, it does so in a way that foreshadows scenes of Stanley Kubrick's *2001: A Space Odyssey* (1968). "Neither I, nor the Engine moved at all, but abode still, as having no manner of weight." Moreover, like many Moon voyages of the time, Godwin's text is an exercise in relativity; the Moon is an opaque body that reflects light but does not emit it, while the Earth assumes "a kind of brightness like another Moon."[5]

Godwin's lunar world, however, bears the traits of simple arcadia where the mental and moral excellence of the inhabitants is in exact proportion to their Brobdingnagian height (Godwin prefigures Swift again when the lunarians are said to live more than a thousand years, like Swift's immortal Struldbruggs). The happy creatures communicate in tunes, that is, some universal language that derives its meanings from various tone pitches. As in most philosophical tales, the traveler from Earth and the lunarians express their mutual surprise at what must appear to be the strangest idiosyncrasies on either side.

Also in 1638, John Wilkins published his lunar treatise, *Discovery of a World in the Moone, or, A Discourse Tending to Prove That 'Tis Probable There May Be Another Habitable World in That Planet, with a Discourse Concerning the Possibility of a Passage Thither*. Again,

it is a semiscientific tract combining the latest knowledge with wild fantasy. Wilkins was one of the most influential members of the Royal Society, advocating the Copernican idea of a heliocentric system. In careful detail, he maintained that some twenty miles beyond the Earth the "sphere of magnetical virtue" ceased to operate, and he estimated the distance to the Moon at 179,712 miles (the actual distance varies between 220,968 and 238,328 miles). He foresaw the problem of creating the initial force to raise a machine, and he exercised rare self-constraint when discussing the possibility of inhabitants on the Moon: "I dare not myself affirm any things of these selenites, because I know not any ground whereon to build any probably opinion. But I think that future ages will discover more, and, our posterity perhaps may invent some means for our better acquaintance with those inhabitants."[6]

Influenced not only by Galileo and Copernicus but also by the recent religious wars that fostered a strong desire for arcadian harmony, the French poet and soldier Cyrano de Bergerac wrote his *Comical History of the States and Empires of the World in the Moon* (1642, published in 1656). Cyrano's Moon is a *locus amoenus* where strife is resolved in philosophic disputes quite differently from the scholastic quarrels on Earth. The lunarians live off the mere smell of food, make payments with poetic verses, and communicate by means of musical notation. However fantastical the tale may be, it features details of astonishing foresight. Cyrano, for example, described his Moon travelers as hardly treading the ground, a prescient anticipation of Newton's theories of gravity, first formulated in 1665–66 and refined in the 1680s. Cyrano also introduced an early prototype of the multistage rocket. When the lunar voyager first throws magnetic bowls filled with morning dew into the air to lift the iron machine by force of attraction, the experiment fails. But when his flying machine is used by silly soldiers for a bonfire, the rockets ignite and fall off as soon as they are burnt (fig. 4).

In the third book of Swift's *Gulliver's Travels* (1726), the float-

Fig. 4
Cyrano de Bergerac. *Comical History of the States and Empires of the World in the Moon.* 1642

ing island of Laputa, "shining very bright from reflection of the sea below," descends from heaven and is governed by the magnetic mainland of Balnibarb below. Laputa is composed of mineral and made to rise and fall by means of "a loadstone of prodigious size."[7] As Nicholson has noted, Swift "neatly turned the tables" by refusing to send his traveler on a voyage through interstellar space and instead transformed the planet into a huge flying chariot peopled by crazy pseudoscientists.

In Daniel Defoe's *The Consolidator; or, Memoirs of Sundry Transactions from the World in the Moon* (1705), a monarch and his entourage make a lunar voyage using "a certain Engine formed in the shape of a Chariot, on the Backs of two vast Bodies with extended Wings, which spread about 50 yards in Breadth, compos'd of Feathers so nicely put together, that no Air could pass. . . . The Cavities were filled with an ambient Flame, which fed on a certain Spirit, deposited in proper quantity to last out the Voyage." Even though Defoe thus anticipates the internal combustion engine, he bridges the inexplicable gaps of the voyage by providing the travelers with a sleeping potion that makes them drowsy until they reach the Moon. They are sent back to Earth by the *"Vis Centrifuga,"* while loosing "the Screw that was fixed to the Moon's Attraction" and traversing "the vast Abyss, or Vacuum between the Moon and us."[8]

In the nineteenth century, scientific plausibility supplanted mere speculation. Edgar Allan Poe claimed for himself "an attempt at *verisimilitude,* in the application of scientific principles." Thus his Moon-travel novelette *The Unparalleled Adventures of Hans Pfaall* (1835) is full of astronomical information (however erroneous) that is typical of the age of positivism. Pfaall frequently uses meteorological instruments, oxygen apparatuses, and even some kind of pressurized cabin.[9] Only fifteen years later, supported by increasingly realistic stories, Thomas Cook, inventor of the package tour, developed the idea of ticket sales for voyages to the Moon.[10]

Poe anticipated Jules Verne's "exact method" in *From the Earth to the Moon Direct in Ninety-Seven Hours and Twenty Minutes* (1865),

in which he depicted the ballistic spaceship fired from a deep hole in Florida. Though the journey lasts 97 hours and 20 minutes, one of the passengers anticipates projectile carriages that allow comfortable traveling in the foreseeable future. Verne does not hold back the more negative attendant phenomena such as mass hysteria, intrigues, sensationalism, and the possibility of technical failure (the travelers miss the landing on the Moon). Like Kepler, he describes the Moon as a dead planet divided into two zones, one of blazing, intense light, the other "dark, dark, dark." Hermann Oberth, one of the pioneers of spacecraft technology, devoured the book as a twelve-year-old, and he honored Verne's farsightedness by naming one of the Moon craters after him. Science fiction could no longer separate the spirit of adventure from technical realism.

Though heavily indebted to Jules Verne, H. G. Wells's "scientific romance" *The First Men in the Moon* (1901) departed from Verne's naive certainties by enriching the fantasies of science fiction with a serious discussion of sociobiological and evolutionary hypotheses. The story has two characters, one a speculator and adventurer, the other a dotty scientist who invents a glass-lined steel globe with a "Caborite" exterior, a material that neutralizes gravitation. Verne balked at the comparison of Wells's work to his:

No, there is no rapport between his work and mine. I make use of physics. He invents. I go to the moon in a cannonball, discharged from a cannon. Here there is no invention. He goes to Mars in an airship, which he constructs of a metal which does away with the law of gravitation. That's all very well but show me this metal.[11]

Wells's trip, however, is not a conjecture for actual space travel but rather a pretext for exploring a place full of beauty and terror. Lush vegetation grows to immense heights in a single lunar day. The selenites erect an alien society based on the vision of ant- or beelike states. Wells shows a fascination for the harmony of the "cosmic garden," but he also warns against the concentration of power in a hermetically closed world.

Figs. 5, 6
Georges Méliès, director. *Le Voyage dans la lune* (*Voyage to the Moon*). 1902

Fig. 7
Fritz Lang, director. Still from *Frau im Mond* (*The Woman in the Moon*). 1929

Subsequent explorations of space in film relied heavily on lunar narratives of the past. Georges Méliès's early *Le Voyage dans la lune* (*Voyage to the Moon*) (1902) still plays with the elements of the fairy-tale and crude comedy, but it employs the new medium to make fun of the new apparatuses, creating awe-inspiring illusions of space machinery and "aéro-buses." Bearded scientists look like magicians, a Follies chorus-line pushes the projectile into a cannon, and the spacecraft finally lands in the eye of the Man in the Moon (figs. 5, 6). Fritz Lang's *Frau im Mond* (*The Woman in the Moon*) (1929) employs the genre elements of a triangle love story, the spy film, and the golddigger melodrama (fig. 7; see plates 2, 3). Lang is reported to have been inspired during a journey in which he slept in a berth no larger than the cockpit of a spaceship. In order to heighten the dramatic suspense, the lifting of the rocket was accompanied by "counting down" instead of "counting up," which, as the story goes, led to the countdown. Despite Lang's cooperation with scientists like Oberth and Willy Ley, the movie is less impressive for its techno-logical vision than for its Art Déco contribution to modern sci-fi design, which reflected a sense of modernity absent from the tale itself.

There have been comparatively few Moon voyages in subsequent decades. *Things to Come* (1936), directed by William Cameron Menzies after a script by H. G. Wells, has become a classic of the sci-fi genre not only because of its overt affirmation of technological progress, but also because of its representation of European modernism. (Producer Alexander Korda and art director Vincent Korda had hired László Moholy-Nagy, later director of the New Bauhaus in Chicago, as a design consultant.) Following a devastating thirty-year-long world war, the twenty-first-century inhabitants of Everytown – a streamlined, underground city of gleaming white – debate the risks and advantages of launching a rocket to the Moon. There is hardly a film from this period that shows the influence of Raymond Loewy's aerodynamic "space cabs" more impressively.

Fig. 8
Irving Pichel, director. *Destination
Moon.* 1950. Set design by Chesley
Bonestell

Fig. 9
Popular Mechanics cover.
May 1950

Destination Moon (1950), directed by Irving Pichel and based
on the novel *Rocketship Galileo* by Robert A. Heinlein, owed much of
its impact to the architectural talents of Ernest Fegte, the special
effects of Lee Zavit (who set Atlanta on fire in *Gone with the Wind*),
and the decorative designs of lunar landscapes of Chesley Bonestell
(see figs. 8, 9). Producer George Pal hired rocketeer Hermann Oberth
to ensure the scientific accuracy of the enterprise. Built upon the
premise that whoever controls the Moon would also control Earth,
the film foreshadowed the Apollo/Sputnik era of competition
between the United States and the Soviet Union. A young industri-
alist organizes and finances a journey to the Moon, "in the name of
the United States and for the benefit of mankind."

In the 1950s, as travel to outer space began to materialize, films
started to reflect the realities of space travel, not just the fantasy of
it. Movies about space travel referred to the threat of nuclear war,
the red scare of communism, and the U.S.'s loss of its monopoly in
space science. By the 1960s and 1970s space reality had become more
exciting than space fiction, at least in regard to lunar journeys. As
the Moon was discovered to be inhospitable to human life, popular
imagination shifted, using the Moon as a mere take-off point and
turning its attention to interstellar expeditions. While the realms of
deep space and cyberspace have provided fertile ground for celluloid
fantasies, they have also at times redirected our attention to the spaceship Earth, and the quality of life here on the beautiful blue planet.

I wish to thank Prof. Hermann J. Real and the
Ehrenpreis Institut für Swift Studien in Münster
for invaluable assistance.

1. Quoted in Ron Miller, *The Dream Machines: An
   Illustrated History of the Spaceship in Art,
   Science and Literature* (Malabar, Fla., 1993), p. 5.
2. Marjorie Hope Nicholson, "Cosmic Voyages,"
   English Literary History 7: 2 (1940), p. 95.
3. Lucian, *Veraie Historiae,* trans. A. M. Harmon, 1
   (London, 1913; repr. Cambridge, Mass., 1961),
   p. 259.
4. John Lear, *Kepler's Dream* (Berkeley, Cal., 1965).
5. Quoted in Nicolson, p. 101.
6. Quoted in Marjorie Hope Nicolson and Nora M.
   Mohler, "Swift's 'Flying Island' in the *Voyage to
   Laputa,*" *Annals of Science* 2 (1937), p. 421.
7. Jonathan Swift, *Gulliver's Travels* (1726), ed.
   Paul Turner (London, 1971), p. 152.
8. Daniel Defoe, *The Consolidator; or, Memoirs of
   Sundry Transactions from the World in the
   Moon* (London, 1705).
9. Edgar Allan Poe, *The Unparalleled Adventures
   of Hans Pfaall*, in *Complete Tales and Poems*
   (New York, 1975), pp. 3–41.
10. Thomas Cook's tour to the Moon is mentioned
    in Sylvia Strasser and Wolfgang Wuerker, *Sonne,
    Mond und Sterne* (Munich, 1996), p. 166.
11. Quoted in "H. G. Wells and His Critics," H. G.
    Wells, *The First Men in the Moon* (London,
    1993), p. 189.

SCOTT W. PALMER

Red Stars and Rocket Ships:

Space Flight and the Cosmos in Early Soviet Culture

With the launch of Sputnik, the first unmanned space mission, in 1957, and Vostok, the first manned vehicle to reach outer space, in 1961, Russia's pioneering postwar space program gained international recognition. The subsequent voyages of the Soyuz and Salyut spacecraft in the 1970s solidified Russia's leading role in space exploration. More recently, the space station *Mir* has dominated international news with reports, first, of its accomplishments as a research base and a testing lab for long-term habitation, and second, of its eventual abandonment. Few people recognize, however, that Soviet culture has sustained a longstanding interest in space dating back to the Bolshevik Revolution at the turn of the century. The years surrounding the Bolshevik uprising of 1917 witnessed a rapid evolution in both the direction and content of Russian culture. The collapse of the Romanov dynasty and the ascension to power of the Bolshevik Party was accompanied by a torrent of social, political, and cultural experiments. At the same time that idealistic leaders of the young Soviet state worked to bring about the immediate transformation of Russia from a backward agrarian nation into a modern industrial state, leading Russian artists and writers sought to realize utopian experiments of their own. An important but little-known aspect of these experiments was the influential role of the cosmos and space flight in shaping contemporary visions of culture and the arts. Although space travel would not become a reality until the 1950s, depictions of space travel flourished as artists and writers used the cosmos to explore the utopian ideals of the early Soviet state.

The origins of Soviet science fiction are conventionally traced to Alexander Bogdanov (1873–1928), a scientist, philosopher, and left-wing political activist who founded the socialist civic-religion of "god-building" in the years that followed the revolution of 1917. Schooled as a physician, Bogdanov proposed a future society organized according to the exact sciences. He elaborated these views in two of Russia's earliest science-fiction novels: *Red Star* (1908) and *Engineer Menni* (1912).

Published nearly a decade before the Bolshevik seizure of power, *Red Star* provided readers with a utopian vision of communism seen through an imaginary account of life on Mars.[1] Combining his idiosyncratic view of science with a liberal dose of ideological didacticism, Bogdanov chronicled the experiences of the Bolshevik activist Leonid, who travels with a Martian companion, Menni, to the red planet. Disheartened by the social inequalities and political repression prevalent in contemporary czarist Russia, Leonid longs to discover a world in which the injustices of modern life have been resolved and peace and harmony reign. He realizes this dream on Mars, where he is treated to a vision of the future in which all social problems have been solved through the application of science and technology.

In Bogdanov's Martian utopia there is no state, nor even a political system. Still, the inhabitants of the planet possess clothing made of synthetic materials, three-dimensional cinema, and a death ray. Martians reside in planned settlements bearing names such as the "City of Machines" and the "Children's Colony," where, in accordance with the Marxist vision of communism, free choice of labor and unlimited consumption are economic realities. Equality, collectivity, and the full emancipation of women are key features of Martian society. Moreover, scientific principles, rather than religion or philosophy, structure the outlook of the planet's inhabitants, and social discord has been resolved through the eradication of rank, deference, and all forms of coercion. The drama of everyday life (once manifested in conflict between individual citizens) is realized by the ongoing collective struggle to master the natural world. To this end, technology provides the Martians with the essential weapons they require to tame the environment. Agricultural production is mechanized and the cultivation of the planet's red "socialist" vegetation provides ample food for its inhabitants.

Red Star provoked a sympathetic response from contemporary Soviet readers. Although the novel predated Russia's communist takeover by almost a decade, it proved most popular after the revo-

Fig. 1
Yakov Protazanov, director. *Aelita.*
1924. Aelita, Queen of Mars, and
Gor, Guardian of Energy, in the
Tower of Radiant Energy, next to
the telescope to Earth

Fig. 2
Yakov Protazanov, director. *Aelita.*
1924. Queen Aelita of Mars in her
Constructivist regalia

lution and was reprinted no fewer than five times. More important, the novel helped to inspire the emerging genre of Soviet science fiction, which, during the decade of the 1920s, witnessed the publication of some two hundred original literary works.[2]

Where Bogdanov's *Red Star* provided Soviet readers with an early literary glimpse into the possibilities of extraterrestrial life, the 1924 feature film *Aelita* (released in the West as *Aelita: Queen of Mars*) supplied Soviet audiences with their first visual images of a fictional cosmos (figs. 1, 2). Based upon a short story originally published by Aleksei Tolstoi, *Aelita* combined interest in outer space with the growing popularity of the new cinematic medium. Directed by Yakov Protazanov (1881–1945), this silent film incorporated innovative set and costume designs derived from contemporary avant-garde styles to create an aesthetically arresting vision of life and politics on another planet. The film is now considered a classic of early Soviet cinema.

Aelita recounts the cosmic exploits of the engineer Loss, who dreams of constructing a rocket ship that will take him to Mars. The film is composed of alternating scenes depicting simultaneous developments on Earth and in space. At home, the engineer suffers through an unhappy domestic life occasioned by frequent spats with his young wife. His marital relationship is further strained by the improper attention given to his spouse by a lecherous capitalist. To escape from his domestic turmoil, Loss immerses himself in the task of constructing a cosmic flying ship. Ultimately, these efforts prove successful and the engineer travels to the red planet, where he encounters the beautiful Martian queen, Aelita. The two fall in love, but trouble soon ensues. Aelita is only a figurehead, controlled from behind the scenes by a cabal of court advisers. These intriguers

oversee the oppression and exploitation of the great Martian proletariat, who are forced to labor like cogs in a machine for the benefit of the planet's ruling class. Upon discovering the desperate plight of the planet's laboring masses, Loss resolves to act. With the help of the queen, he foments a revolution that deposes the advisers and leads to the establishment of socialist harmony on Mars. Following the successful revolution, Loss awakens to find himself back on Earth. His encounter on Mars was only a dream. Stirred from his reverie, the engineer resolves to cast aside his fanciful space project and devote his time instead to repairing his relationship with his wife and contributing to the construction of Soviet society.

In many respects, *Aelita* followed the formula earlier established by *Red Star.* Although the film was less overtly didactic than the Bogdanov novel, its central message concerning the triumph of the workers' revolution over the oppressive forces of capitalism placed it firmly within the canon of the early Soviet Republic's official art. Like many feature films produced during the 1920s, *Aelita* served dual purposes: it was intended to entertain audiences with visions of the cosmos while educating them about the need to develop political consciousness on Earth.[3]

No discussion of space and early Soviet culture can omit Konstantin E. Tsiolkovsky (1857–1935). A secondary- and middle-school teacher from the provincial city of Riazan, Tsiolkovsky is known as the father of Russian astronautics for his important, early speculation on the nature and means of interstellar travel. Long before space flight was a practical reality, Tsiolkovsky wrote a number of farsighted theoretical essays that elucidated principles essential to rocketry. His 1903 essay "On the Exploration of the Cosmos by Means of a Reaction Propelled Apparatus," for example, formulated

Fig. 3
Installation view showing
works by Kazimir Malevich in
The Last Futurist Exhibition. 1915.
The composition *Black Square*
can be seen in the upper corner of
the room

the basic equations necessary for jet-powered flight and accurately described the behavior of rockets in a zero-gravity environment. In addition to producing theoretical treatises and scientific sketches forecasting the possibility of space travel, Tsiolkovsky authored several short stories and literary works, including one of the Soviet period's earliest science-fiction novels, *Outside the Earth* (1920).[4] Although many of his stories were peppered with fantastic descriptions of imaginary extraterrestrial aliens, his scientific and fictional writings also provided prescient visions of the space age to come. Decades before space flight became a reality, Tsiolkovsky correctly described such fundamental concepts as the basics of jet propulsion and the physiological effects of weightlessness. He also forecasted such innovations as space suits, liquid fuel propellants, multistaged rockets, and the mechanics of atmospheric reentry.

Early Soviet images of space exploration and the cosmos were not, however, generated solely by writers and theoreticians. Throughout the 1920s, leading figures in culture and the arts found inspiration in the creative possibilities suggested by outer space and interstellar flight. In the years immediately surrounding the Bolshevik insurrection of 1917, the Russian art world underwent a revolution of its own that witnessed the emergence of eclectic artistic theories and schools such as Rayonism and Constructionism. Initially influenced by the European movements of Cubism and Futurism (which rejected established pictorial conventions in favor of a new aesthetics based on movement, speed, and the reorientation of representational space), Russian avant-garde artists increasingly experimented with color, composition, and new materials in an attempt to break free of the static, two-dimensional world of canvas and paint. In line with contemporary speculation on the potential nature of the extrater-

restrial, many artists and designers incorporated cosmic elements into innovative compositions that challenged traditional notions of spatial relations and suggested the new forms and perspectives that would be experienced by future space travelers.

Of all the new avant-garde artists who contemplated the cosmos, none was more important than Kazimir Malevich (1878–1935). The son of a factory worker, born near the Ukrainian city of Kiev, Malevich studied art at Moscow's College of Painting, Sculpture, and Construction before rising to prominence in the late 1910s as one of the most innovative and controversial of Russia's new breed of painters. Influenced by such contrasting styles as Primitivism, Realism, and Cubism, Malevich soon developed his own experimental theories of art that centered on a concept he identified as "Suprematism." Intending to realize the final stage in the development of painting on canvas, Malevich envisioned Suprematism as a universal system of art that would generate new forms, textures, and colors through the unification of painting and architecture. Ultimately, Suprematism exerted a considerable influence on art within Russia and throughout Europe. From its very inception, ruminations on the nature of space and the incorporation of cosmic aesthetics into composition and design were integral features of the movement.[5]

The debut of Malevich's masterpiece *Black Square* at *The Last Futurist Exhibition* in December 1915 marked the beginning of Suprematism (fig. 3). Consisting of a large black quadrilateral set against a white background, *Black Square* was a complete, radical break with earlier artistic forms that ushered in the modern style of abstract, nonrepresentational painting. In stark contrast to traditional methods of representing space in a pictorial fashion (through the variation of objects or the employment of light and shadow),

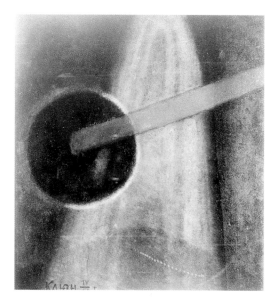

Fig. 4
Ivan Kliun. *Spherical Space*. 1922.
Oil on cardboard, 24 x 21¾ in. State
Tret'iakov Gallery, Moscow, Gift of
George Costakis

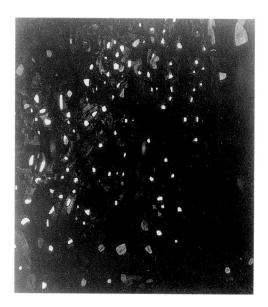

Fig. 5
Boris Ender. *Cosmic Landscape*.
1923. Watercolor on paper,
7⅛ x 6½ in. Collection Zoia Ender-
Masetti, Rome

Black Square utilized the sharp, simple counterpoint of black on white to concentrate space onto a single surface. In effect producing the impression of a spatial infinity opening up into unfathomable darkness, the composition intimated as well the deep void of the cosmos, a fact not lost on Malevich. Although *Black Square* met with mixed reviews by attendees of the exhibition, it soon came to serve as the iconic symbol of the emerging modern art movement.

In addition to spearheading a revolution in artistic aesthetics, Malevich exerted considerable personal influence over the development of numerous Soviet artists. As the director of the State Institute for Artistic Culture in Leningrad from 1923 to 1926, Malevich was instrumental in training a new generation of Soviet painters and graphic designers, many of whom (including El Lissitzky and Nikolai Suetin) openly embraced and expanded upon his theories. Initially patterning their productions after the models established by Malevich, these artists gradually moved away from the absence of perspective that had initially characterized the Suprematist aesthetic towards the use of geometric shapes and the infusion of colors to communicate the sensation of movement through space.

Painter Ivan Kliun (1873–1942) built upon Malevich's artistic theories. A self-taught artist and professor at the First State Free Art Workshops and Higher Artistic Technical Workshops (VKhUTEMAS) in Moscow during the late 1910s and early 1920s, Kliun was responsible for some of the earliest Suprematist works reflecting cosmic themes. His 1922 composition *Spherical Space* (fig. 4), for example, with its nebulaic qualities, hinting at luminous gases and particles of space dust, indicated the presence of a cosmic consciousness that was latent in the designs of many contemporary Russian avant-garde artists. In a similar fashion, Mikhail Plaksin's *Planetary* (1922) and

Boris Ender's *Cosmic Landscape* (1923) intimated the Russian avant-garde's fascination with the extraterrestrial world (fig.5).

If the visual representations depicted in the works of Kliun, Plaksin, and Ender hinted at the role of outer space in the imagination of Soviet artists, then the paintings of Ivan Kudriashev (1896–1972) made explicit the importance of the cosmos in Soviet art of the 1920s. An artist and graphic designer who completed his education under the tutelage of Malevich, Kudriashev was keenly interested in the theories of cosmic flight developed by Tsiolkovsky. A resident of Kaluga province, where Tsiolkovsky taught, Kudriashev had become personally acquainted with the obscure theoretician and corresponded with him for several years. These discussions clearly stimulated Kudriashev's imagination and provided inspiration for a number of innovative artistic creations. Many of his compositions, including *Cosmic Movement* (1924) and *Trajectory of the Earth's Orbit around the Sun* (1926), attempted to serve as visual representations of Tsiolkovsky's scientific conceptions concerning the motion of astral spaces and the dynamics of interstellar light and color (fig. 6).[6]

Notwithstanding his success in leading a revolution in Russian painterly aesthetics, Malevich came to realize that Suprematism had reached a creative terminus. Following the exhibition of his famous "white on white" series in 1918, Malevich withdrew from painting for nearly a decade to devote his energy to the production of what he called an "idealized architecture." Based upon the simple geometric forms that he had pioneered in his early paintings, Malevich's Suprematist architectural projects prefigured the emergence of a new style of architectural design and construction. In much the same way that his nonobjective paintings represented an attempt to break free of the limitations imposed by the two-dimensional

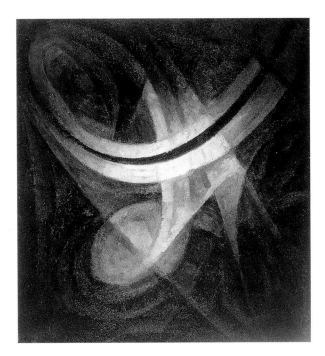

Fig. 6
Ivan Kudriashev. *Trajectory of the Earth's Orbit around the Sun.* 1926. Oil on canvas, 27 x 29¾ in. State Tret'iakov Gallery, Moscow

images produced by canvas and paint, Malevich's architectural experiments represented a reconceptualization of spatial relations that sought to liberate mankind for the possibility of space travel.

Suprematist architecture was built upon the principles provided by a basic form that Malevich called the "architecton." A complex three-dimensional structure that was assembled by joining together smaller geometric subsections, architectons represented Malevich's attempt to fuse the practical concern of the need for living space with an innovative vision of the cosmos. Although these models were limited to two principal variants (one horizontal, the other vertical) by the laws of gravity, Malevich nevertheless envisioned the future construction of extraterrestrial architectons that would provide earthlings with areas of habitation both within and upon the surfaces of these structures. The experimental form of the architecton was clear evidence of Malevich's continuing association of Suprematism with the coming conquest of space. As early as 1920, he went so far as to promote his Suprematist architectural models as the theoretical foundation for a future planetary satellite system, announcing that:

[Between the Earth and the Moon] a new Suprematist satellite can be constructed, equipped with every component, which will move along an orbit shaping its new track. Study of the Suprematist formula of movement leads us to conclude that the rectilinear motion towards any plane can only be achieved by the circling of intermediary satellites, which would provide a straight line of circles from one satellite to another.[7]

Although Malevich's ideas concerning orbiting space satellites produced no practical results, they did inspire a number of his contem-

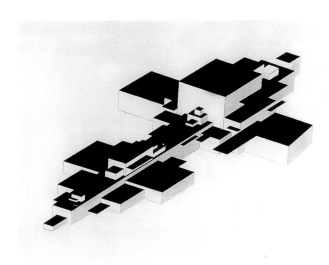

Fig. 7
Il'ya Chashnik. *Design for a Supremolet.* 1927. India ink and pencil on paper, 24⅜ x 30¾ in. Courtesy Leonard Hutton Galleries, New York

poraries to take up the issue of architecture and design for space exploration. Following the lead of his mentor, Malevich, Il'ya Chashnik (1902–1929) devoted considerable time to a series of elaborate sketches of interstellar cities and spaceships. Initially modeling his designs after Malevich's architectons, Chashnik ultimately developed a series of his own cosmic forms called "supremolets," which he incorporated into nearly all of his artistic productions (fig. 7). "Supremolet," a linguistic derivative of the Russian word for airplane (*samolet*), may be roughly translated as "superflyer." More than just the fanciful dreams of a young Soviet artist, these models for space-age constructs bear an uncanny resemblance to modern spacecraft both real and imaginary. In this regard, they suggest the inherent link between the experimental aesthetics of early Soviet artists and the practical designs of contemporary spacecraft.

Early Soviet images of the cosmos and space flight assumed a wide variety of forms. From the revolutionary propaganda of Alexander Bogdanov to the farsighted theories of Konstantin Tsiolkovsky and innovative aesthetics of Kazimir Malevich, political activists, scientists, and artists of differing backgrounds all found inspiration in dreams of outer space. Although these cosmic visions would disappear from public view in the late 1920s, following the rise of Joseph Stalin and the onset of political repression, they remain lasting testaments to the creative impulses and utopian dreams of an earlier, imaginative era in Russia's turbulent history that would be reborn during the postwar period of the 1950s.

1. The novel is available in English translation as part of a three-tale collection that includes the novel's "prequel," *Engineer Menni,* and the short poem "A Martian Stranded on Earth." See Alexander Bogdanov, *Red Star: The First Bolshevik Utopia,* ed. Loren Graham and Richard Stites (Bloomington, Ind., 1984).
2. Richard Stites, "Fantasy and Revolution: Alexander Bogdanov and the Origins of Bolshevik Science Fiction," preface to Bogdanov, *Red Star,* p. 13.
3. For a discussion of the political-educational nature of Soviet cinema during the 1920s, see Peter Kenez, *Cinema and Soviet Society, 1917–1953* (Cambridge, Mass., 1992).
4. *Outside the Earth* can be found in English translation in *The Science Fiction of Konstantin Tsiolkovsky,* ed. David Starchild (Seattle, Wa., 1979).
5. For the best English-language treatment of Malevich's career and the place of cosmic themes in the development of Suprematism, see Larissa Zhadova, *Malevich: Suprematism and Revolution in Russian Art, 1910–1930* (London, 1978).
6. Zhadova, *Malevich,* p. 129 (see n. 19).
7. K[azimir] Malevich, *Suprematism, 34 risunka* (Vitebsk, 1920), p. 2.

DAVID BRODHERSON

Eye on the Sky:

From Astronomy to Astronautics at World's Fairs and Theme Parks

One hundred and fifty years ago, visitors to the first major international fair, the Great Exhibition in the Crystal Palace in London, imagined space through the display of a large telescope and other devices employed in astronomy and celestial navigation (fig. 1). International expositions since 1851 have introduced viewers to the growing field of astronomy through artifacts, demonstrations, and displays.[1] In the eighteenth, nineteenth, and twentieth centuries, the predictability and quantification of the motions of bodies in outer space became useful for an array of endeavors in both the private and public sectors. After the industrial revolution, for instance, telling the time of day or season of the year became increasingly important in coordinating the activities of numerous people involved worldwide in large-scale manufacturing and transportation enterprises. War, commerce, and colonialist expansion all required navigation by the stars across otherwise unmarked oceans. Similarly, mapmaking, essential to Anglo-American exploration, urbanization, and domination of North America, also required measurements based on celestial observation.

With the perfection of a rocket capable of carrying payloads into outer space in the twentieth century, displays of science and engineering at international expositions shifted from astronomical observation and celestial navigation to an emphasis on astronautics or space travel. This shift, a celebration of going into rather than merely looking into space, has appeared in several other aspects of design: research observatories and educational planetaria, murals and sculpture, and amusement rides. By promoting astronomical observation and space travel, these displays, in addition to their value as entertainment, fulfilled numerous purposes: nationalistic, commercial, educational, scientific, political, and even aesthetic.

Opening in Chicago on May Day 1893, the World's Columbian Exposition presented the most diverse display of astronomy of any American fair in the nineteenth century. Foremost among the commercial or educational exhibitors, the recently founded Yerkes Observatory of the University of Chicago showed its already completed forty-inch refracting telescope.[2] The premier American lens-maker,

Fig. 1
The Great Exhibition, Main Avenue,
engraved by N. Bibby from a
daguerreotype by Mayall. J. Tallis
and Co., showing view of telescope
on display in the main hall of the
Crystal Palace, London. 1851

Fig. 2
Henry Ives Cobb. Yerkes
Observatory, University of Chicago,
Williams Bay, Wisconsin. 1897

Alvan G. Clark of Cambridgeport, Massachusetts, ground the "object glass" or main lens. The renowned machine-toolmaker and telescope manufacturer Warner and Swasey of Cleveland, Ohio, mounted the lens.[3] Never before or since has an exhibitor transported such a large, important, and delicate optical instrument for a temporary exhibition. Even today, this telescope, housed at the Yerkes Observatory in Williams Bay, Wisconsin, is the largest instrument of its type (fig. 2). Reflecting the ambiguity and imminent change in the philosophy of science of the 1890s – that astronomy was both part of a liberal arts education and a field of specialization in its own right – the "great refractor" stood in the "Liberal Arts" section of the Manufactures and Liberal Arts Building, designed by architect George B. Post of New York.[4] The telescope sat as prominently as any monumental architectural sculpture, at the terminal vista on the almost-1,280-foot longitudinal axis of Columbia Avenue, the building's main, fifty-foot-wide circulation corridor. The instrument towered over all other displays, enabling fair-goers to see "Chicago's Great Telescope" from almost the whole building.[5]

The master planners of the Columbian Exposition – Daniel H. Burnham, John Root, Frederick Law Olmsted, Henry Codman, and A. Gottlieb – established an adjacent site north of the Manufactures and Liberal Arts Building as a campus for the United States Government to furnish its own buildings and exhibits.[6] Commodore R. W. Meade suggested that the navy occupy another set of buildings adjacent to this parcel.[7] Architect James Windrim, who had worked on the Government Building at the Philadelphia Centennial Exposition, began design of this complex; W. J. Edbrooke, supervising architect in the Treasury Department, replaced Windrim during construction. This work included three small buildings for the United States Naval Observatory: a transit house containing instruments employed to help quantify planetary or satellite movement and determine latitude; an observatory protecting a telescope used in astronomical observations; and a heliograph, a signaling device that used the sun to

send pulses of light in Morse code.[8] These stood near the shore of Lake Michigan and the mouth of the fairground's North Lagoon. The navy "detailed" Lieutenant Winterhalter to oversee and install the exhibits in the three buildings.[9] Under the scrutiny of the curious, crews recorded "observations . . . taken chronometrically, astronomically, and nautically, of the celestial bodies and heavenly phenomena."[10] The observatory, which was the keeper of time for the exposition, employed an unusually accurate electrical clock in its headquarters in the United States capital. From there, the clock transmitted an electric signal via Western Union to the Government Building at the fair, causing "time balls," designed by W. F. Gardner of the observatory, to drop exactly at noon Central Standard Time. One of the three structures, a forty-foot building, housed relics including a ship's chronometer from an 1872 Arctic expedition led by C. F. Hall, as well as photographs and other displays.

The observatory on the Lake Michigan shore, shaped like a cylinder capped by a hemisphere, offered the public an unusual opportunity to use a five-inch equatorial telescope. The fair's observatory staff counted 22,698 people using instruments to view the sun in a month during daylight and another 3,000 observing the heavens at night.[11] To commemorate their visit, fairgoers could purchase any of the many photographic prints of the fair, or the more than one thousand stereographs of the fair from licensed concessionaires, and perhaps even a stereograph of the Moon, such as N. W. Pease's "Full Moon" (fig. 3). Stereographs of the Moon had been widely circulated since the 1850s, and were promoted for their educational as well as entertainment value. In addition to being sold as souvenirs at world's fairs, they were also circulated by mail order, vendors, and shops. A stereoscope is usually and ideally made with two cameras, eye-width apart, or a double-lensed camera, so that when viewed through a stereoscope viewer, a binocular, three-dimensional vision of the subject is produced. In the case of stereographs of the Moon, either two cameras had to be placed a great distance apart –

Fig. 3
N. W. Pease. *Full Moon,* from
the *America Scenery* series.
ca. 1868–78. Albumen stereograph,
3 x 6⅛ in. The Art Institute of
Chicago, Gift of Robert Jesmer

many miles, rather than inches – or a single camera could be used to take pictures over a period of time. Pease's stereoscope of the full Moon was produced roughly between 1868 and 1878, and the pictures appear to have been taken one month apart. Stereograph displays (featuring stereographs and viewers) were frequently placed alongside telescope displays at world's fairs, allowing viewers to look down at a three-dimensional image of the Moon and then look up at the actual Moon through a telescope.[12]

In addition to commercial, educational, and government displays and demonstrations of artifacts and achievements in theoretical and applied astronomy, fair architects incorporated references to the sciences in buildings throughout the exposition through murals, inscriptions, and sculpture. At another location at the Columbian Exposition, John J. Boyle, sculptor for the Transportation Building, designed by Dankmar Adler and Louis Sullivan, represented existing practice in nautical astronomy and added elements presaging achievements in aeronautics and astronautics. The sculptural program for the building, for instance – which was rigorous, classical, and allegorical – narrated the history of transportation. Four major sculpture groups representing four modes of transportation adorned the east side of the building. One of these near the center was a female figure leaning against the wheel of a ship and holding a sextant, an instrument for celestial navigation, in her left hand. In his final report as director of works, Burnham described Boyle's depiction of air travel, the third mode of transportation in the series:

The third group is that of Air, depicted by a youth, standing on an eminence, surveying a globe. . . . On the right is a youth stretching his arms above his head, the attitude of one who is striving for better results; on the left is a youth who, seated on a chimerical flying machine, holds a balloon. This group is representative of futurity and not of actual results, for the time of secure aerial transportation is yet in the dim future.[13]

Single figures stood on the north and south elevations near entrances; one portrayed one of the Montgolfier Brothers, who invented and tested the hot-air balloon in a series of flights in 1783 and 1784. Although at least two balloon ascensions occurred at the fair, designers were skeptical about the technology of flight becoming widespread soon.

With a conservative outlook upon the present and future state of transportation, fair designers were pessimistic about the imminence of aeronautics and astronautics.[14] Yet Burnham and his colleagues admired the appearance of Boyle's sculpture group and somewhat contradictorily approved of this theme in the broader historical context of the whole sculpture program. This attitude is surprising at an event that, in part, was to offer visions of the future. Burnham and his staff called the sculpture program a "highly successful . . . glorification of the evolution of transportation; a climax beginning with the most primitive mode of travel and ending with only the scene of comfort and speed." These remarks indicate that although fair designers were realistic or uncertain about when air transportation would materialize, they were still confident in the future of this means of travel. However, they expressed greater confidence in the conventional, slower-moving, reliable ocean steamship, locomotive, and electric motor as the "best means of modern transportation."[15] Burnham's approval of the sculpture program for the Transportation Building, albeit ambiguous, contrasts with his extreme disapproval of the appearance of the installations inside the Manufactures and Liberal Arts Building, where the University of Chicago displayed its huge telescope. There Burnham criticized the "incongruity of arrangements."[16] Surely the extreme diversity of objects exhibited, the competing styles of their display, and the lack of authority over installation design by individual exhibitors led to his unease about the eventual appearance of the bulding's interior.

The decorative program for Richard Morris Hunt's Administration Building included astronomy-related inscriptions in eight panels

Fig. 4
Pan-American Exposition, Buffalo,
"A Trip to the Moon." 1901

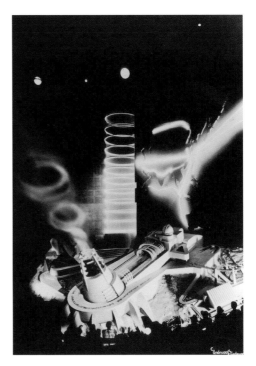

Fig. 5
Raymond Loewy. Rocket Gun at
the New York World's Fair.
1939–40

that set current scientific discoveries within the context of astronomy. These panels depicted "Eight Eras of Scientific Discovery," two of which were defined by events in astronomy. In the fourth period, "Copernicus explained his theory of the Solar System in 1543." In the following era, "Newton published his discovery of the laws of gravitation in 1687." A frieze above the gallery in this building listed five of the world's great astronomers: Claudius Ptolemy, Nicolaus Copernicus, Galileo Galilei, Johannes Kepler, and Sir William Herschel.[17] Copernicus's concept of our solar system, for example, initially published in 1543 as *De Revolutionibus Orbium Coelestium,* overturned the centuries-old Ptolemaic view that the Earth was the center of our planetary system. This theory of a heliocentric system, which by the time of the World's Columbian Exposition was universally accepted, albeit slightly modified by Kepler, had two major ramifications. First, it overturned the geocentric belief, which had been elevated almost to a tenet of Christian dogma, in which the Earth was a symbol of creation. Second, this theory, although modified, became a factual foundation of all planetary science.

Following examples set by nineteenth-century expositions, commercial, educational, and government sponsors continued to promote astronomy through displays of artifacts, demonstrations of various kinds, the design of special buildings, and landscape architecture at fairs throughout the twentieth century.[18] At the same time, the vision and reality of astronautics, or travel, into outer space began to appear at expositions. An amusement ride on the midway of the

1901 Pan-American Exposition, "A Trip to the Moon," was one of the first to shift from astronomy to astronautics for its theme (fig. 4). The main elevation of the asymmetrical building housing the fantasy simulation was a combination of architectural folly and the Spanish Colonial Revival style. A mockup of the airship *Luna* sat on the roof of the building. The exterior of the *Luna* was similar to the typical artist's two-dimensional fantasy of flight of the era – although lacking a propeller, a hybrid of fixed-wing aircraft and lighter-than-air ship. Riders toured the stars and planets in the ship while reclining in steamer chairs and listening to "sweet strains of music." As it approached the Moon, the craft passed through a "sea of sunlit clouds." Guides greeted arriving travelers and led them to an "underground city." Tourists encountered "hordes of queer people . . . [then] the palace of the Man in the Moon, where all are entertained with a revel of the 'Maids of the Moon.'" A Mr. Hugh Thomas and his assistants produced elaborate "electrical effects," which, through some sort of optical projection system, mimicked clouds and simulated or illuminated other anticipated scenes in sequence. This included an electrically created illusion of the *Luna.* The ride, designed by Frederic W. Thompson, an architecture school dropout who claimed to have designed all the principal midway buildings at the Pan-American fair, was one of the leading attractions at the fair. At the close of the fair, Thompson planned to bring the ride to Steeplechase Park at Coney Island in Brooklyn, New York. After a dispute with George Tilyou, the owner of Steeplechase Park, however, Thompson

Fig. 6
Century of Progress Exposition,
Chicago, Electrical Building, detail
of exterior showing "Stellar
Energy" by Ulric Ellerhusen. 1933

Fig. 7
Century of Progress Exposition,
Chicago, high-altitude balloon
ascension at Soldier Field. 1933

designed Luna Park with a similar amusement ride at an adjacent site.[19] Thompson, arguably the Walt Disney of the era, also designed features for the St. Louis Louisiana Purchase Exposition of 1904.

The Depression was a particularly rich decade of expositions with fantasy visions of travel into outer space, in addition to displays documenting actual attempts at flight into the stratosphere. Federal and local governments as well as private businesses expected such large-scale enterprises to stimulate moribund economies and abate the effects of the Depression. The Century of Progress Exposition of 1933–34 in Chicago, the Texas Centennial Exposition of 1936 in Dallas, and the New York World's Fair of 1939–40 (fig. 5) were among these endeavors. Unlike major expositions later in the 1930s, planning for the Century of Progress had begun before the onset of the Depression. Architects Harvey Wiley Corbet and Louis Skidmore oversaw the master plan and architecture of the Century of Progress, which ran for two seasons in 1933 and 1934 (figs. 6–9). Raymond Hood, Ralph Walker, Paul Philippe Cret, Arthur Brown, John Holabird, Edward H. Bennett, and Hubert Burnham assisted.[20] With the advice of Henry Crew, professor of physics at Northwestern University and chair of the fair's Science Advisory Committee, planners decided that the "magnificent" Adler Planetarium, designed by Ernest A. Grunsfeld, Jr., exhibited astronomy so thoroughly that the Hall of Science need not include displays of astronomy (see plate 4). They also agreed with South Park commissioners that the planetarium would be a fee-charging concession. Finally, they felt that incorporation of Chicago's

museums into the fairgrounds "would lend grace and dignity" to the event. To emphasize this relationship and the importance of astronomy as well as other sciences, planners created a major entrance at the north end of the grounds with an east-west circulation axis – a boulevard – terminating at the Adler Planetarium. Sky shows in particular at the planetarium were so popular that, even before the 10:00 A.M. opening, long lines formed for this lecture-demonstration. To accommodate more visitors, the planetarium lecturers shortened the show from one hour to forty minutes.[21] The Hall of Science displayed more historical models and drawings of the sixteenth-century observatories employed by the great Danish astronomer Tycho Brahe, as well as the "Buck Rogers in the 25th Century" show, which was based on the popular book from 1928, and comic strip and radio show, which ran from 1932 to 1940 (fig. 9).

Even though the nearby Adler Planetarium was the main exposition site for exhibitions of applied and theoretical astronomy,[22] the Hall of Science, designed by Cret, housed a craft that marked an important step in travel into outer space: Professor Auguste Piccard's gondola, which rose over 53,000 feet into the stratosphere. Piccard, the inventor of the 300-pound aluminum gondola, and fellow scientist Max Cosyns made their record-breaking flight on August 18, 1932, in order to study cosmic rays emanating from outer space and other phenomena of the upper atmosphere. Cret, who also designed the installation, brilliantly suspended the gondola directly over William Beebe's globular bathysphere in the building's Great Room.

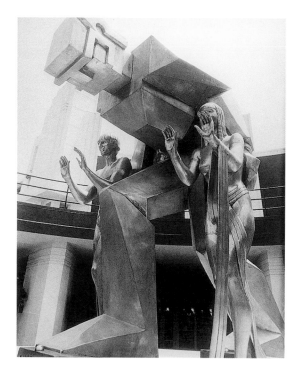

Fig. 8
Century of Progress Exposition,
Chicago, Hall of Science, detail showing *Science Advancing Mankind,*
by Louise Lentz Woodruff. 1933

Fig. 9
"Buck Rogers" attraction at
the Century of Progress Exposition,
Chicago. 1934

The architect located the two disparate artifacts of exploratory science at the north end of the hall on its main axis. His design created a
prominent and extraordinary contrast of shapes and of the sciences
that were plumbing the frontiers of knowledge of the sea and the
edge of space. Also included in the Great Room of the Hall of
Science during the second year of the exposition were a cutaway
model and scientific instruments from a later flight of the balloon
Century of Progress, which navy Lieutenant Commander T. G. W.
Settle and marine corps reservist Major Chester L. Fordney guided to a
record-breaking height of more than 61,000 feet into the upper
atmosphere on November 20, 1933.

In contrast with the completed flights of Piccard, Cosyns, Settle,
and Fordney represented at the Chicago exposition, architectural
murals narrating the history of transportation and a theme ride at the
Texas Centennial Exposition of 1936 both interpreted the future
of astronautics. The 1936 exposition was not an official world's fair,
but it was a major event visited by more than six million people.
When the fair was reincarnated in 1937 as the Greater Texas and Pan
American Exposition, another seven million came.[23] Although the
Dallas fair concentrated on state themes of "Cattle, Cotton, and
Oil," the event also acknowledged issues of worldwide importance,
such as new developments in rocketry. As earlier in Chicago and
later at the New York World's Fair, the Dallas fair boasted murals –
here, adorning the Transportation Building – that narrated the history
of transportation (fig. 10). Dallas architect George Dahl supervised

master planning and design of the building; its location on a main
axis of circulation near the entrance assured its high visibility and
that of its six murals. Dahl had invited the painter Carlo Ciampaglia,
educated at Cooper Union in New York and winner of the Prix de
Rome in 1920, to undertake these and other murals.[24] Ciampaglia's
Art Deco-influenced paintings portrayed attenuated and stylized
muscular figures flanking a Jules Vernian space vehicle rocketing
upward from the Earth. In 1936, *Architectural Forum* described Dahl's
building as "bold and strong; a quality possessed to an unusual
degree by the residents of Texas and the Southwest." The journal
called the fair a "stylistic miscegenation," although it praised certain parts of it. Whatever the case, the "bold and strong" forms of
the building exteriors provided an ideal surface for Ciampaglia's
murals and other surface details. Continuing the theme of transportation, at the southern corner of the exposition was a midway,
where a concessionaire constructed the "Rocket Ride," also known
as the "Rocket Speedway." Imported from England especially for
the fair, the Rocket Ride's simulated journey into space left patrons
"breathless" even though it lasted only a few seconds.[25]

After World War II and during the cold war, travel into outer space
became a reality. Motivated by scientific, nationalistic, and military
goals, the Union of Soviet Socialist Republics beat the United States
into outer space with the launch of *Sputnik 1* on October 4, 1957.
Numerous rockets carrying instrumented satellites and capsules
transporting dogs – and, finally, humans – followed.[26] Consequently,

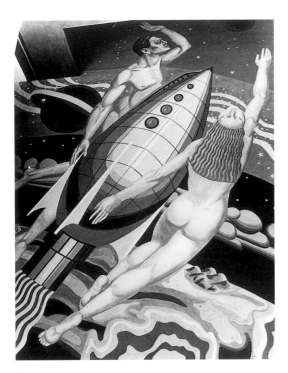

Fig. 10
Carlo Ciampaglia. Transportation
Building mural. Texas Centennial
Exposition, Dallas. 1936

Fig. 11
Postcard showing a model of
Sputnik 2 on display at the Brussels
World's Fair. 1958

the Soviets celebrated this victory at the 1958 Brussels World's Fair, where they showed a model of *Sputnik 2* and other artifacts related to exploration of this "new frontier" (fig. 11).[27] Nevertheless, this exhibition paled in contrast with displays at subsequent fairs; and almost every fair since 1958 has had at least one major exhibit of the equipment and exploits of astronauts and cosmonauts.[28] In January 1958, a United States Jupiter-C missile propelled the *Explorer 1* satellite into space; a failed American launch of the Vanguard satellite followed the next month. Despite the early well-known failures of the American rocket and space programs, the country began celebrating its accomplishments in space exploration over a period of less than four years. Although the Soviets continued to achieve feats in space exploration since the last fair, they refused to participate in the New York World's Fair of 1964–65. To supplement the astronomy displays, Americans prominently exhibited mock-ups, some full scale, and real artifacts of rockets, astronaut capsules, and satellites such as the Saturn V, Mercury, *Gemini 4,* and Tiros, as well as the X-15 airplane (fig. 12). These were displayed in a two-acre Space Park designed by the landscape architecture firm Clarke and Rapuano.[29] Even with the warming of the cold war and the abatement of nationalistic agendas, this new emphasis on space travel continued to supplement and even supplanted fair displays of astronomy.

Whether looking or traveling into the cosmos, scientists and laymen alike have been attracted to the skies for millennia. Many civilizations have regarded cosmologists as priests, scientists, or

explorers. For approximately two millennia explorers, cartographers, geographers, philosophers, sculptors, and scientists have built models of our planet and its relationship to other bodies in space. International expositions, fairs, planetaria, and amusement parks in the nineteenth and twentieth centuries incorporated these astronomical and astronautical discoveries into all aspects of their architectural designs. In turn, these fairs, parks, and amusements helped elevate the stature of astronauts. In fact, a 1999 *Wall Street Journal/NBC News* poll ranked former astronaut and senator John Glenn well above other social and political leaders such as Reverend Jesse Jackson, Christian Coalition president Pat Robertson, President and Mrs. Bill Clinton, and Governor George W. Bush.[30] Although we readily heroicized astronauts as jet jockeys blasting into the unknown, the dangerous reality of space travel contradicts our romantic image. Unlike the first cowboys of the constellations, today's space travelers must be skilled scientists whether their craft are remote-controlled or self-controlled. Almost half a century after humans first traveled on Sputnik, outer space remains both a physical and an intellectual frontier. That astronomy and astronautics have played such a prominent role in the conception and design of international expositions testifies to the importance of the theme of space exploration in discourse of humankind's future. Nothing can compare to the thrill of traveling to space, but the designers of expositions, planetaria, museums, and amusement parks have been trying to convey that thrill, at least vicariously, in their work for 150 years.

Fig. 12
United States Space Park, New York World's Fair, designed by landscape architecture firm Clarke and Rapuano. 1964–65

1. William Whewell, "Lecture I: The General Bearing of the Great Exhibition on the Progress of Art and Science," in Society of Arts, Manufactures, and Commerce, *Lectures on the Results of the Great Exhibition of 1851 Delivered before the Society of Arts, Manufactures, and Commerce at the Suggestion of H. R. H. Prince Albert, President of the Society* (London, 1852), pp. 21–22; James Glaisher, "Lecture IX: Philosophical Instruments, and Processes," in ibid., pp. 327, 328, 337–40, 347–49, 393–96; A. T. Goshorn, *[United States Centennial Commission]: Report of the Director-General, Including the Reports of the Bureau of Administration* 1 (Washington, D.C., 1880), pp. 62, 108, 115, 590–91, 612, and "Synopsis of the Classification," p. 640; Francis A. Walker, *Centennial Exposition. International Exhibition, 1876. Reports and Awards, Groups XXI–XXVII* 7 (Washington, D.C., 1880), pp. 325–26, 384–86, 400–02, 487, 490; Francis A. Walker, *Centennial Exposition. International Exhibition, 1876. Reports and Awards, Groups XXVIII–XXXVI, and Collective Exhibits* 8 (Washington, D.C., 1880), pp. v, vi, 42–44, 49, 52–56, 75, 161, 326, 343.

2. Henry Ives Cobb designed the observatory in a Romanesque Revival style; it was built by the newly established university after the exposition, in 1895–97. D. J. R. Bruckner and Irene Macauley, eds., *Dreams in Stone: The University of Chicago* (Chicago, 1976), pp. 256–71.

3. During a study trip of European observatories, Hale prepared specifications for Cobb's design. For a complete history of the planning, design, and construction of the observatory, see George E. Hale, "Minor Contributions and Notes," *Astrophysical Journal* 3 (Mar. 1896), pp. 213–19; George E. Hale, "The Yerkes Observatory of the University of Chicago: I. Selection of the Site," *Astrophysical Journal* 5 (Mar. 1897), pp. 164–80; George E. Hale, "The Yerkes Observatory of the University of Chicago: II. The Building and Minor Instruments," *Astrophysical Journal* 5 (Apr. 1897), pp. 254–67.

4. John W. Reps, *The Making of Urban America: A History of City Planning in the Untied States* (Princeton, N.J., 1965), pp. 497–502; Moses P. Handy, ed., *The Official Directory of the World's Columbian Exposition May 1st to October 30, 1893: A Reference Book of the Exhibitors and Exhibits of the Officers and Members of the World's Columbian Commission, the World's Columbian Exposition and the Board of Lady Managers: A Complete History of the Exposition. Together with Accurate Descriptions of All State, Territorial, Foreign, Departmental and Other Buildings and Exhibits, and General Information Concerning the Fair* (Chicago, 1893), pp. 224, 366.

5. *Photographs of the World's Fair: An Elaborate Collection of Photographs of the Buildings, Grounds and Exhibits of the World's Columbian Exposition* (Chicago, 1893), pp. 43, 65.

6. Daniel H. Burnham, *The Final Official Report of the Director of Works of the World's Columbian Exposition, in Two Parts,* 1, *Report of the Director of Works* (repr. New York, 1989), p. 36.

7. *Annual Report of the Secretary of the Navy for the Year 1893* (Washington, D.C., 1893), p. 58.

8. Burnham, *The Final Official Report of the Director . . .* 1, p. 58; William E. Cameron, *The World's Fair, Being a Pictorial History of the Columbian Exposition Containing a Complete History of the World-Renowned Exposition at Chicago; Captivating Descriptions of the Magnificent Buildings and Marvelous Exhibits, Such as Works of Art, Textile Fabrics, Machinery, Natural Products, the Latest Inventions, Discoveries, Etc. Etc. with a Description of Chicago, its Wonderful Buildings, Parks, Etc. Embellished with Hundreds of Beautiful Engravings* (Chicago, 1893), p. 472.

9. *Annual Report of the Secretary of the Navy for the Year 1894* (Washington, D.C., 1894), p. 113. In contrast with Burnham's report and Cameron's book, above-noted, pages 111–12 of *Annual Report of the Secretary of the Navy for the Year 1894* credits one F. W. Grogan as "architect of the naval exhibit and principal naval technical expert;" the annual report also explains that Windrim reviewed the plan and found it "original . . . and perfectly practicable."

10. Cameron, *The World's Fair . . .*, p. 485.

11. *Annual Report of the Secretary of the Navy for the Year 1894,* pp. 113–17.

12. See Julie K. Brown, *Contesting Images: Photography and the World's Columbian Exposition* (Tucson and London, 1994). See also Britt Salvesen, "Selling Sight: Stereoscopy in Mid-Victorian Britain," Ph.D. diss., University of Chicago, 1997.

13. Burnham, *The Final Official Report of the Director . . .* 4, pp. 7–9.

14. Ibid., pp. 78, 93, 97.

15. Ibid., p. 7, but see also pp. 8–9.

16. His disapproval was sufficiently intense to make this a larger font or a subtitle or section heading in the Report. Daniel H. Burnham, *The Final Official Report of the Director . . .* 1, p. 15.

17. Presumably Sir William Herschel, although the report does not specify. Ibid., pp. 72–73.

18. See, for example, [Charles Ahrhart], *Official Catalogue and Guide Book to the Pan-American Exposition with Maps of Exposition and Illustrations, Buffalo, N. Y. U. S. A.* (Buffalo, N.Y., 1901), pp. 111–13; Paul Elder, ed., *The Architecture and Landscape Gardening of the Exposition: A Pictorial Survey of the Most Beautiful Architectural Compositions of the Panama-Pacific International Exposition* (San Francisco, 1915), pp. 11, 106, 108, 110, 116; Lenox R. Lohr, *A Guide for Future Fairs: Fair Management –*

The Story of a Century of Progress Exposition (Chicago, 1952), pp. 43, 51; [Century of Progress Exposition Corporation], *Official Guidebook of the Fair 1933* (Chicago, 1934), pp. 42–43, 161; Century of Progress International Exposition, *Official Guidebook of the World's Fair of 1934* (Chicago, 1934), pp. 30, 34, 46, 64; [Century of Progress International Exhibition], *Official Catalog of Exhibits in the Division of the Basic Sciences: Hall of Science* (Chicago, 1933), pp. 19, 52, 133; Jewett E. Ricker, ed., *Sculpture at a Century of Progress: Chicago 1933* (Chicago, 1933), pp. 6–9, 12, 13; Exposition Publications Inc., *Official Guidebook: New York World's Fair 1939* (New York, 1939), pp. 44, 52–54, 148, 174–78; James T. Burns, "P/A Observer: The Busy Architect's Guide to the World's Fair," *Progressive Architecture* 45 (Oct. 1964), pp. 225, 233–35.

19. Ahrhart, *Official Catalogue and Guide Book to the Pan-American Exposition . . .*, pp. 44, 94, 96; Mark Bennitt [ed.], *The Pan-American Exposition and How to See It, A Complete Art Souvenir Edited with a Condensed Guide to Buffalo and Niagara Falls,* Union News Edition (Buffalo, N.Y., 1901); photocopies of clippings from untitled newspapers, "Frederic W. Thompson" and "Trip to the Moon," courtesy of Cynthia VanNess, Special Collections, Buffalo and Erie County Public Library; [Frederic Thompson], *A Trip to the Moon via the Airship Luna* (Buffalo, N.Y., 1901), unpag. For a survey of fair art and architecture, see Joann Marie Thompson, "The Art and Architecture of the Pan-American Exposition, Buffalo, New York, 1901" (Ph.D. diss., Rutgers University, 1980); for brief narratives about Thompson and the "Trip to the Moon" at Coney Island, see Rem Koolhaas, *Delirious New York: A Retroactive Manifesto for Manhattan* (New York, 1978), pp. 32–39, and Richard Snow, *Coney Island: A Postcard Journey to the City of Fire* (New York, 1984), pp. 78, 80-86. The "Trip to Mars by Aeroplane" replaced or supplemented the "Trip to the Moon" at Luna Park.

20. For a brief overview of the history of plans for the Century of Progress Exposition, see Erik Mattie, *World's Fairs* (New York, 1998), pp. 160–65.

21. Lenox R. Lohr, *A Guide for Future Fairs: Fair Management. The Story of a Century of Progress Exposition* (Chicago, 1952), pp. 43, 55, 120, 171.

22. [Century of Progress International Exposition], *Official Guide Book of the World's Fair of 1934,* p. 182; [Century of Progress International Exhibition], *Official Catalog of Exhibits in the Division of the Basic Sciences: Hall of Science,* pp. 10, 14–15, 133; [Century of Progress Exposition], *Official Handbook of Exhibits in the Division of the Basic Sciences, Hall of Science* (Chicago, 1934), pp. 28, 30; Malcolm McDowell, "Gondola of Balloon That Penetrated Stratosphere Will Be Exhibited Here," *Daily News* (Dec. 13, 1932), unpag.; Tyrrell Krum, "A New Stratosphere Record," *Popular Aviation* (Feb. 1933), pp. 89–90. Cret likely was the installation designer in the Hall of Science although I have not yet been able to confirm this in a source supplementary to [Century of Progress International Exhibition], *Official Catalog of Exhibits in the Division of the Basic Sciences: Hall of Science.* I wish to thank Mary Ann Bamberger and John Zukowsky for sharing Century of Progress material with me.

23. David Dillon, *Dallas Architecture, 1936–1986* (Austin, Tex., 1986), p. 196.

24. Willis Winters, AIA, Manager, Planning Design and Construction, Parks and Recreation Department, Dallas, first made me aware of the transportation murals and generously provided me with a photograph of the murals and a copy of an untitled, anonymous, unpublished, summary biography of Ciampaglia, who also had painted at the Chicago Century of Progress Exposition, and copies of other unpublished documents. Ciampaglia's murals are currently being restored. See also "Forum of Events: Texas Centennial Exposition," *Architectural Forum* 65 (July 1936), pp. 9, 62.

25. [Texas Centennial Central Exposition], *The Official Guide Book: Texas Centennial Exposition, June 6, 1936–Nov. 29* ([Dallas], 1936), esp. the pp. that were inserted between pp. 12–13, 31–38, 98, 102.

26. For an excellent history of the space race, see Martin J. Collins and the Division of Space History, *Space Race: The U.S.–U.S.S.R. Competition to Reach the Moon* (San Francisco, 1999).

27. "Expo 58," *Architectural Review* 124 (Aug. 1958), pp. 86, 96; "Architecture at Brussels: Festival of Structure," *Architectural Record* 123 (June 1958), pp. 166, 167; "A Selection of Pavilions Being Erected for the Brussels Exhibition 1958," *Builder* 193 (Aug. 23, 1957), pp. 31, 314; "Brussels 1958," *Architects' Journal* 127 (May 29, 1958), pp. 828–30.

28. See, for example, "Century 21: Seattle World's Fair," *Interior Design* 33 (Mar. 1962), pp. 132–34; Mary Brown, "Century 21 Exposition," *Industrial Design* 9 (June 1962), p. 81; "Soaring Ribbed Vaults to Dominate Yamasaki's Design for Seattle Fair," *Architectural Record* 128 (Aug. 1960), p. 147; "'Lagoon Nebula' Will Star in Spacearium Adventure," *Boeing News* 8 (Feb. 1962), p. 1; "Progressive Architecture News Report: Astronarium-Science Center Proposed for World's Fair," *Progressive Architecture* 42 (May 1961), p. 47; Richard Haitch, "Fair's Space Park 'Tutors' Visitors," *New York Times* (June 14, 1964), p. 79; "Boat Tail," *Boeing News* (Apr. 23, 1964), pp. 1–2; "Satellite to Carry Fair's First Day," *New York Times* (Apr. 12, 1964), sec. 1, p. 84; Warren Weaver, Jr., "U. S. to Show Rockets and Space Vehicles at Fair," *New York Times* (Mar. 9, 1964), p. 3; [Ellen Perry and James T. Burns], "P/A Observer: The Busy Architect's Guide to the World's Fair," *Progressive Architecture* 45 (Oct. 1964), pp. 224–25, 233, 235; Peter Collins, "Expo—and After," *Canadian Architect* 11 (Oct. 1966), pp. 57, 60–61, 68–69; "Bucky's Biggest Bubble," *Architectural Forum* 124 (June 1966), pp. 74–79; "P/A News Report: Cambridge Seven Reveal U.S. Exhibit Plans for Montreal Fair," *Progressive Architecture* 47 (Sept. 1966), pp. 53–54; Editorial Committee of the Second Architectural Convention of Japan, *Structure Space Mankind Expo '70: A Photographic Interpreter,* II (Osaka, Japan, 1970), pls. 78, 126.

29. New York Public Library, Manuscripts and Archives Division, New York World's Fair, 1964–65, Printed Matter, [Fair Corporation], *New York World's Fair, 1964–1965: Information Manual,* photocopy (New York, 1964–65), unpag.; ibid., General Files, Participation Brochures, Museums-U.S. Space Park, press release, "U.S. Space Park" (Apr. 6, 1964).

30. Elizabeth Crowley, "Standard-Bearers? It's the Astronauts, Not the Presidents," *Wall Street Journal* (June 24, 1999), sec. A, p. 10.

Conflict and the
Conquest of Space

View of launch from Test Stand VII,
Peenemünde, Germany. 1943

11
Baugruppe Schlempp. Rendering
of Test Stand VII, Peenemünde,
Germany. Begun 1937

12
Baugruppe Schlempp. Rendering
of Model Factory, Peenemünde,
Germany. Begun 1937

13
Test Stand VII, Peenemünde,
Germany. 1941

14
Klaus Riedel, design leader.
Mobile launch platform. 1945

The V-2 was the world's first long-range ballistic missile. It was initially launched on October 3, 1942. Its famous development facilities at Peenemünde, Germany, were planned and constructed in the mid to late 1930s. After Allied bombing in 1943–44, production was moved to an underground factory in the Kohnstein Mountain in 1944 under the supervision of the SS, or Shützstaffel. Thousands of concentration camp inmates died excavating the caves and working in this factory. Although Hitler and his chief architect and minister of armaments, Albert Speer, originally endorsed the creation of stationary, reinforced-concrete bunkers in occupied France for the launch of V-2s, these not-yet-finished sites were bombed and then overrun by the Allies in the summer of 1944. When mobile launch vehicles and platforms were also developed and adapted from existing vehicles, such as the Krauss-Maffei Km no.11 half-track with an armored launch cabin, the V-2 became the ancestor of today's Scud missiles, which were used in the Gulf War of 1991. The mobile launch platform in plate 14 was designed under the leadership of Klaus Riedel.

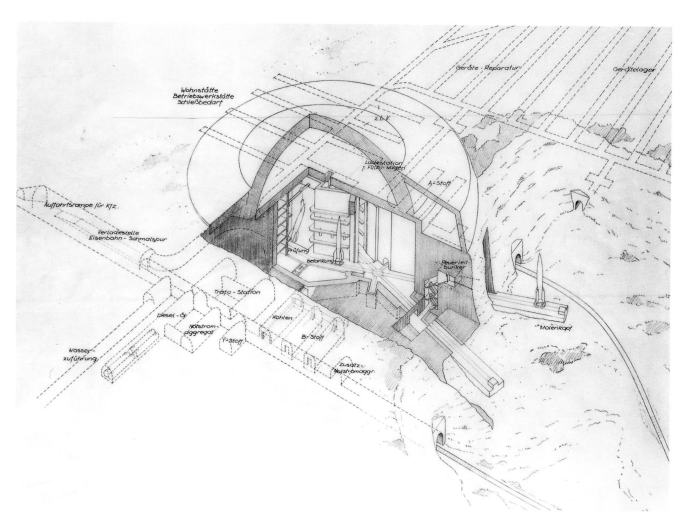

15
Bunker proposed for assembly
and stationary launch of the
V-2 from Wizernes, in occupied
France, detail of cutaway
perspective. August 1, 1944

16
East German poster for the Society
of German-Soviet Friendship celebrating the 41st anniversary of the
October Revolution. 1958

SCOUTING

LOOKS AT SPUTNIK

MAY-JUNE 1958

pages 2-7

17
Scouting magazine cover depicting a red Sputnik casting its shadow over a high-rise American city. May–June 1958

The launch of *Sputnik 1* (Companion) on October 4, 1957, catapulted the Soviet Union into the forefront of a race with the United States for supremacy in space and galvanized the American government and public to commit itself to matching and even surpassing Soviet accomplishments in this area. But this was years away from happening. The Soviet Union capitalized on its early success by promoting this scientific accomplishment in what was called the International Geophysical Year. The poster in plate 16 was commissioned by the government of the German Democratic Republic for the Society of German-Soviet Friendship celebrating the forty-first anniversary of the October Revolution, in 1958. It shows Sputnik, a Moscow skyscraper, and a stylized rocket similar to the Soviet space monument planned at the same time. America's acute awareness of the U.S.S.R.'s accomplishments is echoed in the cover illustration of the May–June 1958 issue of *Scouting* magazine, which depicts a red Sputnik casting its shadow over a high-rise American city. With Yuri Gagarin's first orbital flight aboard Vostok (East) on April 12, 1961, the Soviets again asserted their technical superiority in early space exploration, a situation that did not change until America landed a man on the Moon in 1969. The Vostok capsule was displayed in Moscow in the mid 1960s.

18
Vostok capsule on display in
Moscow. 1965

19
Launch pad 5 at Cape Canaveral's
Air Force Missile Museum, showing
a Redstone launcher. 1953–57

The Army Corps of Engineers laid out the early launch pads at Cape Canaveral, Florida, between the late 1940s and the early 1950s, most probably with the assistance of architect and engineer Maurice Connell. The Noble Company of Oakland, California, a construction company that specialized in oil rigs, was the contractor for the similarly styled, skeletal service towers/launch gantries. The Redstone (1953) was a U.S. Army weapon designed by Wernher von Braun. NASA employed it as a launcher for Mercury capsules, including the May 5, 1961, launch of *Freedom 7*, the spacecraft that was used for Alan Shepard's suborbital flight. Earlier historic flights from the Cape included American answers to Sputnik, such as the Explorer satellite, first launched on January 31, 1958, and the Vanguard on March 17, 1958. Although Vanguard used a navy launcher, Explorer relied on a variant of the Redstone. With this exciting activity taking place at Cape Canaveral, even children's books celebrated it as America's spaceport. Although the earliest facilities have been made into a museum, the Cape is filled with newer launch pads, including 17A and B, two of the newest ones that are used to launch commercial satellites (see plate 58).

20
Launch pad 5 at Cape Canaveral
before a Mercury capsule launch.
April 1961

21
Bell X-1. 1947

22
Proposed Boeing Dyna-Soar.
Begun 1959

23
Me163B Komet. 1943–44

24
Convair advertisement for the
F-102 Delta Dagger. 1955

A long line of rocket planes preceded today's Space Shuttle, such as the Dyna-Soar – the result of a proposal that V-2 General Walter Dornberger made, while he was a consultant to the Bell Aircraft Company in the 1950s, for a space plane to bomb the Soviet Union and shoot down its satellites (see the essay by Roy F. Houchin II in this volume). More tangible precedents in experimental rocket planes range from the famous X-1, which broke the sound barrier in 1947, to the X-15, which took pilots to the edge of space, more than 354,000 feet above the Earth at speeds greater than 4,500 miles per hour. Ironically, these postwar marvels owe their existence, in part, to German rocket planes of the second World War such as the Me163B Komet, a fighter nicknamed the "flying egg" that could climb to its operational altitude of 32,800 feet within a gut-wrenching two minutes. This radical little plane was created by Alexander Lippisch (1894–1976), who became a designer of supersonic delta-wing F-102 and F-106 fighters for the Convair Corporation during the cold war.

Freedom Has a New Sound!

ALL OVER AMERICA these days the blast of supersonic flight is shattering the old familiar sounds of city and countryside.

At U.S. Air Force bases strategically located near key cities our Airmen maintain their *round the clock* vigil, ready to take off on a moment's notice in jet aircraft like Convair's F-102A all-weather interceptor. Every flight has only one purpose – your personal protection!

The next time jets thunder overhead, remember that the pilots who fly them are not willful disturbers of your peace; they are patriotic young Americans affirming your *New Sound of Freedom!*

PUBLISHED FOR BETTER UNDERSTANDING OF THE MISSION OF THE U.S.A.F. AIR DEFENSE COMMAND

CONVAIR
A DIVISION OF GENERAL DYNAMICS CORPORATION

25
Pereira and Luckman. Convair
Astronautics Facility, main lobby,
Kearny Mesa (now part of San
Diego), California. 1955–58 (now
demolished)

26
Charles Luckman Associates, with others, including Brooks and Barr, MacKie and Kamrath, Harvin C. Moore, Wirtz Calhoun Tungate and Jackson, and architect-engineer Brown and Root. Manned Spacecraft Center (now Lyndon B. Johnson Space Center), Clear Lake, Texas. Begun 1962

28
The Austin Company. Boeing Space
Center, Kent, Washington. 1965

27
Harris Armstrong. McDonnell
Space Center and Engineering
Laboratories, St. Louis. 1958

29
Max O. Urbahn, architect, with
Roberts and Schaefer, structural
engineers, and others as part
of URSAM; Seelye, Stevenson,
Value, and Knecht, mechanical,
electrical, and civil engineers;
Moran, Proctor, Mueser, and
Rutledge, foundation engineers.
VAB (Vertical Assembly Building),
Cape Canaveral. 1962–65. The
VAB is shown with the *Apollo 14*
rollout

The space race spawned a number of new complexes, private and public. Two of the most important were designed by Charles Luckman. Dedicated in 1958, the Convair Astronautics Facility was a showpiece factory of 579,000 square feet constructed to build the Atlas, America's first intercontinental ballistic missile (ICBM), of 1954–57. In its heyday the plant housed twelve thousand employees daily. The new facility featured a strikingly modern lobby with a minimalist spiral staircase. Luckman was also in charge of establishing the architectural vocabulary for the new Manned Spacecraft Center, mission control for NASA just outside Houston's city limits. This complex comprised modernist concrete buildings for office, testing, and laboratory use arranged in a university-like campus setting on a 1,600-acre site, with facades incorporating wide overhangs to act as sun screens. The construction of this enormous facility was part of America's commitment to reach the Moon before the Russians, and it was similar to the new buildings at the Kennedy Space Center in Florida, also erected in the early 1960s (plates 30–32). Other striking engineering and test buildings constructed in this era of national support for the space race include a fifty-foot-high satellite testing chamber at Boeing's Space Center in Kent, Washington, and McDonnell's Space Center in St. Louis, which was built to develop the famous Mercury and Gemini space capsules in the early 1960s, and included a thermal testing chamber thirty feet in diameter. Plate 27 shows the Gemini capsule in the testing chamber.

30
Saturn launcher with Apollo capsule being rolled out to the launch site. 1967

31
Launcher crawler-tractor built by Marion Power Shovel Co. 1962–65

32
Space Shuttle *Columbia* on launch
pad 39A. Early 1980s. The architectural firm Giffels and Rossetti
worked on the design of launch
pads 39A and 39B; the launch
facilities were further altered by
Reynolds, Smith, and Hills,
Architects, and Giffels Associates
to accommodate the shuttle

33
Architectura, design architects,
and Morris Architects, with BRC
Imagination Arts, exhibition
design. Saturn V Pavilion, Kennedy
Space Center, Florida. 1996

34
Kevin Craig. Space Camp, Kennedy
Space Center, Florida. 1989

35, 36
Holt, Hinshaw, Pfau, Jones.
Astronauts Memorial, Kennedy
Space Center, Cape Canaveral.
1991. Rendering (top) and photo-
graph of detail (bottom)

37
Hellmuth, Obata and Kassabaum.
Astronauts Memorial Foundation
Space Education Center, Kennedy
Space Center, Florida. 1993

Following President Kennedy's famous 1961 commitment to go to the Moon, the construction of new launch facilities near Cape Canaveral

plunged ahead on what was almost a war-economy footing, with structures such as the Vertical Assembly Building (VAB) being designed

and built in a record eleven months. Of the various buildings erected for space exploration, these are the only ones that received

extensive coverage in the architectural press, including *Architectural Forum* (September 1963 and January–February 1967), *Progressive*

Architecture (March 1965), and *L'Architecture d'aujourd'hui* (September 1967). The Museum of Modern Art, New York, even included

the VAB in its 1964 exhibition *Twentieth-Century Engineering.* When it was finished, the 525-foot-high VAB had the largest cubic vol-

ume of any building in the world. It occupied one million cubic feet of space and accommodated four thirty-story-high Saturn V rockets

designed by Wernher von Braun's team – more cubic space than Chicago's Merchandise Mart and New York's Empire State Building

combined. After the Apollo capsule was placed on the launcher, it moved via an enormous crawler-tractor that also served as a mobile

launch platform to launch pads 39A and 39B, some three miles away. At Cape Canaveral there are two of these vehicles – the largest

tracked vehicles in the world; each one weighs six million pounds when loaded and travels an average speed of one mile per hour. The

same system, buildings, and launch sites, though somewhat altered, are in use today to launch the Space Shuttle missions. Visitors to

the Kennedy Space Center can see these historic structures as well as visit the new Saturn V Pavilion, which houses displays that explain

the Moon race and the Apollo missions that were launched from nearby facilities in the 1960s. Elsewhere on the site, visitors may see a

variety of new buildings, including facilities for educational activities for children and a memorial to the astronauts who have died in

the service of the space program – the latter reminding us all that space launches are still dangerous operations.

SEAN CONNERY IST JAMES BOND

IN IAN FLEMINGS MAN LEBT NUR ZWEIMAL

TECHNICOLOR PANAVISION

Ein MGM / UA Film im Verleih der UIP

38
Lewis Gilbert, director. *You Only Live Twice.* 1967. Lobby card for the German version of the film

James Bond films from *Dr. No* (1962) through *Golden Eye* (1996) have used space themes as part of their plots. *You Only Live Twice* featured sets created by production designer Ken Adams. In the film, arch-villain Ernst Stavros Blofeld, head of the evil organization SPECTRE, steals an American space capsule in an effort to provoke World War III between the U.S. and the U.S.S.R. Blofeld's launch site is a concrete cave comparable to the spaces excavated and planned by the Germans to assemble and launch V-2 rockets; these types of spaces and weapons were highlighted in the thriller *Operation Crossbow* of 1965.

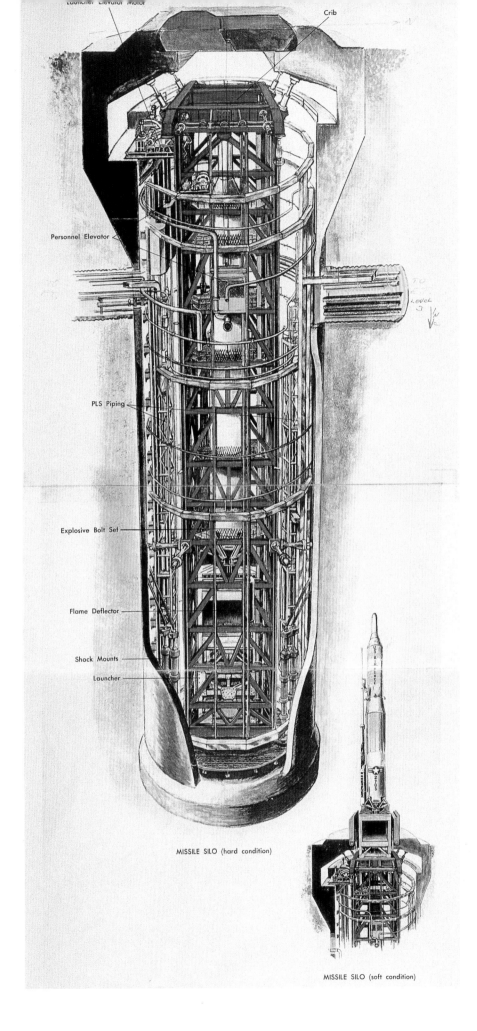

Launcher Elevator Motor

Crib

Personnel Elevator

PLS Piping

Explosive Bolt Set

Flame Deflector

Shock Mounts

Launcher

MISSILE SILO (hard condition)

Crib

MISSILE SILO (soft condition)

39
Daniel Mann Johnson and
Mendenhall. Titan 1 missile silo,
cutaway drawing. ca. 1958

A TRAINLOAD OF SOLID ACTION
WITH A CARGO

45 U.S.M.C.

MINUTEMAN

★ New Minuteman Missile Launching Car
★ New Satellite Launching Car
★ New Exploding Target Range Car
★ Magne-Traction

40
Minuteman missile-launching car
illustrated in a catalogue for Lionel
toys. 1961

41
Proposed Boeing Minuteman
missile railroad launchers being
presented at a press conference.
December 13, 1960

The space race also included a nuclear missile race between the superpowers. The Atlas rocket, developed in the mid to late 1950s, was America's first true intercontinental ballistic missile. It was launched from traditional gantries. The Titan I missile, developed concurrently with the Atlas, was based in underground silos that could withstand a nuclear attack. But because it was a liquid-fueled rocket, it had to be raised from its concrete silo and fueled above ground before launching, making it vulnerable to a second attack (see plate 39, lower right). The Titan II and especially the solid-fueled Minuteman, developed shortly thereafter, had no such liability since the fuels were stored in the missile, making it ready for launching. *Architectural Forum* (September 1960) wrote that with this flexibility silos would be unnecessary, since Minuteman missiles could be launched from mobile platforms, such as trains and trucks. Although silos continued to be adapted and built to house the Minuteman, the popular image of these mobile launchers was captured in a variety of proposals from aerospace companies to toy manufacturers. Boeing planned such a missile train and in 1961 built a test railroad car with the American Car and Foundry company. The shockproof car was 88 feet long and meant to resemble typical railroad freight cars. Ideas for mobile missile launchers continued to surface throughout the cold war – and even into the 1980s, in Sverdrup Corporation's designs with Boeing for rail-based detachments of Peacekeeper missiles and Boeing's proposals for highway-based Midgetman launchers. Because of the classified nature of all of these projects, few architectural journals or books discussed them, with the exception of *Wonders of the Modern World* (1966), by Joseph Gies, who described silo construction in a chapter aptly titled "Hell Hole." Today, with the cold war over, museum displays and buildings themselves present these histories, as, for example, in the exhibit within the new Strategic Air Command Museum near Omaha, and the restored Titan missile silos at the Arizona Aerospace Foundation in Tucson.

42
Leo A. Daly. Strategic Air
Command Museum, Ashland,
Nebraska. 1998–99

43, 44
Paul Verhoeven, director. *Starship
Troopers*. 1996. Special-effects
scenes

Although some films, such as Steven Spielberg's *E.T. The Extra-Terrestrial* (1982), cast aliens in a positive light, many science-fiction movies portray them in a negative or at least ambivalent way. And most, such as the recent *Starship Troopers* (with production design by Allan Cameron), demonize aliens as most World War II-era movies dehumanized the enemy. Designs by artist H. R. Giger for Ridley Scott's *Alien* (with production design by Roger Christian, Anton Furst, and Michael Seymour, and set decoration by Ian Whittaker) and subsequent iterations by other set designers in *Aliens* and *Alien: Resurrection* all fashion these creatures and their architectural environments as hybrids of unappealing anthropomorphic forms and sinister mechanisms, appropriate to their aggressive, life-threatening behavior.

45
Ridley Scott, director. *Alien.* 1979.
Production still

46
Energia-Buran on the launch pad
at Baikonur. 1988

47
Lewis Gilbert, director. *Moonraker.*
1979. The Space Shuttle was
depicted in this film prior to its first
orbital flight

Where all
the other Bonds end...
this one begins!

Albert R. Broccoli
presents

ROGER MOORE
as
JAMES BOND 007

in Ian Fleming's
MOONRAKER

Co-starring Lois Chiles Richard Kiel as 'Jaws'
Michael Lonsdale as 'Drax' and Corinne Clery
Produced by Albert R. Broccoli
Directed by Lewis Gilbert
Screenplay by Christopher Wood
Music by John Barry Lyrics by Hal David
Production Design by Ken Adam
Executive Producer Michael G. Wilson
Associate Producer William P. Cartlidge

ORIGINAL MOTION PICTURE SOUNDTRACK
ON UNITED ARTISTS RECORDS AND TAPES
PG PARENTAL GUIDANCE SUGGESTED
SOME MATERIAL MAY NOT BE SUITABLE FOR CHILDREN

RECORDED IN
DOLBY STEREO
IN SELECTED THEATRES
Filmed in Panavision®
Copyright © 1979 United Artists Corporation
All rights reserved.
United Artists
A Transamerica Company

Title Song Performed by Shirley Bassey

America's Space Shuttle has been a success story of the 1980s and 1990s. Although there was one major accident – when the *Challenger* exploded on January 28, 1986 – the fleet of five space planes (*Atlantis, Challenger, Columbia, Discovery,* and *Endeavor*) has made well over one hundred orbital flights since the first one in 1981. The press had seen mock-ups for the shuttle in the mid 1970s and witnessed atmospheric flight testing in 1977, so that as a result, the public was well prepared for the eventual orbital use of this space plane even when it appeared as one of the stars in the James Bond thriller *Moonraker* in 1979. Afraid of its potential military use, the Soviet Union began its own programs to counter the American shuttle. One was called Uragan (Hurricane), which was an early-1980s prototype for a two-seat space fighter that was intended to shoot down America's shuttle should the United States decide to use it as a bomber against the Soviet Union. Although this Russian space fighter was never implemented, another plan came closer to competing with the shuttle. It was called Buran (Snowstorm), and was designed in the mid to late seventies by Valentin Glushko, who also designed its massive Energia booster. In contrast to Buran, the American Space Shuttle was the work of a variety of designers and engineers and even aerospace corporations, as the contract made its way from theory to reality. Buran was finished in 1984 and looked similar to the American shuttle except for its propulsion system. Unlike the Space Shuttle, which uses its own engines as the final stage into orbit, Buran used the enormous Energia booster alone to place it into orbit. Its first and only orbital flight was an unmanned one in late 1988. With the fall of the Berlin Wall in 1989, and the drastic changes in the Russian and eastern European economies, the Buran program was abandoned in 1993. It was too costly to fully develop as a manned spaceplane. In any case, the Russians already had tried-and-true methods for sending cosmonauts and cargo to their space station *Mir* (begun in 1986) with Soyuz (Union) launchers, the so-called "Model Ts of rocketry," which were based, eventually, on Sergei Korolev's R-7 missile of 1955–57. In fact, the Soyuz launchers still use the same facilities at Baikonur developed by chief civil engineer Vladimir Barmin for the R-7 and early Sputnik launches of the mid to late 1950s. Meanwhile, the American shuttle has found new life in post–cold-war commercial uses, such as carrying freight in its cargo bay, much as commercial airliners do.

48
Soyuz launcher on its Baikonur launch pad. November 15, 1988

49, 50
Lockheed Martin Corporation.
Proposals for unmanned combat
aerial vehicles (UCAVs). 1997–99

Unlike the corporate image for the merger of Lockheed and Martin, which was designed in 1996 by the firm Anspach Grossman, the dynamic new logo for the tactical aircraft division of the Lockheed Martin Corporation is the creation of a team of their staff designers and specialists in corporate communications. Soon after it was designed, the logo won several 1998 Addy or American Advertising Awards from the American Advertising Federation, as well as a Telly Award from the Center for Creativity in Cincinnati, which recognizes non-network television and video commercials. The design team consciously avoided including any of the company's famous existing aircraft, such as the F-16 Fighting Falcon or the F-22 Raptor. Instead, they created a futuristic form similar to aerospace engineer Burt Rutan's conceptual studies for fighters of the future, which were published in *Aviation Week and Space Technology* in 1998, as well as the tailless fighter proposals being developed by Lockheed Martin in the late 1990s. The designs and the logo shape itself resemble the striking, curvilinear Martian spacecraft in the 1953 film *War of the Worlds.*

51
Lockheed Martin Corporation graphic design staff, headed by Michael Roundtree. "Fighter Enterprise" logo. 1997–98

52
Byron Haskin, director. *War of the Worlds.* 1953. Film still

53
Michel Mignot, designer, with
Rainer Turk, engineers. Space
Center Guyana, Ariane Launch
Facility No. 2, Kourou, French
Guyana. 1982–86

54
Christian Tinturier, designer, with
Rainer Turk, engineers. Space
Center Guyana, Rocket Testing
Tower and Concrete Blast Trench,
Ariane Launch Facility No. 3,
Kourou, French Guyana. 1989–95

When Space Center Guyana was developed in the mid 1960s, it was used as the launching site for smaller sounding rockets and small

orbital payloads. Published in *Techniques et Architecture* (September 1969) as a phased, planned city with consistently modernist buildings

for the housing, hotel, offices, and restaurant, the space center has grown considerably since the first launch by the French Space Agency

(CNES) in 1970. With expanded commercial weather, Earth observation, and telecommunications satellite opportunities in the 1980s

and 1990s, the spaceport also grew to accommodate increased launches with the European Space Agency's new launch vehicles: Ariane 1

(1979), Ariane 3 (1984), and the current Ariane 4 (1988) and Ariane 5 (1995). Arianespace, founded in 1980 as the first commercial space

transportation company in the world, has launched more than 155 satellites. Its location near the Equator in a secure area away from

populated settlements made it a strong competitor in the ever-increasing commercial satellite launch business in the 1990s. Illustrated

are an Ariane 4 rocket being launched from the Ariane Launch Facility No. 2 (plate 53), the Rocket Testing Tower and Concrete Blast

Trench of Ariane Launch Facility No. 3 (plate 54), and an Ariane 5 before its launch at Facility No. 3, with lightning-rod towers nearby.

56, 57
Sea Launch, a joint venture of
Boeing Commercial Space with
RSC Energia, NPO Yuzhnoye, and
Kvaerner. 1999

Sea Launch is a post–cold-war commercial satellite launching venture among American (Boeing), Russian (Energia), Ukrainian (Yuzhnoye), and Norwegian (Kvaerner) companies. Managed by Boeing, the Sea Launch homeport is located in Long Beach, California, at a disused navy facility that was remodeled in 1996–98 by San Francisco architects Kellor and Gannon. They built new "clean rooms" (rooms that are dust-free and have strict temperature and humidity control) and administrative facilities so that clients who are launching communications satellites can assemble their payloads at the dock for immediate loading onto an ocean-going launch platform, which was created by Kvaerner, specialists in producing offshore oil rigs. The seagoing launch platform also carries the Russian Energia booster for the final or third stage, which delivers the satellite into orbit, and the larger first and second stages of the Ukrainian Zenit rockets. The assembled launchers and payloads are stored on this self-propelled launch platform along with the accompanying crew ship. Free of the support expenses of a land-based launch site, both the ship and platform can then travel to an optimal latitude for launching the satellite. The system was tested in mid 1999 and implemented on October 9, 1999, with the launch of a DIRECTV satellite.

58
View of a Delta II launch, which delivers a Hughes Thor III satellite into orbit for Telenor Satellite Services. June 9, 1998

The Delta family of satellite launchers is one of the most efficient in space history, having a 94.7 percent success rate since its creation by the Douglas Aircraft Company in 1960. (By contrast, the World War II V-2 had about an 80 percent success rate for its launches.) The current Boeing (which merged with McDonnell Douglas in 1997) Delta II launcher dates from 1989. Its main propulsion system consists of liquid fuel augmented by a cluster of eight solid-rocket boosters; launch is from Cape Canaveral Air Force Station in Florida or Vandenburg Air Force Base in California. The launchers themselves consist of elements that are fabricated at Boeing's Huntington Beach factory, assembled at their Pueblo, Colorado, factory, and shipped to the launch facilities on the east or west coasts. Boeing is planning the next generation of large launch vehicles, such as the Delta III and Delta IV. Both of these will compete in the commercial space market directly with the new Ariane 5 launchers of the European Space Agency as well as with the launchers from the Russian, Ukrainian, and Chinese commercial space programs. In order to fabricate and assemble the components for its Delta III, Boeing hired the Austin Company – architects and engineers who have worked on many Boeing buildings since the 1930s – to build a new factory in Decatur, Alabama, in 1998. It is scheduled for completion by 2000.

59
Delta II liquid oxygen tank being
fabricated in Boeing's factory at
Huntington Beach, California

Landor Associates designed the corporate image for Telenor (formerly Norwegian Telecom) after the deregulation of Norway's telecommunications industry. The new company wanted to project a more customer-oriented structure. In order to compete with other international telecommunications companies and establish a strong identity, Landor suggested the name change to Telenor as well as the idea of featuring the new name in Norway's national colors, red and blue. To emphasize its futuristic business of high-tech telecommunications, bold curves and a lightning bolt were incorporated into the logo. NBBJ, a Seattle-based firm that specializes in high-tech research buildings, designed Telenor's new corporate headquarters on the site of Oslo's old airport. The scheme is made up of modular units, which hold thirty employees each, as Telenor requested, and function as "an office of the future." In all the complex houses six thousand employees. Two boldly curving buildings, reminiscent of forms in Telenor's logo, serve as circulation spaces connecting the office units via bridges. The open spaces of the interior are meant to convey the company's democratic attitude toward its staff, customers, and surroundings.

60
Landor Associates. Telenor corporate
image. 1994–95

61
NBBJ Architects with Peter Pran,
designer, and HUS, associate
architects. Computer-generated
view of model of Telenor
Corporate Headquarters, Oslo-
Fornebu, Norway. 1998–2001

62
Carlson Technologies, Inc. GPS
backpack for the land warrior of
the twenty-first century. 1997

63
Garmin Products. Personal GPS
receiver. 1997–98

With the outbreak of the Gulf War in 1991, architect Steve Carlson of Carlson Technologies,

Inc., was commissioned by the U.S. Army to create a backpack that would provide climate-

control and a secure environment from poisonous gas. He was asked to do this based on his

previous experience adapting space suit technology for cooling Formula One race cars. The air-

conditioned backpack won several design awards in 1994 and 1995. Following the success of

this research and development commission, Carlson proposed equipping the soldier of the

future with a climate-control backpack that is also linked to global positioning system (GPS)

satellites. This GPS backpack also won a Silver IDEA Award in 1997 in the IDSA / Business Week

competition. Nowadays, it is becoming more and more commonplace to be able to buy your

own inexpensive GPS unit for traveling or camping, and there are several automobile compa-

nies that offer these services as well.

In the 1990s, corporations increased satellite launches for commercial space operations such as satellite television and telecommunications, which led them to expand their facilities for the manufacture of satellites and related components. The Hughes Space and Communications Company, an industry leader in satellite design and construction, built the world's largest satellite factory in the 1990s, with more than 600,000 square feet of space and new high-tech features in 41,000 square feet of testing space. This factory, the ISF (plate 65), features a 63,000-cubic-foot thermal vacuum chamber (its arched door alone weighs 105 tons) for testing their popular HS 376, HS 601, and HS 702 satellites. La Cañada Design Group has specialized in a number of high-tech buildings for electronic corporations, including extensive remodeling and redesign work at Rockwell's Newport Beach facilities, where post–cold-war retooling has influenced both defense and commercial applications in the fabrication of semiconductors for fax modems. For Rockwell, La Cañada designed new electronic testing rooms, clean rooms, and a smock room with electronic interlocks to maintain the highest level of cleanliness for the production of silicon chips.

64
La Cañada Design Group, headed by Lance Bird and Veronica West. Interior view of Rockwell Semiconductor System Plant, Newport Beach, California. 1996–98

65
Steven Wooley and Associates.
Hughes Space and Communications
Company, Integrated Satellite
Facility (ISF), El Segundo, California.
1992–98

Shooting the Moon:

Icons of Space Photography

PETER BACON HALES

In 1839, Jacques-Louis Daguerre trained his newly invented camera on the night sky to capture the Moon, and thus to demonstrate the prodigious possibilities of his newly invented photographic process, and perhaps to prove its superiority over the methods of his rival, the Englishman William Henry Fox Talbot. The two had been locked in competition with each other and with the demands of a technologically sophisticated and demanding audience, who wanted the new medium to achieve not just the extraordinary but also what had been previously impossible and seemed now only inevitable. From the first moment, photographers declared and spectators believed that photography could capture the "real" world – both visible and invisible – and viewers wanted to see its miraculous powers trained on the known and the unknown universe. In his first batch of images, Daguerre had included a remarkable photomicroscopic rendering of a spider, one that so thrilled the American painter, scientist, and inventor Samuel F. B. Morse that he wrote back to the U.S. that Daguerre's discovery "is, therefore, about to open a new field of research in the depths of microscopic Nature. We are soon to see if the minute has discoverable limits."[1] For Daguerre, capturing the Moon's image would prove he had succeeded in the spectacular and could now use his tool to photograph not only the microscopic but also the infinite.

Daguerre was wrong. He could not do what he promised. His process was too slow, too insensitive, and his knowledge of the intricacies of astronomy too rudimentary. His failure was a harsh blow, made all the more bitter by the success just a few months later of the American scientist John William Draper. One of the first American daguerreotypists and a close friend of Morse, Draper saw Daguerre's process in much the same light as did the inventor himself. Draper looked to the medium to merge science and art, and he developed a method that, he bragged, "adds not a little to the magic of the whole operation."

The combination of technology, science, art, and magic characterized the new medium and fed the fantasies of a universe-scaled empire that were already percolating in the popular imagination of citizens in Europe and America. Though it was still more than two decades until Jules Verne would publish his remarkable work of science fiction, *From the Earth to the Moon Direct in Ninety-Seven Hours and Twenty Minutes* (1865), the notion of capturing the Moon via the new photographic technology developed out of the larger impulse to apply technology to explore nature, to capture its fugitive elements and bend them to human use.

In its earliest stages, the photography of space did not follow Draper's purely scientific bent, but combined science, art, philosophy, and something close to the spiritualistic. Certainly the greatest of daguerreian Moon-shots was the one made by the scientist-daguerreotypist team of Harvard astronomy professor William C. Bond and the Boston daguerreotypist John Adams Whipple (fig. 1). Laboring over a period of three years, Whipple finally succeeded in making an image that was, critics agreed, both scientifically accurate and aesthetically pleasing – in Whipple's own words, "a clear, well-defined, beautiful Daguerreotype of the Moon."[2] The small silver plate was also, however, a strange amalgam of transcendentalist spirit-travel and a form of, not theft exactly, but something deliciously close to it, in which, by the agent of light (fugitive light, many critics and photographers called it), the unreachable was captured and held.

That the Moon or stars might be so possessed was an especially intriguing idea. Most popular descriptions of the new photographic process proposed some mystical quality of the *sun's* rays that linked viewer and subject into a secret marriage. That the Moon and stars could do so as well suggested a new form of mystery and magic. Richard Rudisill has written brilliantly of the combination of scientific discovery and mystical mumbo-jumbo that characterized the early years of this process; he reported that the discovery that Moon, star, and sunlight could all activate the photographic process represented a scientific breakthrough that was understood as both philosophical and mystical: all things in the universe were in some way bound together, alike.[3]

Fig. 1
John Adams Whipple. *Moon.*
1850–51. Daguerreotype. National
Museum of Photography, Film,
and Television/Science and Society
Picture Library, London

We may consider the early daguerreotypes that captured the Moon just as their makers, critics, viewers, and possessors did: as an early form of space travel, in which the spirit rather than the body did the traveling, or, more mundanely, in which the technology of the moment made it possible to hold, even to own, a piece of the universe otherwise unattainable. This was the first stage of space travel: a product of Romantic impulses and intuitions, combined with the nineteenth century's belief in the progressive power of technologies, and linked to the larger impulse toward exploration, acquisition, and imperial domination over the known and, eventually, the unknown universe. This was Verne's ideal, and it even set the terms for the twentieth century's more pragmatic and instrumentalist campaigns to conquer space.

And yet for a process so heralded in the 1850s, the capture of the heavens made little progress for nearly a century. The interruption in space photography that ensued between Whipple's accomplishment and the cold war seems a vast chasm, but this is only the result in part of the peculiar nature of photography and its reputation, both popular and elite. Within the evolving history of photography, this hiatus did not occur because it was impossible to conceive of space travel, space destinations, or space imagery. On the contrary, popular literature was full of such imaginings, and so was the imagery it engendered, from book illustrations to the wonderful hyperbole of serial stories published in the forerunner journals of science fiction and fantasy. But these images were pointedly overwrought. They were not simply stylized in their rendering. They were also stylized to declare that they *were* renderings, that we were entering the realm of goal-directed dreaming, of imagination that might then excite action – the making of a generation, then two, then three, of spacemen and spacewomen who would grow up yearning for the stars and would, over time, make that yearning over into active campaigns, by becoming engineers and physicists and test pilots, as

well as by paying taxes enthusiastically to support the budding programs that appeared after the end of World War II.

But space imagery was not photography, nor did it strive to resemble photographs. Photography had to be "true," and its visual evidence had to draw straight from the physical world; to fabricate photographs of space, even with the seamless artfulness of the Victorian collages of O. G. Rejlander or Henry Peach Robinson, would have been dismissed with contempt. Instead, photography of space remained within the grasp of astronomy, as larger and larger telescopes combined with more and more sophisticated photographic technologies to produce spectacular images of the planets and the galaxies. These nestled nicely within the dreamlike fantasies of space travel, and they no doubt formed the space-scapes upon which millions of those young dreamers painted their images of space travel, exploration, and settlement.

All this would change rapidly in 1957, when the Soviet Union announced its successful launching of *Sputnik 1* and then, four years later, the appearance of Yuri Gagarin in the inner reaches of outer space. On the global stage of public drama, the space race seemed increasingly to belong to the enemy in a war of images and image, photographs and propaganda.

Looking at the next iconic moment in the visual imagining of space travel, we must also remember that the postwar space boom was for Americans at least in part a campaign of atonement, meant to upend the dark visions of atomic warfare and Promethean excess and turn them into a benevolent expansionism in which all citizens of the globe cooperated, all were conquerors looking down from above, none the conquered looking up at the agents of their doom.[4] In science fiction, especially, this theme of redemptive extraterrestrial imperialism is prominent, but it is also found in the den-and-workshop magazines of American men after the war, such as *Popular Science, Popular Mechanics,* and the like. There, the illustrations

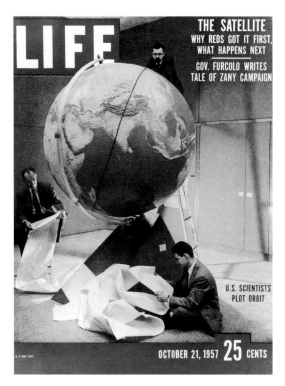

Fig. 2
"U.S. Scientists Plot Orbit,"
cover of *Life* magazine.
October 21, 1957

Fig. 3
"Astronauts' Wives: Their Inner
Thoughts, Worries," cover of *Life*
magazine. September 21, 1959

began to change, becoming less dramatically fictitious and more and more photographic as the editors, authors, and readers began to conceive of space travel as an act not of the imagination but of the nation. Soon, photographs depicted the launch pads, space ships, Moon, and stars – the ever-expanding Empire Terra.

The go-go years of the American space program began with the launching of *Sputnik 1* on October 4, 1957, and NASA's rush to respond. From that moment on, the marketing and photography of space travel intertwined tightly. Here, too, we can credit the cold war, for it was the culture of secrecy, forged on the Manhattan Project and brought to a fine edge by the vision of a Soviet arsenal dominated by intercontinental ballistic missiles carrying megawarheads of atomic and then hydrogen super bombs, that impelled the space program and made control of its image an essential part of that space war. From the first, NACA (the National Advisory Committee for Aeronautics) and then NASA regulated the image of American space travel, first by limiting and controlling access to the sites where space travel was being tested, and then, as it became real, by subtly and sometimes blatantly setting forth the script according to which photographers worked. The photographs were real, they were true, but they created and promoted a more and more complex and complete mythology of space travel as an American triumph of scientific prowess, technological know-how, and democratic zeal over a hostile and powerful natural space-scape. Even as American

scientists, politicians, and military men faced the fact that the Americans lagged behind the Soviets in the space race, the publicity and public information officers and their cadres sought to create the opposite impression. To do this successfully required photographs, that is, a medium by now steeped in celebrations of the facts of ordinary life in a democratic society full of prosperity and hope.

But, again, photography's reputation for truth and the depressing fact that no American could be photographed in space until May 1961 made American space photography a matter of wish or promise rather than fulfillment, although not for lack of will. Until 1957, *Life* had presented only a few photographs of American space programs on the magazine's interior, and no covers. The week of the Sputnik launch, the magazine was reduced to a cover picture (albeit striking from our distance) of American scientists poring over printouts of the Russian orbit in front of a giant globe (fig. 2). For all of 1957, there were three *Life* covers dedicated to space; in 1961, the year of Gagarin's first flight, the number doubled. Once America truly entered the race, in 1962, the numbers peaked and then steadied – eight in 1962, then an average of three a year, as the targeted events unfolded with the regularity of a script written by NASA's public relations cadre – suborbital, orbital, spacewalk, Moon landing, and Moonwalk.

Still, these monumental otherworldly events appeared in the larger context of the American story as part of the narrative of democracy ascendant, of benevolent globalization abroad and

Fig. 4
Launch of *Apollo 11*. July 16, 1969

nuclear families at home. And so the images of American space travel retained the sense of ritual commemoration that dominated most of postwar photojournalism, particularly as it appeared in the immensely popular picture magazines that offered up weekly interpretations of current events and brought the homely issues of individual and family into the light of democratic universality.

In part this shift to more personal narratives was simply a matter of practicality. As the autumn of 1957 brought *Sputnik 1* to the American skies, and as NASA rockets exploded on their launch pads or moments after liftoff, NASA officials sought new and more appealing images to counter these pictures of failure. Up to this point, the predominant settings for the photography of space had been the shiny, gadget-strewn labs of the scientists, the vast assembly plants for the rockets, and the launch pads. Now NASA shifted the focus to the particular, the personal, and the heroic – to the astronauts who would travel to space, to the Moon, and to the stars.

NASA's decision in 1961 to grant *Life* magazine sole access to the astronauts and their stories – and those of their wives and families – was simultaneously a deeply conservative act and a brilliant stroke on the agency's part. By the later 1950s, *Life* effectively owned mass-market photography, having acquired or invented the central themes and genres of the medium over the period from its founding in the midst of the Depression through World War II and into the postwar era. Taking its cues from the documentary photography of the 1930s and the propaganda photography of the war years,

Life remade mass-market photography as a medium of hope, unity, and reconciliation, and it was a program ideally suited to the needs of America's space program.

During these golden years, between 1957 and 1969, *Life* presented a series of iconic photographs of space travel: the first astronaut team; the astronauts and their families at their homiest, barbecuing or sitting in their ranch-home living rooms or saying grace at the supper table (fig. 3); the launch, with its dramatic explosions and its massive rocket poised just off the launch pad (fig. 4); the pickup at sea; then the spacewalk, with its balletic floating tubes and tools and the ungainly but radiantly pure white spacesuit and the cowl reflecting the Earth, the Sun, or – most commonly – the space capsule; and then, finally, those culminating images of the lunar module flying across the bleak terrain, of the landing, of the footprints on the surface of the Moon, of Buzz (Edwin) Aldrin portrayed by Neil Armstrong's spaceproof Hasselblad camera, walking, or standing with the American flag waving improbably – impossibly – beside him (figs. 5, 6, 8).

The last image may have represented the height of space photography, but it was also the first artifact of its demise. More than any other journal, *Life* made exultant declarations on its covers for *Apollo 11*'s triumphant affirmation of sovereignty over the Moon. "Barnstorming the Moon" read the June 6, 1969, cover, and then the words "Leaving for the Moon" were overlaid upon an image of Armstrong in his flight suit waving as he walked to the launch on July 25; on the cover for the August 8 issue, "On the Moon: Footprints and Photographs by Neil Armstrong and Edwin Aldrin." But even that was not the end: two days later, *Life* put out one of its special editions, titled "To the Moon and Back," with a tightly cropped image of the space conquerors, one shown reflected in the faceplate of the other.

Still, the spectacular images of footprints and brilliantly reflective technological surfaces – meant to signify the ultimate imperial declaration, the culmination of that promise of technology and

Fig. 5
Buzz (Edwin) Aldrin engaged in
extravehicular activity, *Apollo 11*.
Photograph taken by Neil A.
Armstrong with a 70mm lunar
surface camera. July 1969

Fig. 6
Flag on the Moon. July 19, 1969

democracy united in photography and in the impulse to reach out to the Moon, planets, stars, and galaxies – conveyed a quality that was both hyperphotographic and postphotographic. Too clear, too brilliantly lit, too dramatically colored, they declared themselves constructions and not documentary captures, and these constructions had about them a ring of falsehood, of undeliverable hyperbole. For many viewers, it was the flag that tipped the balance from satisfying truth to uncomfortable propaganda. But it wasn't simply that someone had manufactured a flag that could stand out from its pole in the airlessness of the Moon's non-atmosphere. It was that Aldrin was unable to fully extend the flag, and as a result it almost convincingly mimicked the effect of earthly wind on a Fourth of July display in small-town America (see fig. 6). In a stroke of splendid, if unintended, verisimilitude, a generation was made to doubt the truth of the photograph, even as, at that same moment, they grasped with the zeal of aficionados the brilliance of the spectacle that resulted.

These pictures were the culmination and the end of the long trajectory that began with Daguerre's promise that he could shoot the Moon with his photographic invention; now photography had captured the Moon and then gone further – had reconstructed it, reinvented it, and in the process had turned photography from the medium of truth, the only medium capable fully of communicating the triumph of technology and democracy over Nature, and transformed it into the new medium of brilliant and distracting fiction.

The photography of space travel after that moment moved predictably from spectacle to expectation, and then to saturation and

normalcy, and finally to boredom. When the *Challenger* exploded on January 28, 1986, tragedy struck a crew handpicked for its publicity value – a crew that comprised not people but types – the types NASA hoped to present as the amalgam that is America. Hundreds of thousands of people, many of them schoolchildren, saw the event, but not through the lens of the photographic camera. They were watching on the television monitors in their classrooms at 11:40 A.M., as their teachers, persuaded by the presence of one of their own colleagues on the crew, tuned it in for an extracurricular activity meant to end not in fiery immolation but in another inevitable step forward of the American empire in space. By then, television had long replaced photography as the medium best suited to the scripted narratives of American glory put forth by the publicity department at NASA. So also with the inquiry afterward, and with the legendary image of physicist Richard Feynmann demonstrating the fatal flaw of the O-ring: video, not photograph. Now the glories and the ignominies of space travel would be the province of new media – first television, then, more recently, the Internet, where NASA maintains *NASAWeb* (fig. 7), a continually rejuvenated high-tech extravaganza mixing film clips, speeches by NASA's administrator, official history, Freedom of Information releases, even *NASA for Kids,* and *Women and NASA,* a cheerily demographic-driven apologia-and-redress subpage. The result is great entertainment, and that is the new theme of space travel: no longer grand heroic exploration, the human spirit reaching to the stars, but instead space as spectacle, as theater, or, more modestly, as a bit of this evening's diversion. In this realm

Fig. 7
Astronaut's footprint made
on lunar soil during *Apollo 11*
mission. July 19, 1969

Fig. 8
View from *Apollo 8* of Earth
rising. 1968

of entertainment, photography plays its role. No longer a medium of truth, no longer the master of Nature, now it is simply a tool in the manufacture of an Einsteinian theme park: Spaceland.

Still, there is a coda to this story, or, one might more accurately say, a recurrent fugitive image, a persistence of vision. It is a picture made from space, and one that most of us remember perhaps more vividly than the most spectacular of spacesuit-and-Moonflag shots. It is a photograph not of the conquering of space and the leaving of Earth but of turning back, with longing, with regret, with profound doubt about the enterprise of mastery that has redesigned our sense of human relationship to the planet. It is the image of Earthrise, of the planet seen from Apollo, in its blue and green lush tenderness, by the men and machines leaving Earth, perhaps not to return (see fig. 8).

In one of the greatest of cold-war science-fiction novels, Robert Heinlein's *Foundation,* readers first encounter Earth as it would exist in the far-future, when most of humankind had long left the planet behind: as a biologically dead sphere, layered with metal superskins, one upon the other, within which could be found the residences of those who remained on the mother planet to administer to the galactic empire that technology, democracy, and the vaunting ambitions of humankind had produced. In one scene, a visitor from a far corner of the galaxy takes his vacation moment to ride from sub-metallic interior up to the surface, and in the process meets up with others who, like him, are seeing Earth for the first time. They are residents. They have come up for air, for space, but they are uncomfortable with it. Earth is dead, and they don't regret it.

This is the space-imperial future that lies behind George Lucas's *Star Wars* series, in which Earth has not simply disappeared under the weight of technology – it has disappeared altogether, even from the memory of humankind. Against this picture of planetocide is posited the other photograph that space travel offers, of Whole Earth – fragile, delicate, beautiful, the sum of our longings and representing the completeness we have sought to embrace throughout human history – now made possible, real, and true with a Hasselblad camera trained through a spaceproof sheet of glass by an astronaut in a white space suit who is about to plant, or has just returned from planting, the simulation of that most delicate of events, wind-raised cloth – not sailing across the Atlantic, but waving above hay-smelling Earth far away, perhaps too late to be loved and saved.

1. Morse's comments are quoted in Richard Rudisill, *Mirror Image: The Influence of the Daguerreotype on American Society* (Albuquerque, N.M., 1971), p. 77.
2. Quoted in Rudisill, *Mirror Image,* p. 86.
3. Ibid., pp. 88–89.
4. This phenomenon, the cold-war myth of a one-world government devoted to extraterrestrial imperialism, is one of the now-lost themes of American culture, and one I deal with at some length in a forthcoming study of the period.

On the Threshold of Space:

Norman Rockwell's *Longest Step*

ANNE COLLINS GOODYEAR

In the early 1960s, as the United States competed with the Soviet Union to be the first country to land on the Moon, the National Aeronautics and Space Administration (NASA) established a program by which it would invest in artwork as a means of establishing a cultural record of space exploration. Norman Rockwell, whose iconic images of American life had come to shape the way the nation viewed itself, was one of the artists chosen to participate in the program. He turned his attention to space exploration at the moment when it shifted from being the stuff of fantasy to a tangible political and human contest, and responded with characteristic sensitivity to this transition. As is particularly evident in Rockwell's painting *The Longest Step* (fig. 1), NASA found in this beloved artist a perfect vehicle to present a heroic, yet human, view of the burgeoning space program.[1]

The NASA Artists' Cooperation Program was initiated with the encouragement of NASA's second administrator, James Webb. In March 1962, having been presented with a portrait of Alan Shepard by artist Bruce Stevenson (fig. 2), Webb recommended that NASA "consider in a deliberate way just what [it] should do in the field of the fine arts to commemorate the past historic events, such as [Alan] Shepard's and [John] Glenn's flight, as well as future historic events that we know will come to pass."[2] After appropriate consultation with the Fine Arts Commission and the director of the National Gallery of Art, Washington, D.C. – a gesture intended to forestall criticism of the program both inside and outside of NASA – the art program was entrusted to the joint leadership of Hereward Lester Cooke, curator of painting at the National Gallery, and James Dean, director of NASA's Educational Media Division. The purpose of the art program was to grant American artists free access to NASA's facilities and events so that they could interpret the significance of America's forays into space. Cooke summarized the program's underlying philosophy in his letter of invitation to artists: "NASA is commissioning your imagination, and we want records of fleeting

impressions and poetic by-products of thought as much as precise documents of optical experience."[3] Significantly, as Cooke explained to them, the space agency rejected exclusively using photography, itself a product of science and technology, as a visual record of early attempts at space exploration. Art, especially when it reflected the artist's hand, provided a vital means to express the human significance of the space program.[4]

Due to concern over the potential political implications of spending federal money on the arts, the initial steps the NASA art program took were conservative ones. Although in principle artists were free to select any subject matter that interested them and to depict it in any style they pleased, the first artists selected by NASA were realists. In a January 1964 editorial, Cooke reassured readers of the *Cape Kennedy Spaceport News* of his intention to avoid commissioning abstract art, explaining, "We feel the material here is abstract enough."[5]

Among the first artists to participate in the NASA art program was Robert McCall, who had gained recognition for the paintings of World War II he made for *Life* magazine.[6] McCall's meticulous observation and craftsmanship glorify humankind's technological achievements and anticipate the moment that human beings might make space a common habitat. In McCall's images, space age technology assumes a human dimension. As Cooke observed, "[McCall] has the quality and scope of imagination to travel in space, and carry us, the spectators, along with him in full confidence that we are in the hands of a competent guide. Many of his pictures portray events which man could never see or photograph and which, without his talents, would remain in the realm of words, mathematical formulae and taped electronic signals."[7] It was precisely this aspect of McCall's work that led film director Stanley Kubrick to commission him in 1967 to create the four oil paintings that would serve as the basis for publicity posters for his science fiction film, *2001: A Space Odyssey* (see plate 70).

Like McCall, Rockwell represented an ideal choice for Cooke and Dean. As a well-known American artist whose prestige would bolster

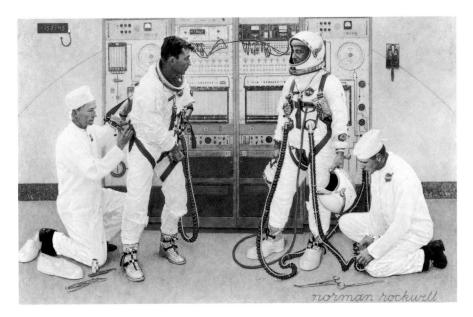

Fig. 1
Norman Rockwell. *The Longest Step (Astronauts Grissom and Young Suiting Up).* 1965. Oil on canvas, 35 x 55 in. National Air and Space Museum, Smithsonian Institution, Washington, D.C.

Fig. 2
Bruce Stevenson. *Alan B. Shepard, Jr.* 1962. National Air and Space Museum, Smithsonian Institution, Washington, D.C.

the art program, Rockwell could be counted upon to create images that would engage their audience. In a memo to Dean, Cooke gushed: "Mr. Rockwell is perhaps the best known illustrator in America, and has expressed great interest in the assignment. I think NASA would do well to make every effort to obtain his services. . . . His drawings or paintings could be given very wide circulation and would reflect great credit on the NASA program."[8] Although Cooke may not have known it, Rockwell's images of American life had already been associated with the space program by a journalist who praised Glenn and his family as a "Norman Rockwell original."[9] Given Rockwell's impact on American culture and the wholesome image NASA went out of its way to convey, his association with the space program was a natural development.[10]

Rockwell's career as an illustrator for popular magazines, however, posed one unexpected hurdle for the organizers of NASA's art program: *Look* magazine, with whom Rockwell had recently signed a contract, wanted to publish the paintings that resulted from Rockwell's association with the NASA art program.[11] NASA's proposal to commission Rockwell using the same contract as other artists – providing an $800 honorarium and the opportunity to witness space history in exchange for the donation of resulting sketches and finished works to NASA – had to be revised.[12] Officially, Rockwell would be considered a member of the press, working on a story about NASA, and *Look* would retain the right to be the first to publish the images Rockwell produced.[13] One contemporary photograph of Rockwell on site at Cape Canaveral shows the artist wearing his press badge (fig. 3).

In addition to appeasing *Look* magazine, this arrangement benefited the interests of the space agency. Rockwell's paintings would be guaranteed instant circulation to a wide popular audience, fulfilling the art program's mission to help educate the American public about the "aims and accomplishments" of the space program.[14] Indeed, the publication of Rockwell's space paintings in a popular magazine was very much in keeping with the history of "space art." During the 1950s, the work of space artist Chesley Bonestell had reached a large segment of the American public through its publication by *Collier's* magazine in a series of issues devoted to the prospect of space flight (see the essay by Frederick Ordway in this volume).[15] As the political scientist Howard McCurdy has argued, images such as Bonestell's went a long way to making "[the prospect of] space flight seem real."[16] A decade later, Rockwell's popular illustrations would be called upon not to help convince the public that space travel was possible, but rather to convince Americans that it was a worthwhile investment.

Following his visits to the Manned Space Center (MSC, now the Johnson Space Center) in Houston in the summer of 1964, Rockwell completed *The Longest Step,* his first space-related painting, in the spring of 1965. The painting was created to celebrate the first manned Gemini mission, *Gemini 3,* flown by astronauts John Young and Virgil (Gus) I. Grissom. Project Gemini represented the intermediary step between the Mercury and Apollo programs, providing NASA the opportunity to gain experience with maneuvers that would be required for the Moon-bound Apollo mission, such as Extravehicular

Fig. 3
Norman Rockwell atop the Vehicle
Assembly Building at Cape Kennedy,
Florida. ca. 1969

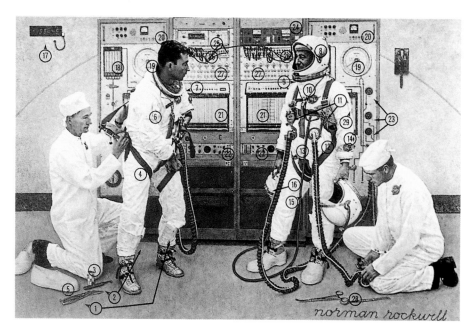

Fig. 4
Diagram of Norman Rockwell's
The Longest Step featured in *Look*
magazine. April 20, 1965

Activity (EVA) and orbital rendezvous. Published in full color in the April 20, 1965, issue of *Look,* Rockwell's *Longest Step* appeared as a two-page spread, sandwiched between Ben Kocivar's short essay about the painting and a diagrammatic reproduction of it (fig. 4), which numbered and identified every piece of equipment pictured, down to a pencil included in a small pocket on the left sleeve of Grissom's space suit. Just as Rockwell, *Look,* and NASA had agreed, *The Longest Step* served as the basis of an educational publication about the space program – complete with Rockwell's enduring representation of it. Perhaps most important, Rockwell's image accentuated the dedicated teamwork that lay behind the space program, featuring, in addition to the description of the space age hardware, brief biographies of each of the four men pictured. The suit technicians, Joe W. Schmitt and Alan Rochford, received the same attention as the two astronauts.

As was typical of Rockwell's practice of the time, the artist relied upon multiple photographs to construct his composition. Yet, as Rockwell stressed in his autobiography, the photographs were compiled strictly as aids to record vital information he would need for the painting, such as poses and costumes: "I don't copy photographs. . . . They are guides, nothing more. The essential ingredient in every one of my finished paintings is me – my feelings, ideas, skills."[17] The photographs, shot by Rockwell's photographer Brad Herzog during a special session with the astronauts at MSC, show the artist taking on his customary role as director, encouraging the astronauts to assume the pose that seemed most appropriate. A collection of dozens of photographs, some annotated to indicate appropriate colors,

demonstrates Rockwell's careful attention to detail, down to the very instruments casually arrayed by the feet of the assisting technicians.[18]

One snapshot in particular, complete with Rockwell's pointing hand, captures the essence of the image Rockwell would paint (fig. 5). In this image Rockwell placed the astronauts standing and facing one another, apparently engaged in a moment of speechless communication. Their poses nearly mirror each other, a visual pun on the name of the project, "Gemini," which refers to the twin stars of Castor and Pollux in the Gemini constellation.[19] Young seems to look at Grissom with a mixture of expectation and anticipation. Grissom's pose is slightly more relaxed, and the veteran smiles calmly back at his protégé. Rockwell retained these expressions and postures in his painting and made at least two critical adjustments to accentuate the wordless exchange. First, he painted in wire connectors in the console behind the astronauts, visually connecting their heads. In this way Rockwell playfully suggested that Grissom was mentally encouraging the rookie.[20] Rockwell further conveyed Grissom's friendly mentorship by placing a helmet on Grissom's head, thereby implying that the helmet in his hand, as seen in the source photo, is for his partner.

Unlike the photograph, Rockwell's painting does not depict a dress rehearsal (so to speak), but instead the main event.[21] In the left corner of the painting, Rockwell added the countdown clock he had observed on another wall of the room, and indicated that just over two hours remained before launch.[22] He also included yellow booties on Grissom's feet as well as a pair behind Schmitt, who assists Young, suggesting that the astronauts were preparing to be walked outside to their waiting spaceship.

Fig. 5
Snapshot of Norman Rockwell
directing astronauts John Young
and Virgil I. (Gus) Grissom. 1964

Fig. 6
Domenico Veneziano. *Madonna and
Child with Saints,* St. Lucy altarpiece,
main panel. Mid 1440s. Tempera on
panel, 6 ft. 10 in. x 7 ft. 1 in. Galleria
degli Uffizi, Florence

Rockwell's control, however, included not only posing the astronauts, but also choosing the moment at which to represent them. His
decision to show the astronauts putting on their space suits has particular significance when seen in the larger context of his career. As
an illustrator accustomed to working with models, Rockwell had a
particular sensitivity to the transformative potential of costume. His
paintings often picture children trying on new clothes as they strain
to grow up and assume a particular identity, or occasionally show a
misfit wearing completely inappropriate attire.[23] In his autobiography,
describing his youthful attempts to be part of "high society," Rockwell
remarked that "clothes were vital."[24] By picturing Grissom and
Young putting on their gear, Rockwell epitomized the moment of
transformation of these men into astronauts. This liminal moment,
by extension, metaphorically records the transition of the American
space program from the realm of the imagination to that of reality.

Significantly, in 1964 the space program placed special emphasis
on the suits that Rockwell chose as part of his subject. As the astronauts entered the new phase of the Gemini program, they would
no longer rely entirely upon their space capsule for protection against
the elements. Instead, the suits themselves would provide this protection as the Gemini astronauts ventured from their capsules into the
vacuum beyond. The importance of the suit was alluded to in Kocivar's
discussion of Rockwell's painting: "During one of [the Gemini mis-
sions], our astronauts will do what the Russians have already done:
get out of their capsule and move about in space. Their protection for
that leap is the space suit and its almost unbelievable ability to support
life where it has never gone before."[25] Grissom and Young would not

venture out of their capsule as the astronauts in following Gemini
missions would do, but the *Gemini 3* flight inaugurated this new era
and the use of the new suits. Indeed, when Rockwell visited the astronauts' dress rehearsal, the space suit's design was itself in the midst
of a transformation. Photographs show Young wearing what appears
to be a white G3C pressure suit, while Grissom seems to be pictured
in the silver G2C training suit.[26] In fact, Rockwell's desire to represent
accurately the new Gemini G3C suit led to an unprecedented concession from the space agency: in response to his repeated requests,
NASA permitted the top-secret suit to be brought to Rockwell's
Stockbridge, Massachusetts, studio under the protection of Schmitt,
the elder of the two suit technicians portrayed in the painting.[27]

In a letter of thanks to Rockwell for a charcoal sketch of the
composition, Herzog told the artist, "I can see my photograph in
each case but at the same time the whole portrait has been subjected
to a marvelous and wonderful translation so that your signature is
really superfluous."[28] Some of the "transformations" that Herzog
alluded to have already been discussed, but there are other, still
more significant changes that Rockwell made to his final painted
image. Perhaps most significant is the formal arrangement of the
painting: its pyramidal composition recalls the classical composition
of Italian Renaissance altarpieces, such as Domenico Veneziano's
Madonna and Child with Saints (fig. 6). The positions of Young and
Grissom recall those of saints paying homage to the Madonna and
Christ; the kneeling figures of Schmitt and Rochford seem to provide a link between these exalted astronauts and those of us who
must admire their feats from afar. At the apex is the computer,

Fig. 7
Raphael. *School of Athens.* ca.
1510–12. Fresco. Stanza della
Segnatura, Vatican, Rome

Fig. 8
Norman Rockwell. *Man on the
Moon (United States Space Ship on
the Moon).* 1967. Oil on canvas,
70⅝ x 46 in. National Air and Space
Museum, Smithsonian Institution,
Washington, D.C.

whose strong vertical seam combines with the horizontal panels of
switches, linked by wire connectors, to suggest a cruciform shape.[29]
In his final version of the painting, Rockwell nearly doubled the
area occupied by the computer by adding two consoles – each of
which enabled him to include a halolike juxtaposition of a large dial
behind each astronaut's head. Although Rockwell – in typical fashion – had received a photograph of such a computer configuration,
a preliminary sketch of the painting showing only two computer
panels suggests that this expansion was a later conceptual development. Indeed, the gentle protrusion of an arch from beneath the
outer two consoles in the finished work suggests that the decision
to increase the area of the computer was undertaken during the
final stages of the picture's completion.

The composition's similarity to Renaissance altarpieces offers a
gentle pun: the astronauts (and the Soviet cosmonauts) represented
the first people in history to escape Earth's atmosphere, literally
achieving a new communion with the heavens. The technology celebrated in the center of the composition made this all possible. At
the same time, the implications underlying this celebration are somewhat ambiguous: had technology indeed replaced the spirit as an
object of worship in contemporary society? Four years after the painting appeared in *Look,* Richard Nixon would refer to the events of
the Moon landing as "the greatest week in the history of the world
since Creation."[30]

Rockwell's painting also resonates with another Renaissance
masterpiece, Raphael's *School of Athens* (fig. 7). In the background,
a blue arch unifies the composition. Rockwell's source photographs
reveal no obvious inspiration for the arced line in his painting aside
from formal considerations; its integral role in the composition
appeared in an early oil sketch. Just as Raphael's use of architecture
organizes the activity of the *School of Athens,* so Rockwell's arch

contains the activity of the astronauts and their assistants. Here
Grissom and Young serve as counterparts to Raphael's Plato and
Aristotle, and the suit technicians function as their devoted followers.
Rockwell must also have noticed that the blue arch suggested the
curve of Earth itself, which the astronauts would, of course, be able
to observe from space.

By associating his painting of Grissom and Young with well-known
Renaissance masterpieces, Rockwell integrated the space program
into a historical tradition. Viewed through Rockwell's representation
of it, the space program does not appear as a break in human history,
but rather as a glorious continuation of human aspirations toward
sublime accomplishments. Despite the "flashing arena of electronic
consoles and out-of-this world instruments" that Rockwell observed
in Houston, Kocivar observed: "One thing has not changed. Rockwell
sensed the romance was still there, in the individual courage of the
spacemen, and painted the first Gemini team as 'idealists in the old
romantic sense, dedicated and devoted to their mission.' "[31] The title
of the painting itself ties the space program back to the early days of
flight, as Kocivar explained: "In the barnstorming days of flight, veteran parachutists used a classic quip on beginners: 'Watch that first
step. It's a long one.' The longest step of our time is Project Gemini."[32]

The Longest Step would inaugurate a series of four major paintings by Rockwell devoted to the American space program.[33] Yet, in
many ways, the first one would be his most successful, since it permitted the artist to work within a mode that felt particularly comfortable. Whereas his later space-related paintings, particularly *Man
on the Moon (United States Space Ship on the Moon)* (fig. 8), would
frustrate Rockwell with their demands for technical accuracy, *The
Longest Step* enabled him to focus on the human significance of
space exploration: the transformation of regular men into astronauts,
a terrestrial species into cosmic voyagers.

I would like to thank Richard Shiff, Linda Henderson, Dom Pisano, Tom Crouch, and James D. Dean for their encouragement during this project. I would also like to thank Pamela Mendelsohn, curatorial assistant at the Norman Rockwell Museum, Stockbridge, Mass., for her gracious assistance with my archival research.

I have used the following abbreviations in my notes: NASA: National Aeronautics and Space Administration; NASM: National Air and Space Museum, Smithsonian Institution, Washington, D.C.; NGA: National Gallery of Art, Washington, D.C.; NRA: Normal Rockwell Archives, Norman Rockwell Museum, Stockbridge, Mass.; SI: Smithsonian Institution, Washington, D.C.

1. Norman Rockwell's painting is now owned by NASM, where it is known by the title *Astronauts Grissom and Young Suiting Up.*

2. James Webb, memorandum to Hiden Cox, Mar. 16, 1962, Art Dept. Files, Aeronautics Division, NASM, SI.

3. Hereward Lester Cooke, letter of invitation to artists, quoted in Hereward Lester Cooke and James D. Dean, *Eyewitness to Space* (New York, 1971), p. 11.

4. For a more detailed description of the foundation of the NASA art program and a discussion of how art was used to humanize the space program, see Anne F. Collins, "Art, NASA, and the Moon Quest," in Belena Chapp, ed., *One Small Step: Exploring America's Adventures in Space, 1959–1999,* exh. cat. (Newark, 1999), pp. 11–26; and Collins, "Art, Technology, and the American Space Program, 1962–1972," *Intertexts* 3: 2 (Fall 1999), pp. 124–46.

5. Hereward Lester Cooke quoted in "Counting Down with the Editor," *Spaceport News* 3 (Jan. 30, 1964), p. 8. Cape Canaveral, which houses the Kennedy Space Center, was known as Cape Kennedy from 1963 to 1973 (Helen T. Wells, Susan H. Whiteley, and Carrie E. Karegeannes, *Origins of NASA Names,* The NASA History Series [Washington, D.C., 1976], p. 149).

6. The first group of artists commissioned by NASA witnessed the *Mercury 9* launch of Gordon Cooper in May 1963. These artists were Robert McCall, Mitchell Jamieson (who covered Cooper's Pacific recovery), Peter Hurd, John McCoy II, George Weymouth, Lamar Dodd, Paul Calle, and Robert Shore.

7. Hereward Lester Cooke, foreword, Phoenix Art Museum, *Robert McCall: Space Artist,* exh. cat. (Phoenix, 1972), unpag.

8. Hereward Lester Cooke, memorandum to James D. Dean, Mar. 18, 1964, Hereward Lester Cooke Papers, Gallery Archives, NGA.

9. Gay Talese, "Glenn Family Calm Amid Cheers and Confetti," *New York Times* (Feb. 24, 1962), p. 13. Cited by James L. Kauffman, *Selling Outer Space: Kennedy, the Media, and Funding for Project Apollo, 1961–1963* (Tuscaloosa, Ala., 1994), p. 61.

10. On NASA's attempt to convey a positive image of itself, see Kauffman, *Selling Outer Space,* esp. ch. 4, "*Life:* NASA's Mouthpiece in the Popular Media"; see also Howard McCurdy, *Space and the American Imagination* (Washington, D.C., 1997), esp. ch. 4, "Apollo: The Aura of Confidence."

11. Letter from Allen F. Hurlbut to James D. Dean, July 17, 1964, box 16, "Astronauts File," NRA. Rockwell resigned from the *Saturday Evening Post* in June 1963 and soon thereafter went to work for *Look* (Karal Ann Marling, *Norman Rockwell* [New York, 1997], p. 137).

12. On the original terms of the contract and their revision, see the following exchange of letters: Carl M. Grey, letter to Norman Rockwell, June 9, 1964; Rockwell to Grey, n.d.; James D. Dean, letter to Rockwell, July 27, 1964. All correspondence, "Astronauts File," box 16, NRA.

13. Telephone interview with James D. Dean, Mar. 1, 1999.

14. On the educational aim of the NASA art program, see James Webb, quoted by Shelby Thompson, "First Drawings Received from NASA's Artists' Cooperation Program," draft news release (June 20, 1963) (news release made public June 25, 1963), Art Dept. Files, Aeronautics Division, NASM, SI.

15. On the significance of *Collier's* space series, see McCurdy, *Space and the American Imagination,* pp. 37–41, and David E. Nye, *American Technological Sublime* (Cambridge, Mass, 1994), pp. 225–26.

16. McCurdy, *Space and the American Imagination,* pp. 29–51.

17. Norman Rockwell, as told to Tom Rockwell, *My Adventures as an Illustrator* (New York, 1994), p. 292.

18. See box 63 (photographs), NRA.

19. Lloyd Mallan, *Suiting Up for Space* (New York, 1971), p. 218.

20. Telephone interview with James D. Dean, Mar. 1, 1999.

21. Although Rockwell had witnessed the astronauts dressing at the Manned Space Center in Houston, they would in fact have dressed at Kennedy Space Center at Cape Canaveral the morning of the launch. Rockwell's depiction of the ready room is based on what he saw in Houston.

22. Photographs taken during Rockwell's session with the astronauts indicate that the countdown clock was located on another wall. Sketches in his files demonstrate that Rockwell was particularly intrigued by the clock and by how to represent it. (See box 63 [photographs] and box 16, "Astronauts File," NRA.)

23. One study of Rockwell's attention to clothing has been carried out by Eric J. Segal, who offers an insightful account of how Rockwell's use of clothing in early illustrations of boys and young men signifies appropriate gender roles. See Eric J. Segal, "Norman Rockwell and the Fashioning of American Masculinity," *Art Bulletin* 78 (Dec. 1996), pp. 633–46.

24. Rockwell, *My Adventures as an Illustrator,* p. 232.

25. Ben Kocivar, "The Longest Step, Painted for *Look* by Norman Rockwell," *Look* (Apr. 20, 1965), p. 109.

26. Lillian D. Kozloski, *U.S. Space Gear: Outfitting the Astronaut* (Washington, D.C., 1994), pp. 58–59, figs. 4.6, 4.7. According to Kozloski, the G3C suits were first "delivered to MSC in August 1964." Rockwell must have witnessed one of the first dress-rehearsals with the new suit. Ultimately Young and Grissom would both wear the G3C space suits.

27. Telephone interview with James D. Dean, Mar. 1, 1999.

28. Brad Herzog, letter to Norman Rockwell, Sept. 2, 1964, "Astronauts File," box 16, NRA.

29. Observation of Dana Bell based on an unidentified essay, personal communication, Mar. 31, 1999.

30. Quoted from *New York Times* (July 25, 1969), by Nye, *American Technological Sublime,* p. 250.

31. Kocivar, "The Longest Step . . .," p. 109.

32. Ibid.

33. In addition to *The Longest Step,* Rockwell painted the following space-related paintings for *Look*: *Man on the Moon (Portrait of an Astronaut),* 1967; *Man on the Moon (United States Space Ship on the Moon),* 1967; *Apollo and Beyond (Apollo 11 Space Team),* 1969; *The Final Impossibility: Man's Tracks on the Moon,* 1969.

DEANE SIMPSON

The Vostok Cosmonauts:

Training the New Soviet Person

New Soviet people will conquer cosmic space.
— Nikita Khrushchev, "The First Flights of Man into Cosmic Space"

Far from assimilating the tool with the body according to the mechanistic tradition of cartesian dualism, we must conceive tool and instrument "like a second sort of body, incorporated into and extending our corporeal powers." It then becomes possible and even necessary to logically invert the terms of our proposition on the role of architecture. The incorporation of technology is not effected by "imagining" a new environment, but by reconfiguring the body itself, pushing outward to where its artificial extremities encounter "the world." It is not so much imagining houses for cyborgs then, but rather of redesigning and literally recrafting our instrument enhanced and equipped body, so that it can "inhabit" the world.
— Georges Teyssot, "Body Building: Toward a New Organicism"

The individuals selected to be the first Soviet cosmonauts, trained in 1960–61, were thought to exemplify the highest manifestation of the New Soviet Person. They were the spiritual children of Soviet premier Nikita Khrushchev, the realization of his dreams of Soviet heroism and futurism, and the first fruits of the scientific and technological revolution engendered during his seven-year plan (fig. 1). The Soviet cosmonaut represented the ongoing project of the modernization of the human organism, whose goal was a new, prototypical human subject. The cosmonaut training program comprised both unprecedented experimental design research, which applied science and technology to the testing and retooling of the human organism (fig. 2), and a course of political and ideological education. The outcome of this project was a series of new performative limits for the human organism through the incorporation of various modes of technology by the body.

In 1959, Soviet authorities began to recruit military pilots for

possible cosmonautic training. By February 1960, they had selected twenty pilots, and the first training session was held on March 14, 1960, under the direction of Colonel General N. P. Kamanin, cosmonaut training director, and Colonel E. A. Karpov, deputy director. Since the tasks of a cosmonaut were then seen as a natural extension of those of an air force pilot, cosmonaut training was modeled to a large extent on the pilot's current training program. A number of the techniques and apparatuses used to train cosmonauts were further developed from existing practices in the field of aviation medicine (a field in which Karpov had considerable expertise). The cosmonaut program, however, intensified existing methods and developed new ones in a more comprehensive and extreme fashion.

The cosmonauts were housed in a building at Khodynskoye Field within the Frunze Central Airfield, near Moscow. By the middle of 1960, the top six candidates – Valery Bykovsky, Yuri Gagarin, Grigory Nelyubov, Andrian Nikolaev, Pavel Popovich, and Gherman Titov – were selected for advanced training.[1] By early April 1961, Gagarin was named as the prime cosmonaut for the first manned flight, with Titov as his back-up. On April 12, 1961, Gagarin carried out his history-making flight aboard Vostok (East), which propelled him into a single orbit around Earth in a flight that lasted 108 minutes before landing inside the Soviet Union.

Despite the secret nature of the Soviet space program, a large amount of material documenting the entire program was, in fact, published by the Soviet Academy of the Sciences in Moscow in 1963. A report entitled "Pervye Kosmicheskie Polety Cheloveka" ("The First Flights of Man into Space") recounted the scientific results of biomedical research conducted in preparation for and during the orbital flights of spacecraft satellites Vostok and *Vostok 2*.[2] This text constituted the official record of early cosmonaut activities. Translated passages from this publication may form a partial catalogue of biotechnical advancements of this period of the program. According to

"The First Flights of Man into Space," the specific methods of cosmonaut training were based upon a detailed analysis of human responses to the conditions of spaceflight, which, in certain cases, were extrapolated from existing medical aviation data and upon the results of medico-biological research carried out during the Sputnik program of the 1950s.

The main principles of the cosmonaut training program were to increase resistance to the unfavorable conditions of spaceflight, and to acquire the working skills for on-board operations and theoretical preparation for spaceflight. The unfavorable conditions of spaceflight were divided schematically into three areas: 1) the conditions of space as a unique uninhabitable environment, such as the condition of total vacuum; ultraviolet and infrared radiation; and extreme temperatures; 2) the conditions of the dynamics of spaceflight, including noise, vibration, weightlessness, and increased gravitational pressures (that is, weightedness); and 3) conditions related to the occupation of the spacecraft cabin, which were more wide-ranging and included the microclimate of the space vehicle; isolation in a confined space with severe restraint upon movement; nutrition, clothing, and work schedule; the extreme nervous and psychological tension caused by novel surroundings; new time-space relations; and the awesome responsibility for one's own actions in an environment in which mistakes could be disastrous. While the unfavorable conditions of space were largely addressed by the architecture of the spacecraft, the latter two categories are of particular interest here as they refer to the intention of retooling the body, or of modifying the architecture of the human organism itself through the concept of incorporation and training.

The training program itself was divided into three main components: first, a theoretical component, which covered the rudiments of rocket and space technology, the construction of Vostok, astronomy, geophysics, and the basics of space and aviation medicine; second, a general physical conditioning component; and third, a special training component, which included aircraft flights to simulate weightlessness; prolonged stays in isolated chambers; parachute jumping; centrifuge and vibri-stand training; training in the thermal chamber with thermal pressure; and flight simulation in the Vostok capsule model.

General physical conditioning focused upon the human body as a highly malleable entity. The goal of the conditioning was to improve overall body mobility and plasticity of the central nervous system; and to develop the functional ability of the whole human organism – in particular, to increase resistance to inner-ear irritations, changes in atmospheric pressure, and a lack of oxygen. Moreover, general physical conditioning provided an excellent way to build the body's resistance to unfavorable environmental conditions created by radiation, poisonous chemicals, infection, or exposure to temperature extremes.

Through regular examinations, doctors monitored and tested the cosmonauts' emotional and physical responses during this general physical conditioning. In addition, the cosmonauts monitored their own activities, such as heart rate, sleep and sleep patterns, appetite, and general well-being. The physical conditioning of the trainees improved considerably as the training period progressed. For example, the exercises on the looping wheel improved the level of body coordination. The cosmonauts also began to show an increased ability to manipulate the body in reduced gravity, as well as a greater resistance to the disorientation and discomfort caused by changes in vertical and horizontal positioning, gained through the training of the inner ear.

General physical conditioning also provided the context for exploration into the reserve possibilities of the main physiological systems,[3] because the cosmonauts demonstrated that the exercises altered their performative capabilities and significantly expanded the limits of their endurance or tolerance. Adaptive incorporation of technology by the body provided certain elastic zones in what we

might call their "performance envelope." The development of physiological conditions (through specific muscular training, for example)
also allowed for an increased resistance to black-out and blurred
vision during centrifuge training.

The special training component developed more specialized skills
and involved more experimental incorporative systems. The red-
and-black chart test, for instance, was performed daily in conjunction
with prolonged periods of testing (ten to fifteen days) in an isolation chamber. The purpose of the test was to investigate the performative limit of the human nervous system in relation to positive,
negative, and zero stimuli. The trainee was asked to count red and
black squares that appeared in random combinations on a digital
chart, counting black in ascent and red in descent (fig. 3). During
the chart tests, the trainee was exposed to various external irritants
and stimuli, including sirens, pulsing lights, sharp noises, musical
rhythms, and the voice of the speaker reading from the same chart.

Throughout the training program, Gagarin performed extremely
well, exhibiting a high level of resistance to irritants and maintaining such individual characteristics as his sense of humor and good
nature through prolonged periods of isolation. He was able to relax,
fall asleep quickly, and wake up in a set time, and maintain a sustained work schedule. Although occasionally suffering from light
drowsiness, he reacted quickly to irritants.

Another test in the special training program, the centrifuge,
introduced the human body to a different kind of stress, increased
gravitational forces or weightedness, and tested the trainee's ability
to adapt or manufacture resistance to the effects of such weightedness (fig. 4). The centrifuge tested the cosmonaut's physiological
reactions to prolonged vertical acceleration and acceleration according to a set trajectory. The facial reactions and expressions of the
cosmonaut were then monitored and filmed (fig. 5). When the cosmonaut exhibited symptoms such as chest pains, distortions of sight,
and severe breathing impediments, the test was terminated.

The centrifuge test monitored a number of physical attributes
including heart rate, breathing rate, blood pressure, electrical charges
in the brain, reactions to stimulation by light, and gas circulation
(respiratory or digestion function). The test revealed that heavy
mechanical pressure on the chest and stomach hindered breathing
during back-chest acceleration. As the increasing speed of the centrifuge and its resulting gravitational forces required cosmonauts
to breathe faster and to involve additional muscles (in the shoulder,
neck, and stomach), a kind of altered panting resulted. Ultimately,
the act of breathing was relearned to accommodate altered weightedness, densities, speeds, and temporal and spatial conditions. Altered
limits of performance were defined through the reorganization and
redistribution of the body.

*During centrifuge training, Titov reported experiencing a feeling
of great pressure over his entire body, especially chest and stomach.
With acceleration at 7G and 9G it was difficult to raise his head, to
lift up his body from the chair. It was difficult to move his arms and
legs. But even with the greatest acceleration it was possible to move
fingers and the lower part of the arm. He experienced great diffi-
culty in breathing as the pressure increased, along with an increase
in general abdominal and leg muscle tension. . . . Titov reported
that this increase in muscle tension helped reduce a worsening of
blurring and greying of vision. Titov also reported that the types
of acceleration during actual spacecraft takeoff and re-entry were
much easier than those simulated in the centrifuge.*[4]

The thermal chamber was designed to test and develop the cosmonaut's resistance to high temperatures in case of an emergency,
such as a malfunction in the spacecraft cabin's cooling systems. The
thermal chamber tests were also intended to educate the cosmonaut and facilitate his ability to monitor his own state in conditions
of overheating. During these trials, a cosmonaut would be placed
in a 70° C. chamber, at 30 percent humidity with 5 feet per second of

Fig. 4
Cosmonaut Gherman Titov in the
centrifuge. 1961. Video stills

air movement for a period of 30, 40, 50, 60, and 70 minutes at two-
to three-day intervals. The test was terminated at the cosmonaut's
request, or when his pulse rate reached 120–130, or his body temperature rose by 2.5 to 3.5° C. A number of tests were conducted before,
during, and after heat exposure: pulse rate; body and mouth temperature; skin temperature on the chest, back, hip, inside the helmet, and between clothes and underwear; pulse rate after standard
physical exercise (fifteen sit-ups); and sweat/water loss (scales).

*During Gagarin's stay in the thermal chamber . . . he perfectly per-
formed all of the tasks of the supervisor. After ten minutes, he had
slight perspiration, after 20 minutes, overheating became apparent,
he started sweating, by this time his temperature rose to 37.5 deg C,
pulse 75–80. By the 40th minute of the test, heavy sweating, body
temperature 38 deg C, 100 pulse . . . Gagarin exhibited a good ability to resist the effects of overheating. The limits here were high,
but Gagarin was used to furnaces and had always been fond of the
Russian sauna bath. Titov read during these tests . . . and, upon his
own demand, prolonged his stay in the chamber for twice as long
as required of the test.*[5]

Prior to the initial 1960–61 training period, a number of other
experiments had also been carried out. One particular series of experiments into weightlessness occurred in the express elevator at Moscow
University. The elevator car – mounted with scientific instrumentation
and volunteer subjects aboard – was placed in free-fall from the
twenty-eighth floor of the building. The end of its fall was cushioned
by air brakes at the base of the shaft, of course, but during the trial,
the subject's feet were attached to the floor for less than one second
before being suspended between the floor and ceiling (in free-fall)
for a limited period of weightlessness. This particular test seems to
be an excellent illustration of the program's tendency to develop
alternative practices for existing technology, resulting in this case in
a bizarre twist on Otis's original demonstration of his safety elevator.

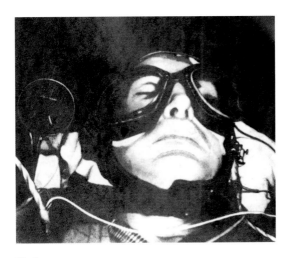

Fig. 5
Titov in the centrifuge. 1961

Fig. 6
Yuri Gagarin in a plaster cast for
the fabrication of a customized
launch seat. 1960

Working from the position that new architectures could be generated first through the reconfiguration of our own bodies rather than through the reimagining of new worlds, it is possible to view the Soviet space program as a strategic site of architectural activity (fig. 6). The program created a prototype for a new subject, reimagining what the human organism could do through the integration of larger social and technical systems and strategies. Seen as a mode of architectural production that reconfigured or redesigned the body itself, the practices of the cosmonaut training program prefigured such fields as deep-sea diving, sports medicine, aviation, extreme sports, and the circus. For instance, David "The Bullet" Smith, the world-record-holding "human cannonball," is an example of the deliberate retooling of the body. Through a number of specific training techniques and various technologies, Smith developed the ability to withstand up to eight times the force of gravity in propelling himself distances of 170–180 feet out of a thirty-two-foot-long cannon barrel. Endeavors such as these confront the commonly understood (natural) performative limits of the human body. Through the incorporation of various modes of technology by the body, the cosmonaut training program initiated an exceptionally sophisticated scientific version of such efforts (fig. 7).

The ability to use a tool or instrument is learned through a process of "incorporation." The word "incorporation" is derived from the Latin *corpus*, meaning to bring within a body. The process of incorporation occurs in both temporal and spatial terms. Temporally, it enables us to perform new activities, which, through repetition over time and through the formation of habit, become imperceptible. Spatially, tools and instruments are incorporated as components of an equipment structure that forms our environment.[6] The philosopher Maurice Merleau-Ponty explained incorporation this way: "The blind man's stick has ceased to be an object for him, and is no longer perceived for itself; its point has become an area of sensitivity, extending the scope and active radius of touch, and providing a parallel to sight."[7] In other words, the blind man temporally and spatially incorporates the stick as a part of his body through repetition of use.

In a wider sense, "incorporation" has been described by Jonathan Crary and Sanford Kwinter as "encompass[ing] the integration of life into larger social and technical systems and strategies."[8] Such a definition is aptly suited to the scientific, technical, social, political, and ideological processes that occurred within the framework of Soviet technological modernization. For example, the production of the New Soviet Person was accordingly defined in Communist Party doctrine as a progressive scientific and technological incorporation.[9]

The modernization of the Soviet state was grounded in the opposition of the technical, scientific, and artificial to the natural. Technology represented the triumph of socialism over nature, and it had long been the state religion.[10] Within such a framework the human body did not operate as an essential natural entity, but rather as a completely impressionable biotechnical arrangement constructed through its relationship to technologically and socially engineered systems. Thus, Soviet modernity promoted Soviet techno-scientific fantasies of achieving total control over nature (and the human organism) – a program in which the discipline of design extended into the realm of the human body and its performance. As present on its sports fields as it was in its factories, this realm of Soviet life was typically identified under the blanket term "Physical Culture."

This project of centralizing control of human organisms through techno-rationalist logics verges precariously on the brink of the absurd and the irrational. In the 1994 film *Serp i molot* (Sickle and Hammer), Russian director Sergei Livnev explored this theme of the artificial. It is a work that tells the bizarre story of sex-change under the Stalinist motto, "If the fatherland needs soldiers, we make soldiers. If it needs mothers, we make mothers."[11] Clearly, here the body was perceived as a malleable or flexible entity, generated and controlled by the state. The transformation was both medical/biological and social/political.

Fig. 7
A cosmonaut being propelled on a
"rocket pole." 1960. Video stills

Soviet cultural historian Vladislav Todorov has described the campaign of mass social engineering that took place in the Soviet Union in this way: "Through labor, the bodies were remade in the factories. Through labor, bodies were corrected in the camps. Camps and factories were the grand laboratories for reinventing the human physique."[12] The factory became an intense site of social engineering, operating as a location "for the production and formation of an altogether new 'type' of human being."[13] The body here operated as the product of an embodied knowledge acquired through vigorous training.

Amid the glut of contemporary texts focusing on the notion of the modern body, the typical portrayal is that of a mechanized and regimented entity. The Soviet body, particularly the factory worker, is frequently described in those terms. However, it is possible to view a project of incorporation within the Soviet space program through a slightly different lens, one in which it would be possible now, from a distanced temporal (as well as social and political) perspective to view aspects of the program as potentially productive design strategies or tendencies. If the factory can be considered as the site of the instrumentalization of the human organism, then the training of cosmonauts for the Soviet space program seems to be the site of the most extreme manifestation of this syndrome. In this regime, the body is transformed through an incorporation of the apparatuses and programs themselves, to the extent that the modernization of the body operates through the preparation for spaceflight, rather than through the event of spaceflight itself. The centrifuge, for example, enables this modernization, not because it accurately simulates the dynamic forces experienced inside the vehicle during liftoff and reentry, but because it produces outcomes related to the incorporation of the actual training apparatus by the body. It and the other experimental training procedures opened up the possibility not of conquering new environments but of redesigning the body to inhabit the existing one while Vostok remained fixed on the ground.

1. For an overview of the program, see Phillip Clark, *The Soviet Manned Space Program* (New York, 1988).
2. N. M. Sisakyna and V. I. Yazdovskogo, "Pervye Kosmicheskie Polety Cheloveka" (Moscow, 1963). In writing this text I have worked from an unpublished English translation by Nadia Mishustina, 1999.
3. *Izvestia* (Apr. 24, 1961), pp. 3–5.
4. Sisakyna and Yazdovskogo, "Pervye Kosmicheskie . . . ."
5. Ibid., p. 91.
6. Georges Teyssot, "The Mutant Body of Architecture," in Elizabeth Diller and Ricardo Scofidio, *Flesh: Architectural Probes* (New York, 1994), p. 15.
7. Maurice Merleau-Ponty, *Phenomenology of Perception* (London, 1962), p. 143.
8. Jonathan Crary and Sanford Kwinter, eds., *Incorporations* (New York, 1992), p. 12.
9. Donald D. Barry and Carol Barner-Barry, *Contemporary Soviet Politics: An Introduction*, 2d ed. (Englewood Cliffs, N.J., 1982), p. 58.
10. Matthew J. Von Bencke, *Politics of Space: A History of U.S.–Soviet/Russian Competition and Cooperation in Space* (Boulder, Col. 1994), p. 13. Von Bencke further writes of the place of technology in modern society: "But its most important icon was no longer the tractor, the hydroelectric plant or even the hydrogen bomb. It was the rocket" (ibid.).
11. *1998 Rotterdam Film Festival Catalogue*.
12. Vladislav Todorov, *Red Square, Black Square: Organon for Revolutionary Imagination* (Albany, N.Y., 1995), p. 70.
13. Sanford Kwinter, "Virtual City, or the Wiring and Waning of the World," *Assemblage 29* (Apr. 1996), p. 96.

Airpower Doctrine and Hypersonic Technology:

A Political History of the Dyna-Soar

ROY F. HOUCHIN II

In spring 1952, with the war in Korea still raging, the Bell Aircraft Company and the United States Air Force started talking about aerospace bomber capability – the ability to operate in the single continuous field of air and space.[1] There were two primary reasons for replacing existing weapon systems, such as the outdated B-17 that had been developed in the 1930s: to increase range of flight and to decrease vulnerability.[2] Yet, even with jet engines, the conventional aircraft of 1952 could not fly nonstop from the American to the Soviet heartlands; and even with aerial refueling – a capability still in development – it would still take the B-52 (see plate 80), the most advanced bomber in the Department of Defense (DoD) pipeline, more than ten hours to reach Moscow from Omaha. Whatever the range, studies also suggested that by 1965 the B-52 and its follow-ups, the B-58 and B-70 bombers, would not be able to strike their Soviet targets without the use of decoys and electronic countermeasures. Thus, early in 1952, Bell Aircraft, creators of the famed X-1 rocket plane (see plate 21), which first broke the sound barrier, urged the air force to consider the development of a hypersonic "boost-glider" that would extend the service's airpower doctrine into space by developing a vehicle that could fly much faster, higher, and farther than any intercontinental jet bomber (or guided missile) and be capable of discharging an atomic bomb to a Soviet target.

At the instigation of Walter Dornberger, the former commander of Nazi Germany's rocket installation at Peenemünde and now a missile design consultant for Bell, Bell initiated a boost-glide program.[3] The envisioned technology incorporated the hypersonic flight and reentry of a spaceplane that had been boosted into its flight trajectory by a missile. Dornberger's bomber-missile (BOMI) concept offered the air force planners an opportunity to extend the service's airpower doctrine into the edge of space. The air force was, therefore, eager to study Bell's idea. As General Donald L. Putt, deputy chief of staff for development and director of the air force's Scientific Advisory Board, stated, "We have always strived to try to fly higher and higher. One could control the atmosphere by just being able to fly a bit higher than the other fellow. So I think the same thing will occur in space."[4]

Subsequently, Bell conducted a five-year program of feasibility studies in hypersonic boost-glide technology. One of the most significant outcomes was the Boeing Company's Dyna-Soar, a military forerunner of today's Space Shuttle (fig. 1; see plate 22).[5] In similar aerodynamic fashion, air force planners proposed using Dyna-Soar (whose name was an acronym for Dynamic Soaring), as a reusable shuttle to perform orbital reconnaissance routinely or act as a strategic deterrent by performing nuclear bombardment missions.[6] As early as 1960, air force planners also began investigating the possibilities of an antisatellite subsystem for Dyna-Soar. Yet, as a weapon system, Dyna-Soar represented a direct military threat to the Soviets. As a result, both the Eisenhower and Kennedy administrations permitted only research on Dyna-Soar; they preferred the development and deployment of automated reconnaissance satellites through a highly classified and compartmented organization ultimately known as the National Reconnaissance Office (NRO).[7] To protect these valuable national intelligence resources, the Eisenhower administration fought to gain international legal acceptance of reconnaissance satellites, rather than military spacecraft. Consequently, air force attempts to incorporate hypersonic boost-glide technology into an aerospace doctrine no longer suited administration officials, and Secretary of Defense Robert S. McNamara announced the cancellation of Dyna-Soar on December 10, 1963. Even though officials in the Office of the Secretary of Defense (OSD) gave other reasons for Dyna-Soar's cancellation, in reality, the air force and OSD disagreed over international space policy; the air force's belief in the promise of routine manned military access to space, as well as Dyna-Soar's operational nature, adversely influenced the program's prospects, and prevented the air force from introducing hypersonic technology into its traditional airpower doctrine.[8]

Fig. 1
General Roscoe C. Wilson and
the Boeing Company's Dyna-Soar
program manager George H.
Stoner with Dyna-Soar model.
ca. 1962

By implementing part of his "New Look" program in 1953, President Dwight D. Eisenhower hoped to harness defense spending and reduce East-West tensions through arms control. In order to realize such an ambitious program in a cold-war environment, Eisenhower needed accurate intelligence to evaluate Soviet military forces, their number, and disposition. He considered the CIA-operated U-2 spy plane a temporary solution, believing that space-based satellites would eventually acquire long-term intelligence. Responding to the intelligence demand, the services – especially the air force – felt justified in requesting fiscal support for research and development of technologies to fulfill Eisenhower's program. Indeed, the need to verify Soviet nuclear strike capabilities warranted a continuous and accurate strategic reconnaissance system. Since international conditions necessitated an intelligence-gathering system, air force planners believed doctrinal logic also dictated a space weapons system. Because space technology in the 1950s had scarcely advanced since the 1910s, air force leaders like General Curtis E. LeMay had long felt the service could anticipate the development of more capable space systems in the same way that aircraft in World War I led to the development of more capable fighters, bombers, and reconnaissance planes for World War II. Similarly, air force leaders knew their cold-war global responsibilities would require evolutionary technology and believed that the high frontier of space justified a similar response.[9] "To control space," noted air force chief of staff General Thomas D. White, "we must not only be able to go through it with vehicles that travel from point to point, but we must stay in space with human beings who can carry out jobs efficiently."[10] Although

acknowledging a concern for the defense of space assets, Eisenhower sought a diplomatic solution to the problem through negotiations with the Soviets and through international agreements at the United Nations. In the process, he established the nation's policy of "freedom-of-space" and, with the creation of NASA, "space-for-peace."

Prior to the exigency of formulating a response to Sputnik (fig. 2), air force leaders envisioned three separate hypersonic boost-glider programs for what would become Dyna-Soar by 1972. Developing these parallel programs, however, could not be accomplished under Eisenhower's budgetary constraints. Thus, on December 10, 1957, the rise of Dyna-Soar became both a political and economic expedient through the consolidation of three previous air force feasibility studies: Hywards (first proposed in March 1956), Brass Bell (first proposed in January 1956 as a focused continuation of Bell Aircraft's 1952 BOMI proposal), and Rocket Bomber (or ROBO, first proposed in February 1956).[11] The first developmental phase of Dyna-Soar, like Hywards, involved testing a piloted vehicle to obtain aerodynamic, structural, and human-factor data at speeds and altitudes significantly beyond the reach of the X-15 research aircraft (fig. 3). Dyna-Soar would operate at speeds up to 10,800 mph and up to an altitude of 350,000 feet, compared with the X-15's 4,000 mph and 250,000 feet. In addition, the first developmental phase would provide a means to evaluate military subsystems.

In gathering test data and establishing criteria for Dyna-Soar, air force leaders made a clear distinction between experimenting with a research prototype and developing a conceptual test vehicle. Unlike the X-15, which was designed to provide information for general application, air force engineers designed Dyna-Soar to provide information and hardware for an operational weapons system. The second developmental phase of Dyna-Soar, like Brass Bell, would produce the operational hardware to fulfill a manned reconnaissance mission by using a spacecraft capable of reaching an altitude of 170,000 feet over a distance of 5,000 to 10,000 nautical miles at a maximum

velocity of 13,200 mph. The third phase incorporated the ROBO
bombardment mission by using a more sophisticated vehicle able to
obtain an orbital altitude of 300,000 feet and a speed of 15,000 mph.
Additionally, during this phase Dyna-Soar would become an operational weapons system capable of accomplishing the air force's
traditional roles of reconnaissance, interception, logistics, and bombardment in the aerospace medium. The service's planners believed
this type of mission flexibility made the boost-glider a logical and
attractive weapons system for the early 1970s.[12]

When the Soviets launched *Sputnik 1* on October 4, 1957, the
question of establishing an international legal precedent for satellite
overflight disappeared in the repercussions of the event. The orbiting
of Sputnik shocked, then galvanized, the American people (see plate
17) and Congress into committing vast resources to the nation's missile
and space programs. In turn, air force leaders believed that their doctrine, as well as concerns for American prestige and security from Soviet
space threats, called for the development of military countermeasures
like Dyna-Soar. The administration, however, advocated and directed a
peaceful civilian response to the Soviet incursion into space. To placate
the proponents of space weapons systems and to provide some technological insurance, OSD's Advanced Research Project Agency (ARPA)
and all three services pursued research on space weapons; but funding
restrictions and space policy directives from Secretary of Defense Neil
H. McElroy and Herbert F. York, the director of Defense Research and
Engineering (DDR&E), permitted only feasibility studies on the kinds of
space-based weapons that air force visionaries considered as exten-
sions of the service's traditional doctrine.[13]

As their early feasibility studies began to reach technological
fruition in the latter years of the Eisenhower administration, air force
leaders requested support for continued development and deployment of their projects in support of the service's doctrine.[14] As such,
in 1957, Dyna-Soar's proponents believed the hypersonic vehicle
would continue the air force's traditional quest for weapon systems

that would perform at higher altitudes, faster speeds, and over
longer ranges than their predecessors – even into space. "In addition
to requiring no [aerial] refueling," they suggested, "it promises
global range, multiple attack trajectories, a 3000' CEP [circular error
probable], the capability of recall, and detection warning time of
three minutes as compared to the fifteen minutes for ICBMs." As
such, it would exceed the abilities of the Strategic Air Command's
(SAC) existing and near-term bombardment aircraft, as well as
match the SAC's ICBMs. Air force leaders also felt that Dyna-Soar's
reconnaissance subsystems would be "extremely vital" for SAC.[15]
They believed a "high order" of photographic, ferret (electronic
eavesdropping), radar, and infrared intelligence as well as a capability for detecting and identifying "hard targets" within the Soviet
Union would be required to provide the nation's decision-makers
with timely reconnaissance information immediately following the
initiation of hostilities. Even though peacetime requirements might
be met by other advanced reconnaissance satellite systems, air force
planners considered the objectives of their boost-glide manned
reconnaissance system and those of the automated reconnaissance
satellites to be quite different. Reconnaissance satellites were
designed to collect intelligence data through routine surveillance.
On the other hand, they envisioned hypersonic boost-glide spaceplanes collecting more "detailed technical intelligence" because they
could fly for "short flight times over areas as desired . . . at compara-
bly lower altitudes (25 to 50 miles versus 300 miles), hence containing
more detailed information." Additionally, the vehicles and their
reconnaissance payloads were designed to be fully recoverable and

Fig. 3
A North American X-15 research rocket plane, which was used to collect data on the upper atmosphere

reusable. As such, air force leaders considered the two means of intelligence gathering as complementary rather than competitive, and they pressed for the development of both capabilities – automated satellite surveillance and manned boost-glide reconnaissance.[16]

On November 9, 1959, Secretary of the Air Force James H. Douglas, Jr., announced the Dyna-Soar contractors. The Boeing Airplane Company won the competition and was awarded the system contract. The Martin Company was named associate contractor with the responsibility for booster development.[17]

Within six months after the American public learned of these contractual decisions, Nikita Khrushchev's threats of Soviet retaliation against American intelligence activities became a reality when the Soviet Union shot down a U-2 reconnaissance aircraft, resulting in the cancellation of these missions. Three weeks after the curtailment of these overflights, a new generation of American early-warning satellites made their debut with the launch of MIDAS II (Missile Defense Alarm System). On August 10, 1960, the successful launch and recovery of the thirteenth Corona reconnaissance satellite (*Discoverer 13*) seemed to promise the emergence of timely photographic intelligence and a means of filling the vacancy left by the cessation of U-2 overflights. While the information provided by these new technologies confirmed Eisenhower's beliefs about the Soviet Union's technological potential, their operational success – like similar missions envisioned for Dyna-Soar – represented a military threat to the Soviet Union. Subsequently, many members of Congress, the public, and the air force believed the Soviets would attempt to eliminate American reconnaissance satellites by military means.[18] Based on their demonstrated abilities, the Soviet's verbal threats to develop an antisatellite system capable of destroying the administration's new intelligence-gathering satellites seemed quite credible. Proponents of hypersonic boost-glide technology again thoroughly examined the historic precedent for the evolutionary development of a weapons system to protect American space-based

assets. This belief fostered renewed action to advance Dyna-Soar and provided fuel for the political fires of the ongoing presidential race. Informed by overhead reconnaissance, Eisenhower discounted these Soviet threats and continued to seek passage of an international agreement to legalize satellite overflights.[19]

When John F. Kennedy took office in January 1961, Eisenhower's secretive Corona reconnaissance satellite program was already providing vital strategic information about the Soviet Union to select elements of the president's senior leadership, including officials within the OSD. At the same time, Soviet threats to disrupt these systems became increasingly frequent and shrill. In reaction to America's technological developments in satellite reconnaissance hardware, the Soviets publicly refuted the previous administration's notions about the nature of their space systems by demonstrating a number of new capabilities. In February 1961, they placed a large spacecraft (weighing more than 14,000 pounds) into orbit to serve as a launch platform for a planetary explorer to Venus. This action pinpointed American concerns about a growing Soviet ability to launch weapons from space against Earth and space targets.[20] Worried about the U.S.S.R.'s military space potential, Kennedy officials within the State Department advocated a continued reliance on Eisenhower's legacy of space-for-peace through a policy of openly disclosing American launch activities. While the political embarrassment of the U-2 incident in May 1960 represented a classic case of the consequences of non-sanctioned territorial overflight, some OSD officials disagreed with the State Department's policy of open disclosure. Subsequently, the Kennedy administration vacillated over the legitimacy issue of reconnaissance overflights; ultimately, they opted to implement a black-out policy. In the fall, as the crisis over Berlin escalated, the president gained additional appreciation for the political importance of reconnaissance satellites.[21]

As this international drama unfolded, NASA administrator James E. Webb and defense secretary McNamara signed an agreement.

Fig. 4
Artist's rendering of Dyna-Soar
landing

Among other things, the agreement enumerated McNamara's desires to control air force research and development, to carry out his plans for cost-accounting reforms, and to initiate his policy of defining the need for any new space program through competition. His policy would make each burgeoning project fiscally competitive with all other DoD and NASA space programs.[22] Implementing McNamara's policy would be a difficult job for the air force's project managers, especially when they did not have the clearances required to know about the highly classified and compartmented details of the NRO's programs. Because the need for new weapon systems was based on the premise that they would be the best means of combating enemy weapons systems not yet in existence, these new projects received severe scrutiny under McNamara's policy. Indeed, research and development programs such as the "pinpoint" guidance system designed for Dyna-Soar's space-to-surface missile became prime targets for the secretary of defense's budget-cutting process because the intensity of future threats was subject to verification, to changes in enemy perceptions about America's military abilities, and to varying political opinions.[23]

In September 1961, air force leaders issued their plan for future (over the next ten years) space operations. Space systems, they argued, promised breakthroughs in a number of key doctrinal and technological areas, including the ability to make fast strategic retaliatory strikes from hypersonic bombers traveling through low Earth orbit. The plan specifically highlighted the need "for the development of reusable space vehicles which would be able to make aerodynamic landings within specified geographical areas after performing space missions" (fig. 4). Finally, all evidence suggested a role for man in space. As Lieutenant General James Ferguson, General LeMay's deputy chief of staff for research and development, stated, "Man has certain qualitative capabilities which machines cannot duplicate. . . . Thus, by including man in military space systems, we significantly increase the flexibility of the systems, as well as increase the proba-

bility of mission success."[24] McNamara and Dr. Harold Brown, York's successor at DDR&E, did not accept the air force's doctrinal explanation for military space operations. Instead, McNamara led other OSD officials in an investigation of alternatives to Boeing's Dyna-Soar in an attempt to cut spiraling defense costs and eliminate his concerns about the possible duplication between the air force's project and NASA's newly approved Gemini program. In addition, OSD officials initiated the secretary's Planning-Programming-Budget System (PPBS) and created five-year plans for research and development, weapons procurement, and cost reductions.[25]

Accompanying these new economic and managerial policies were a new nuclear defense strategy and the complete tightening of all public information regarding reconnaissance satellites; these actions adversely affected the development of Boeing's Dyna-Soar and the service's plans to extend their aerospace doctrine into space. Throughout 1961, air force officials were specifically barred from mentioning the SAMOS (another type of reconnaissance satellite) program by name or mission and were prevented from making public statements dealing with satellite reconnaissance unless they obtained prior approval from the administration.[26] By the end of the year, it was as if "SAMOS and MIDAS never existed," insofar as open government publications were concerned. Shortly thereafter, the administration's "blackout" policy was even extended to *Discoverer,* the cover story for the NRO's Corona satellite. In keeping with this policy, McNamara told the Dyna-Soar program managers to rename their project to highlight its initial research phase and publicly deemphasize its military potential.[27] As the administration's information security policy altered public perception about the importance and nature of military space operations, the secretary of defense introduced his no-cities, "counterforce" nuclear strategy to Congress. Because this strategy called for a force second to none, it did not last long. Following the Cuban Missile Crisis in October 1962, the Soviet Union began a concerted effort to attain full retaliatory capability

Fig. 5
Test pilots with Dyna-Soar mock-up. 1962

with the U.S. In turn, McNamara began to replace "counterforce" with "assured destruction." Under the strategy of "assured destruction," the NRO's reconnaissance satellites emerged as proven, stabilizing, and cost-effective assets to national defense. To tamper with their security by deploying what OSD officials considered to be unproven, destabilizing, and expensive manned systems – such as Dyna-Soar – seemed imprudent.[28]

The implications of these international and domestic events coincided with Brown's views of the air force's attempts to extend its airpower doctrine into space. Like York, Brown was ambivalent about a manned military role in space because, according to him, a military requirement for Dyna-Soar did not exist.[29] He further pronounced a systematic "building block" approach to meet any possible contingency and "to provide insurance" should a need for a manned military space weapons system arise. In addition to defining specific air force missions according to Eisenhower's legacy of space as a sanctuary, Brown believed these efforts would shorten any time lag should OSD approve full-scale development of Dyna-Soar's military subsystems and their subsequent integration into the air force's aerospace doctrine.[30] This OSD policy continued to restrict the Dyna-Soar program to its initial research phase despite the service's detailed assessments of the utility of manned military space missions, such as bombardment, reconnaissance, and logistics. On October 9, 1962, Brown's deputy for defense research and engineering, John H. Rubel, stated that although new ideas for military operations in space might be forthcoming, "technical and policy decisions concerning the development of systems for military use were not being made on general or philosophical grounds or in furtherance of abstract doctrinal concepts. . . . Doctrinal abstractions such as 'sea power' or 'air power' or 'aerospace power' are often useful for analysis and discussion of the patterns as history reveals them. But these doctrinal abstractions do not translate well into new programs and projects."[31] Given this continued domestic climate, support for Dyna-Soar's exis-

tence outside the air force community was eroding even though the test pilots were already chosen and the mock-up completed (fig. 5).

Yet the successful integration of Boeing's Dyna-Soar into the air force's aerospace doctrine depended less on military necessity and more on political acumen. A change of attitude had occurred within the Kennedy administration about the military uses of space and the nature of the threats in the medium. The October 1963 United Nations preliminary settlement between the United States and the Soviet Union renounced "weapons of mass destruction" and formalized these pledges in U.N. Resolution #1884. In addition, both nations now had operational reconnaissance satellites providing vital intelligence information and neither side wished to jeopardize that balance.[32] Because Dyna-Soar had been conceived as a delivery platform for nuclear weapons and eventually considered as a satellite interceptor, two of the military justifications for its existence had been politically compromised. Preempted by treaties limiting the military use of space, Soviet efforts to prohibit American reconnaissance satellite activities with an operational weapons system ended when both nations tacitly accepted existing territorial overflights in outer space.[33]

Through two administrations air force leaders had steadfastly supported the necessity for human military space systems and argued for their inclusion in the service's inventory as a logical extension of its traditional doctrine. Unfortunately, this policy conflicted with the space policies of both the Eisenhower and Kennedy administrations. In turn, each administration used its OSD officials to help ensure the legitimacy of unmanned reconnaissance satellites by restraining the air force's manned military space weapons system to its research phase. As international diplomatic efforts secured the limitation of nuclear weapons in space, the question of overflight became moot when both nations possessed operational reconnaissance satellite systems. The consequences of the administration's previous decisions surfaced on October 23, 1963, in Denver, Colorado, during what had been originally scheduled as a routine status briefing by the Dyna-Soar system program office to OSD officials as published in *Boeing News,* March 21, 1963.[34] In reality, McNamara and Brown wanted answers to three broad questions: "What does the Air Force want to do in space, what is the relative cost effectiveness of manned and unmanned space systems [specifically SAMOS], and how do these two approaches to military space operations compare with other means of doing the job?" Because none of the Dyna-Soar representatives had been briefed about OSD's intentions, they were ill-prepared to answer these pivotal questions; nor did Bill Lamar, the program's chief engineer, or any of the other corporate or military representatives have the special clearances required to present such a comparative and comprehensive briefing about the highly classified space-based assets of the NRO. Thus, McNamara and Brown left the briefing convinced of the cost effectiveness of existing unmanned systems to perform the reconnaissance mission, but unconvinced of the necessity for Dyna-Soar to perform either the bombardment or satellite inspection missions. Neither OSD official addressed what proponents highlighted as the cost-effective logistical consequences of Dyna-Soar's routine access to, and from, space. On December 10, 1963, the Johnson administration announced the cancellation of Dyna-Soar.[35]

Two months later, before the Senate Subcommittee on Department of Defense appropriations, secretary McNamara summarized his reasons for Dyna-Soar's demise:

The X-20 [Dyna-Soar] was not contemplated as a weapon system or even as a prototype of a weapon system. . . . It was a narrowly

defined program, limited primarily to developing the techniques of controlled reentry at a time when the broader question of "Do we need to operate in near-Earth orbit?" has not yet been answered. . . . I don't think we should start out on a billion dollar program until we lay down very clearly what we will do with the product, if and when it proves successful.[36]

Contrary to McNamara's statement, air force leaders specifically defined Dyna-Soar's role as a weapons system and its potential for routine access to space within the context of their aerospace doctrine. In fact, OSD officials denied the air force an opportunity to extend its aerospace doctrine hypersonically into space because they believed the program's military objectives were incompatible with the administration's space policy and duplicated the ability of existing reconnaissance satellites. When the United States and the Soviet Union began formal negotiations to limit the military use of space, having informally insured the mutual acceptance of satellite overflight, Dyna-Soar represented a threat to international stability in the minds of OSD officials. The air force lost its spaceplane, and the opportunity to inhabit the ultimate "high ground," because of a doctrinal rivalry with OSD and because of the operational capabilities of the NRO's reconnaissance satellites. Dyna-Soar's fall was certain when air force leaders, consistently pressing for a manned role in space, failed to persuade McNamara of the spaceplane's ability to out-perform or complement existing unmanned reconnaissance assets. These automated diplomats had become so crucial to administration officials that they could not afford to allow anything to threaten their operation.[37] Not until the beginning of NASA's shuttle operations in the 1980s would the air force once again have an opportunity to explore the hypersonic regime of human military operations in space and to integrate this technology into its "higher, faster, farther tradition" of airpower doctrine.

This essay was published in a different form in *1998 National Aerospace Conference Proceedings* (Dayton: Wright State University, 1999), pp. 266–74. The views expressed in this paper are those of the author and do not reflect the official policy or position of the United States Air Force, the Department of Defense, or the United States Government.

1. As early as March 1958, air force chief of staff Gen. Thomas D. White officially sanctioned the term "aerospace" by using it in his article "Air and Space Are Indivisible," published in *Air Force*. It would be incorporated into the air force's doctrinal manual, *Air Force Manual 1–2*, in 1959.

2. Air Research Development Command, *Abbreviated Systems Development Plan, System 464L – Hypersonic Strategic Weapon System* (Wright-Patterson Air Force Base, Oh., Oct. 10, 1957), pp. 9–10. This is the first Air Research and Development Command-approved development plan for Dyna-Soar. It highlights what proponents believed were the reasons why the Strategic Air Command needed a hypersonic weapons system to eventually replace existing manned bomber and reconnaissance systems. It also suggests that a complementary relationship existed between the command's proposals for unmanned reconnaissance satellites (contained in Weapon System 117L) and manned systems like Dyna-Soar.

3. Dornberger's work stemmed from the A-9/10 research and the A-11/12 studies undertaken while he commanded the Peenemünde rocket faculty. While he was aware of the research done by Eugene Sänger and his wife, Irene Sänger-Bredt, their efforts did not shape Dornberger's designs. Indeed, the two approaches were fundamentally different. The Sängers envisioned a rocket-sled that would push their spaceplane on long rails to begin its initial phase of flight. Using A-4 (V-2) technology, Dornberger put his spaceplane on top of a multistage rocket to boost the vehicle directly into its suborbital flight.

4. Quoted in Gen. Thomas D. White, "Space Control and National Security," *Air Force Magazine* (Apr. 1958), p. 80.

5. Although the Bell Aircraft Company initiated hypersonic studies for the air force, the Boeing Company was selected as the prime contractor for Dyna-Soar on Nov. 9, 1959 (Martin would develop the booster). Directorate of Systems Management, "Weekly Activity Report" (Wright-Patterson Air Force Base, Oh., Nov. 13, 1959);

Directorate of Systems Management, TWX RDZSXB-31261-E (Wright-Patterson Air Force Base, Oh., Nov. 13, 1959).

6. Although Dyna-Soar never flew, air force and Boeing engineers spent three years developing specific military versions of Dyna-Soar to fulfill the second and third phases of the program. The facts and figures presented in this article are from the following detailed sources: R. E. Douglass, *Dyna-Soar Step IIB Reconnaissance Subsystems* (Seattle, Wash., 1961); L. P. Bershad and M. L. Reeves, *Dyna-Soar Step IIB Reconnaissance Subsystems, Engineering Program Report* (Seattle, Wash., 1961); J. F. Toomey and E. E. Spear, *Dyna-Soar Step IIA Planning and Analysis* (Seattle, Wash., 1961); J. Harry Goldie, *Dyna-Soar Step IIA Planning and Analysis: Preliminary Information for System Package Plan* (Seattle, Wash., 1961); J. F. Toomey and E. E. Spear, *Dyna-Soar Step IIA Planning and Analysis Second Interim Report: Preliminary Information for System Package Plan, Addendum* (Seattle, Wash., 1961); J. Harry Goldie, *Dyna-Soar Step IIA Planning and Analysis System Package Program for Dyna-Soar Step IIA Final Report* (Seattle, Wash., 1962); William G. Miller, *Dyna-Soar Step II Program Cost Estimates* (Seattle, Wash., 1962); Lou Bernstein and J. D. Israel, *Dyna-Soar Step II Program Plan* (Seattle, Wash., 1962); D. W. Thurlow, *CNN 50 Program Plan* (Seattle, Wash., 1963); G. E. Ledbetter, J. F. Milton, and J. Harry Goldie, *X-20 Military Capability, Appendix* (Seattle, Wash., 1963); Col. Walter Moore and William E. Lamar, *Manned Orbiting Station and Alternatives, Vol. IV, Report to the President's Scientific Advisory Committee, Space Vehicle Panel* (Dayton, Oh., 1963). While there are additional documents from other contractors, these serve to illustrate the depth and breadth of the air force's continuing commitment to Dyna-Soar's military potential. Dyna-Soar would be flown by a single pilot. In addition, because the vehicle had more than 1,000 cubic feet of usable volume within the vehicle and its transition section, proponents envisioned having the flexibility to deploy a two-man bomber or antisatellite subsystem, a four-man logistical subsystem, or a self-contained space station (the final versions of these variations are summarized in the last two documents). In its station configuration, a crew of three would be able to stay in orbit for 74 days (that included 14 days for reserve).

Additional information was also obtained from the personal files of William E. Lamar, Dayton, Oh., Dyna-Soar's chief engineer and the deputy director of engineering for the program.

7. R. Cargill Hall, "Origins of U.S. Space Policy: Eisenhower, Open Skies, and Freedom of Space," *Exploring the Unknown* (Washington, D.C., 1995), ch. 2; Hall, "Postwar Strategic Reconnaissance and the Genesis of Corona," *Eye in the Sky: The Story of the Corona Spy Satellites* (Washington, D.C., 1998), pp. 86–119; Gerald Haines, "The National Reconnaissance Office: Its Origins, Creation, and Early Years," in Dwayne A. Day, John M. Logsdon, and Brian Latell, eds., *Eye in the Sky*, pp. 143–57; Curtis Peebles, *The Corona Project* (Annapolis, Md., 1997); David N. Spires, *Beyond Horizons* (Colorado Springs, 1997).

8. C. H. Uyehara, "Dyna-Soar Antecedents," unpublished manuscript, pp. 35–36. In his press conference the day he canceled the program, Secretary of Defense Robert S. McNamara said it lacked attainable objectives, it became too costly, and it duplicated NASA efforts.

9. Charles C. Alexander, *Holding the Line: The Eisenhower Era* (Bloomington, Ind., 1975), pp. 16–37; Lawrence Freedman, *Evolution of Nuclear Strategy* (London, 1981), pp. 74–96; U.S. Congress, *DOD Appropriations for 1960* (85th Congress, 1st Sess., Pt. 1, 1959), pp. 391–92; Robert F. Futrell, *Ideas, Concepts, Doctrine: Basic Thinking in the U.S.A.F., 1907–1960* (Maxwell Air Force Base, Al., 1989), p. 215.

10. Gen. Thomas D. White, *Astronautics and Space Exploration* (85th Congress, 2nd Sess., 1960). pp. 109–11.

11. Air Research Development Command, *Abbreviated Systems Development Plan, System 464L, Attachment 3, Technical Analysis,* pp. 1–20. In attachments 1, 2, and the body of the text, three additional aspects of the program are provided: first, a summary of technical reports (through Oct. 1957), definitions, and a detailed explanation of the program's development; second, the additional research that would be required; and third, the cost estimates. Throughout the life of the program, air force officials stressed the need for Dyna-Soar to perform these military missions. As early as November 1958, the question of how best to present these capabilities to OSD officials arose. Overemphasizing the vehicle's military potential might mean a quick death, given the administration's stated

and unstated space policy. Clarence Geiger, an air force historian, wrote the first official (initially classified secret) two-volume history of the program. His work provides an understanding of what air force officials intended for the program and some of the obstacles they faced. Geiger's two additional volumes of primary source supporting documents are invaluable. *History of the X-20A Dyna-Soar* (Andrews Air Force Base, Md., 1963) and *Termination of the X-20A Dyna-Soar* (Andrews Air Force Base, Md., 1964). More recently, Curtis Peebles has written a four-page summary of the program that highlights a few of the issues Geiger raised in 1964, provides additional interpretation, and places the program in the context of other air force space systems. Curtis Peebles, *High Frontier* (Washington, D.C., 1997). Using recently declassified documents and interviews with the participants, Roy F. Houchin II's unpublished doctoral dissertation (Auburn University, 1996) goes even further in placing Dyna-Soar's development in context.

12. Uyehara, "Dyna-Soar Antecedents," pp. 35–36; Richard P. Hallion, "Saga of the Rocket Ships," *Air Enthusiast* (Mar.–June 1978), pp. 90–91; *Ad Hoc Committee for the Evaluation of Contractor Proposals for System Requirement 126 Report* (Oct. 1, 1957), p. 3, attachment 1 (definitions), pp. 6–7. SR 126 outlined the requirement for Rocket-Bomber (ROBO). The Ad Hoc Committee was formed on June 20, 1957, and consisted of representatives from these air force agencies: Air Research and Development Command, Wright Air Development Center, Cambridge Air Force Research Center, Air Material Command, and the Strategic Air Command. In addition, representatives from the National Advisory Committee for Aeronautics and the Office of Scientific Research also attended.

13. Paul B. Stares, *The Militarization of Space: U.S. Policy 1945–1984* (New York, 1985), pp. 25–51; James R. Killian, Jr., *Sputnik, Scientists, and Eisenhower: A Memoir of the First Special Assistant to the President for Science and Technology* (Cambridge, Mass.,1977), pp. 1–19; General B. A. Schriever, "The USAF and Space," *Air Force/Space Digest* (May 1964), pp. 161–62; Houchin, unpublished doctoral dissertation, chs. 6, 7.

14. White, "Air and Space Are Indivisible."

15. Air Research Development Command, *Abbreviated Systems Development Plan, System 464L Attachment 3, Technical Analysis,* pp. 9–10.

The authors were referring to the time it would take the Soviets' radar to detect the two types of approaching vehicles. In turn, they based their mathematical computations on national and service intelligence estimates that suggested what kinds of radars the Soviets were capable of fielding.

16. Ibid. Regarding altitudes, early Dyna-Soar flights were scheduled to be "once-around," suborbital missions; after being launched from Cape Canaveral, Fla., they would land at Edwards Air Force Base, Cal. As such, these initial flights would demonstrate the viability of the vehicle and provide a solid foundation for the operational phase of the program. Later flights would be orbital and longer in duration, giving program engineers an opportunity to expand on the vehicle's military potential.

17. Directorate of Systems Management, "Weekly Activity Report"; Directorate of Systems Management, TWX RDZSXB-31261-E.

18. Stares, *The Militarization of Space,* pp. 138–61; Phillip J. Klass, *Secret Sentries in Space* (New York, 1971), pp. 98–120.

19. Gerald M. Steinberg, *Satellite Reconnaissance: The Role of Informal Bargaining* (New York, 1983), pp. 2–23; Lt. Gen. Howell M. Estes, letter to Gen. Bernard A. Schriever (Sept. 28, 1961); Stares, *The Militarization of Space,* pp. 43–65.

20. George B. Kistiakowsky, *A Scientist in the White House* (Cambridge, Mass., 1976), pp. 380–84; Jeffery T. Richelson, *The U.S. Intelligence Community* (Cambridge, Mass., 1985), pp. 10–16. The Office of Missile and Satellite Systems was established on Aug. 31, 1960, followed by the NRO in Sept. 6, 1961. Walter R. Dornberger, "Arms in Space: Something Else to Worry About," *U.S. News and World Report* (Oct. 9, 1961), p. 76. Interestingly, the Kennedy administration, having used it as political grist for the election campaign, publicly put to rest the missile gap debate. On Feb. 6, 1961, McNamara staged an off-the-record news briefing in which he admitted that the United States and the Soviet Union had about the same small number of ICBMs. Republicans satirically "congratulated" Kennedy on closing the missile gap in just eighteen days. Reporters doggedly pursued this issue for six more weeks, but it was ultimately buried in the aftermath of the Bay of Pigs and the space race. Walter A. McDougall, *The Heavens and the Earth* (New York, 1985), pp. 328–29.

21. Steinberg, *Satellite Reconnaissance,* pp. 37–55; Klass, *Secret Sentries in Space,* pp. 65, 108–14. The policy – begun in Jan. 1961 – would be extended and tightened. As a result, internal conflicts over the nature of military space systems would become less and less prevalent in the media. The lack of public debate indirectly helped shape U.S.-U.S.S.R. space policy relations.

22. Charles D. Bright, *The Jet Makers* (Lawrence, Kan., 1978): pp. 68–74; U.S. Congress, House, *Space Posture, Hearings before the Committee on Science Astronautics* (88th Congress, 1st Sess., 1963), pp. 174–75. The subtle ability of the PPBS process to inhibit the technological innovation of programs that were open to public debate (as opposed to "black" programs, which were highly compartmented) is detailed in Sir Michael Howard and John F. Guilmartin, Jr., "The Revolution in Military Affairs: Defining an Army for the 21st Century," *Fifth Army Conference on Strategy* (Carlisle Barracks, Penn., 1994), pp. 22–25, 34–36. Additional insights on the direct and indirect effects of the PPBS process can be found in Robert S. McNamara, *Essence of Security* (New York, 1968); McNamara, *Blundering into Disaster* (New York, 1986); McNamara, *Out of the Cold* (New York, 1989); McNamara, *In Retrospect* (New York, 1995); Debra Shapley, *Promise and Power: The Life and Times of Robert McNamara* (Boston, 1993); Barton C. Hacker and James M. Grimwood, *On the Shoulders of Titans: A History of Project Gemini* (Washington, D.C., 1977); and Futrell, *Ideas, Concepts, Doctrine.*

23. Goodyear Aircraft Corporation, *Pinpoint Guidance for a Dyna-Soar Air-to-Surface Missile* (Akron, Oh., April 4, 1961). Presentation made to the Dyna-Soar management and engineering staff at the Wright Air Development Division, Wright-Patterson Air Force Base, Oh. From the personal files of William E. Lamar. The debate over the costs, risks, and probability for a successful mission is still alive today. For some of the more recent details on whether the DoD should rely more heavily on the Space Shuttle or continue with its current reliance on expendable launch vehicles, see the remarks of Rep. Dave Weldon (R-Fl) in the May 17, 1999, issue of *Space News;* Sig Christenson, "Future Military Missions May Utilize Space Shuttle," *San Antonio Express* (May 21, 1999); and Warren Ferster and Brian Berger, "U.S. Air Force Weighs DSP Shuttle Launch," *Space News* (June 14, 1999).

24. U.S. Congress, House, *Department of Defense Appropriations for 1963* (87th Congress, 1st Sess., Pt. 2, 1961), pp. 476–89.

25. U.S. Congress, Senate, *TFX Contract Investigation, Hearings before the Permanent Subcommittee on Investigations of the Committee on Government Operations* (88th Congress, 1st Sess., Pt. 3, 1963), pp. 756–58; Memo for Record, Zuckert, Korth, and McNamara, Nov. 21, 1962, in *TFX Contract,* Pt. 4, pp. 1030–34; Department of Defense News Release No. 1907-62, Nov. 24, 1962 (U.S. Air Force Historical Research Agency, Maxwell Air Force Base, Ala.); McNamara, *The Essence of Security,* pp. 85–96; Alain Enthoven and K. Wayne Smith, *How Much Is Enough? Shaping the Defense Program, 1961–1969* (New York, 1971), pp. 24–36.

26. Klass, *Secret Sentries in Space,* p. 110; Steinberg, *Satellite Reconnaissance,* p. 43.

27. Dyna-Soar gained an additional designation on June 26, 1962. Five months earlier, secretary of defense McNamara had directed Dyna-Soar program manager Col. Walter Moore to create a new designation that would reflect the system's Step I research phase rather than its military potential. This policy was in keeping with the administration's decision to impose a blackout on the public disclosure of reconnaissance activity. As this blackout policy (begun in Jan. 1961) was extended and tightened, internal conflicts over the nature of military space systems became less and less prevalent in the media and the lack of public debate indirectly helped shape U.S.–U.S.S.R. space policy relations. Subsequently, Dyna-Soar was also referred to as X-20 after June 1962. But, in keeping with the spirit of McNamara's intent, it is incorrect to suggest that the name X-20 represents the entire program after June 1962. Indeed, X-20 should never be used in reference to the program prior to June 1962 and should only be used to refer to the Step I research phase of the program after June 1962. Similarly, the name Dyna-Soar more correctly refers to the military aspects of the program after June 1962. Ironically, most people still associate the name X-20 with the program rather than Dyna-Soar, although the name Dyna-Soar was never dropped and the air force always viewed the project as a multiphased program that would yield a weapons system. For more on the informal bargaining process, see Steinberg, *Satellite Reconnaissance.*

28. William W. Kaufmann, *The McNamara Strategy* (New York, 1964), pp. 114–21; Henry L. Trewhitt, *McNamara: His Ordeal in the Pentagon* (New York, 1971), pp. 110–16; McDougall, *The Heavens and the Earth,* pp. 329–41.

29. U.S. Congress, Senate, *NASA Authorizations for FY 1963, Hearings Before the Committee on Aeronautical and Space Sciences* (87th Congress, 2nd Sess., 1962), p. 343.

30. Ibid., p. 335.

31. John H. Rubel, "Rubel Spells Out Space Philosophy," *Missiles and Rockets* (Oct. 22, 1962), pp. 37–38.

32. New York Department of Public Information, United Nations, *Yearbook of the United Nations, 1963* (Washington, D.C., 1963), pp. 101–2, 133–34.

33. Walter C. Clements, Jr., *Outer Space and Arms Control* (Cambridge, Mass., 1966), pp. 31–54; Steinberg, *Satellite Reconnaissance,* pp. 64–67, 86–87. The Soviets used their own passive military reconnaissance satellites after the launching of *Cosmos 4* on Apr. 26, 1962.

34. William E. Lamar, Director of X-20 (Dyna-Soar) Engineering, J. Harry Goldie, Boeing Project Representative, and Col. Walter L. Moore, Program Director, *After Action Reports,* Oct. 24, 1963 (Wright Patterson Air Force Base, Dayton).

35. McNamara Press Release, Dec. 10, 1963 (U.S. Air Force Historical Research Agency, Maxwell Air Force Base, Ala.).

36. U.S. Congress, Senate, *Subcommittee of DOD Appropriations of 1964* (88th Congress, 2nd Sess., Pt. 1, 1964), pp. 171–75. For a historical overview of hypersonic research from 1924 through 1995, see Richard P. Hallion, ed., *The Hypersonic Revolution: Case Studies in the History of Hypersonic Technology* (Washington, D.C., 1998), 3 vols.

37. Garret Mattingly, *Renaissance Diplomacy* (Boston, Mass., 1955). Mattingly chronicles the stabilizing role that diplomats played as each provided valuable intelligence about their host states to their sponsors. Just as diplomats provided for the stability of nation-states during the Renaissance, I posit that reconnaissance satellites began to perform a similar stabilizing role for the United States and the Soviet Union in the early 1960s, hence the phrase "automated diplomats."

Selling Space:

Corporate Identity and Space Imagery

LEONARD RAU

Space and corporate identity have a common ground in contemporary society: both are semiabstract concepts created by the communication systems that surround them. Space is a concept constructed to rationalize the place of the Earth in a wider system. Corporate identity is also a concept, created and refined over the past one hundred years to enable corporations to build and enhance emotional value, either within or outside an organization. This essay assesses how companies have used space imagery to enhance their corporate profile. My objective is to ascertain why and how the use of space-related imagery has had an impact on both high- and low-technology-oriented companies.

Space imagery began to infiltrate the realm of corporate identity during the late 1970s, when space travel and related culture were heavily promoted. For instance, NASA's space program, begun in 1958, gained expanding public support in 1981 with the launch of the Space Shuttle. Meanwhile, films such as the *Star Wars* trilogy (1977, 1980, 1983), *Alien* (1979), the James Bond film *Moonraker* (1979; see pl. 43), and the cult classic *Bladerunner* (1982) increasingly portrayed a world familiar with space exploration and the products of space-related research, as well as the concept of mass travel. Both the NASA launch and the cinematic portrayal of space travel have arguably shaped the idea, meaning, and future of space exploration. Many corporations interested in expanding or redefining their corporate identities began to associate themselves with the latest space technology.

Before considering how corporate identities have been shaped by space imagery, it is necessary to define the terms of discussion. "Corporate identity" is defined as the brand name, logotype, trademark, and other marks that are used to represent the meaning and purpose of an organization or company, and it is executed through an "implementation system," a method for applying the logotype to corporate products, buildings, or services. Through the use of the logotype, combined with distinctive colors and typefaces, a company can develop a tone of voice for communication, termed a "corporate expression."[1] Both corporate identity and corporate expression are long-term, strategic marketing activities undertaken by companies to differentiate themselves from competitors, build emotional meaning, and demonstrate a company's value.

Space, "the immeasurable expanse in which the solar and stellar systems, nebulae, and so on are situated,"[2] has almost magnetically drawn human interest. H. G. Wells explained its appeal: "There is no way back to the past. The choice is the Universe – or nothing."[3] Understanding space and its opportunities is part of the future, albeit in a distinctly different way now than thirty years ago. Reflecting this interest in space, numerous companies have employed space imagery to help define corporate identity. Four are of particular interest: Boeing and Lockheed Martin, both directly involved in the exploration of space; Netscape Communications, which introduced a new technology and a new communications medium associated with space; and the Saturn Group, a General Motors car company whose product does not directly relate to space technology at all. Each of these four companies has benefited from using space imagery to develop or enhance its corporate identity, especially in an increasingly future-focused society, dominated by the rise of the Internet and global branding.

Boeing, the world's largest aircraft manufacturer, has a distinct corporate identity, developed by its own graphic artists in the 1940s,[4] featuring a word mark written in the Stratotype typeface especially developed for the Boeing Company in 1947.[5] In 1997, Boeing commissioned Rick Eiber, a Seattle-based corporate identity consultant (whom they had hired once before in 1987), to design a new logotype to represent the merger between Boeing and McDonnell Douglas.[6] Boeing's strategy was both to modify the existing word mark and logotype and to develop a new implementation system to popularize its use. The new logotype was developed to evoke "the global Boeing

Fig. 1
Rick Eiber, designer. Corporate identity for the Boeing Company, 1997, as applied to the administration building of Boeing Plant 2, East Marginal Way, Seattle, Washington

Fig. 2
Enterprise IG, designer. Logotype for Lockheed Martin, 1995, as applied to NASA's X-33 reusable launch vehicle, shown in a computer-generated image by John Frassanito and Associates. 1997

markets in commercial, defense, and space flight"[7] and to represent the ambition and form of the merger between Boeing and McDonnell Douglas (fig. 1). The new logotype, a redesign of the McDonnell Douglas logo (developed in the 1960s), comprises symbolic space-related elements: the globe as viewed from space, a wing motif to characterize the physical equipment that Boeing manufactures, and a "swish" around the globe to represent movement and dynamism. The word mark and logotype can be used in either a stacked or single-line application.[8]

Lockheed Martin, one of the world's leading diversified technology companies, appointed the design consultancy Enterprise IG in 1995 to develop a visual representation of the merger between Lockheed and Martin Marietta.[9] Based on a stylized development of the old identities, the new logotype comprises two highly simplified and stylized arrows, one passing horizontally, the other pushing up at an angle of 70 degrees, combined with the word mark "Lockheed Martin" drawn in a proprietary typeface, that is, one that was developed for Lockheed Martin's exclusive use (fig. 2). The arrows indicate movement, precision, focus, and direction – all core values of the organization.[10] Daniel Tellep, chairman and chief executive officer of Lockheed Martin, explained that the identity change was intended to align business strategy with identity strategy. As with all corporate

identities, a key component of theirs was the implementation system, which included using the logo on everything from signage to starships, such as the proposed X-33 VentureStar. Tellep proclaimed that the new corporate identity was contributing to Lockheed Martin's success: "We maintained our leadership role in defense and aerospace, while solidifying our position in our high growth information, materials, and energy businesses, giving us the platform we need for continued strong financial performance."[11]

Unlike the identities of Boeing and Lockheed Martin, which evolved from previous identities, the corporate identities of Netscape and Saturn were developed to meet the needs of newly formed companies. Both were designed by Landor Associates of San Francisco, who also were experienced in developing, in the late 1980s through the 1990s, corporate identities for several telecommunications and technology companies, such as GE Communications and Telenor (see plate 60), as well as Alcatel, France Telecom, and AT&T's WorldNet (figs. 3–5).[12]

Netscape Communications, a software company famed for its development of the Internet browser Netscape Navigator, had specific needs for its corporate identity.[13] Principally, the logo needed to be suitable for application both on and off screen as well as on packaging, browser windows, and corporate merchandise. The Netscape

Fig. 3
Landor Associates, designer.
Corporate identity system for
Alcatel. 1987

Fig. 4
Landor Associates, designer.
Corporate identity for France
Telecom. 1993

Fig. 5
Landor Associates, designer.
Corporate identity for AT&T's
WorldNet. 1995

logotype features an oversize letter "N" on a crescent formed by the curvature of the Earth (fig. 6). The "N" is framed by a square box and surrounded by stars, which are animated for on-screen application to indicate invisible electronic data movement. Secondary elements, such as a lighthouse motif, were developed to allow brand expression. Landor aimed to develop an "identity for Netscape [that] articulates its user-friendly attributes and, seen worldwide by millions of users daily, serves as a recognizable, durable, and permanent billboard on the Web."[14]

In 1983, when General Motors established its new automobile manufacturing division, the Saturn Group, Landor Associates was commissioned to develop its corporate brand and corporate identity, reflecting the credo, "Saturn – a different kind of car/company."[15] Landor's solution was to interpret the Saturn Corporation name literally, developing a corporate identity that relied heavily on space imagery (fig. 7). The name Saturn was used to represent the planet as well as the Saturn rockets used in the Apollo program.[16] Its typeface was a conscious modification of that used in an earlier NASA logo. The logo also drew upon Saturn's red color to represent not only Saturn but also the heat and power of the Sun. Two curved lines represent the curvature and outer ring that symbolize Saturn. Landor consistently applied the new logo to every aspect of the company's production, including the car, corporate and dealership signage, letterhead and stationery, and even the car key itself.[17]

It is interesting to note that even though Saturn's logo is the most distinctive of the four identities examined here, the company is furthest away from space in terms of its product. Instead of visualizing a direct connection to space, Landor used motifs and representative imagery to incorporate the key values or concepts associated with space into Saturn's corporate identity: technological ambition, achievement, success, development, speed, transportation, and direction. Whereas the Saturn Group has followed the semiliteral path by explaining the key point of difference between their cars and others'

through the application of "out-of-this-world" imagery, Boeing and Lockheed Martin have developed literal representations of space. Meanwhile, Netscape has followed the abstract path, developing an animated, on-screen identity that represents the aspirations of space exploration: discovery, new technology, and real-life applications.

As demonstrated by these four examples, the values associated with space can communicate the values of an organization in a positive and dynamic way. Corporate communications influence the perception of a company among all audience groups – shareholders, customers, and employees. To increase the power and potency of corporate communications, a clear idea, message, and delivery mechanism need to be in place. Increased competition makes it imperative that companies distinguish themselves from one another in all ways. The traditional methods of using proprietary technology, product availability, or pricing to distinguish oneself are easily copied and often bettered; therefore, companies such as these are looking to differentiate themselves from others through the corporate brand, often with emotional meaning. Space as a concept has numerous strong characteristics to which many companies aspire: it is infinite and unknown; it requires precise and sophisticated calculations; and it offers challenging opportunities.

National identity plays an important role in the development of corporate identities that use space imagery. According to recent research published by Interbrand Newell and Sorrell, New York, the leading corporations using space imagery in their corporate identity are predominantly American-based.[18] Space programs are a clear result of national policy and world status.[19] For instance, General Motors chose the name Saturn because of the national importance of the Saturn rocket in the Apollo space program. Saturn wanted their corporate image to reflect the same triumph of technology that the Apollo mission achieved in retaliating against Russia's successful launch of the first satellite, *Sputnik 1*, in 1957 and its first manned mission, with cosmonaut Yuri Gagarin, in 1961. Or, in the

Fig. 6
Landor Associates, designer.
Corporate identity system for
Netscape. 1994

Fig. 7
Landor Associates, designer.
Corporate identity for Saturn, as
applied to a car key. 1987

words of Saturn's marketing group: "General Motors wanted to launch a small car project that could create vehicles, designed and manufactured in the United States, that could beat foreign competition in a marketplace which, at the time, was dominated by foreign imports. Therefore, the project was dubbed *Saturn* from the early days, in memory of the Saturn rockets."[20]

The expression of national identity is evident at all levels in companies operating in the global marketplace; from NASA product endorsement (both official and unofficial) to leading corporations such as Boeing, who have introduced space technology into aircraft, most recently with its 1999 Airborne Satellite Television System, to small local companies such as the British company SureLoc, with its advanced range of structural and industrial adhesives.[21] Using national identity in a strategic manner to drive communications has proven to be a powerful marketing tool for a variety of companies including Swatch, whose logo incorporates the Swiss flag, drawing on the reputation of Swiss watchmakers for precision and fine craftsmanship.

Corporate expression that embraces the power of space imagery to enhance a company's reputation in the customer's mind can help to introduce a new technology. Products such as Tefal's non-stick pans based on teflon technology, Nestlé's freeze-dried coffee, and, most recently, a new Russian yogurt using cultures extracted from cosmonauts' saliva have all been developed from space-related technology.[22] This interest in space technology has not been manifested directly into a corporate identity, but through forming a subtle relationship with space in order to facilitate corporate or product communications.

Corporate logos associated with the forward-thinking, delivery-driven culture of space generate the perception of a corporation's ambition and ability to change and articulate the unknown. For instance, the use of Saturn borrows space imagery as part of its strategic corporate identity development.[23] Corporations that adopt space imagery for their corporate identities have also acknowl-

edged its benefits inside the company. Space imagery is a powerful tool in attracting new employees and making a company a more attractive place to work. Developing a culture based on ground-breaking work can motivate an organization to succeed. Innovative companies such as Saturn, for example, use product development as a key stimulus of the business culture.

Although not a direct part of a corporate identity, drawing on imagery of space in the widest sense can fulfill a key role. Rolex has consistently sent watches into space with astronauts and then used the resulting coverage as part of a corporate advertising campaign. The meaning is clear: a Rolex watch operates without gravity and is so accurate that even astronauts can rely on the technology.[24] The consumer, who will probably never enter space, still knows and believes that the object has the possibility to outperform other watches; this increases the perceived value of the Rolex brand. Thus, through strategic communications, companies such as Tefal and Rolex have shown that the corporate brand of an organization can be built to use "space" values to inspire confidence in investors, employees, and customers alike. This will probably increase as more activities develop in space.

Michio Kaku, professor of theoretical physics, argues that the future will introduce "a fourth ingredient that makes up our understanding of the universe: spacetime."[25] Commercial success will continue to be driven by research and development, albeit in a much shorter time frame. This view of the future raises questions regarding existing corporate identities and the basis on which they were developed, literal or abstract. For example, the current identity of AT&T represents space imagery through its portrayal of the globe symbol, which denotes the passing of information across a network (although still through wires).[26] The identity has longevity. In contrast, British Telecom indicates its focus on voice-based telephony by featuring a human piper on its logo, revealing a reluctance to develop corporate identity to represent the challenge of the digital age.[27]

Fig. 8
Advertisement for Langenscheidt's
bilingual Russian-English dictionary
featuring American astronaut
David Wolf aboard the Russian
space station *Mir*. From *Publisher's
Weekly,* January 31, 2000

The *Mir* space station and the forthcoming International Space Station will enhance the potential of space to impact corporate identity.[28] By placing a product physically on the space station, numerous companies are trying to achieve what Tang did when astronauts were featured consuming its powdered drink. Echoing this strategy, Langenscheidt advertised its Russian-English dictionary being used by an American astronaut aboard *Mir,* with the tag line: "Don't leave Canaveral without it" (fig. 8). The increasing role of product placement in colonizing space will thus benefit companies that do not have products that are directly space-related.

It would be naive to look at the potential communication benefits relating to space and corporate identity without considering the ethical dimension. There are many positive implications of association with space, as presented in this essay, but, as with military technology, the benefits could also bring negative implications. As the ethical concerns of investors or consumers are likely to increase, we should consider whether being associated with technology developed for warfare or environmental destruction will be acceptable. This question will increasingly become an issue, following the already vocal public reaction to the brand disasters that Shell faced with the Brent Spar oil rig disposal[29] or Nike's purported exploitation of child labor in Asia. Taxpayers will determine the level of investment available to build a habitable space station in near or far space. Although not a direct influence on the future of corporate identity, it is clear that a negative connotation could result from being linked to space – it may be seen as a waste of time and money. The justification for government spending is likely to come from two areas, each of which will significantly aid corporate identity. The first will be the stimulation of research and development to foster new products that will stimulate the economy and raise the standard of living.[30] The second will be the justifiable funding of academic research, albeit through corporate-led joint initiatives.[31]

Public perceptions of space have traditionally been formed based on a combination of news reports of space exploration and science-fiction movies. Representations of space are both literal and abstract in nature. This is becoming evident throughout several local, international, and global organizations, such as Texaco, Philips, and Star Alliance. The increase of space-related imagery in corporate identity will influence the wider public's view of space. Swayed by this information, people may believe that Netscape is enhanced by its relationship with space, or that Lockheed Martin has introduced state-of-the-art space-related technology into the domestic environment,[32] or that Saturn cars are "above the earthly competition."

The greatest change in emphasis regarding space and corporate identity will come from the benefit in emotional terms that space exploration brings. Space research is facilitating the introduction of invisible technology, such as telecommunications, into modern society. Similar to space technology, telecommunications products focus on facilitation and ideas; their corporate identity, therefore, will be an important vehicle in delivering these messages, over the traditional benefit of focusing on materials, technology, and the idea of "progress."

The successful organizations of the future are going to be those companies that are flexible, idea-oriented, and responsive to customer needs, all characteristics demanded by space exploration (the astronaut as customer). A society focused on ideas and service will demand that companies use design to build corporate identity that has meaning. Peter Gorb, a professor of design management, has argued that corporate identity is the visual manifestation of corporate strategy, and that therefore "design is a corporate weapon."[33] Companies will use space imagery to support strategic marketing activities to continue to build competitive advantage, communicate company values, and attract and excite customers.

1. Unpublished internal document, 1999, SAS Design Consultants, London.

2. *The Shorter Oxford English Dictionary,* 3d ed. (Oxford, England, 1954, repr. 1970).

3. Quoted in Michio Kaku, *Vision* (Oxford, England, 1998), p. 295.

4. See *http://www.boeing.com/news/releases/1997/news.release.970801.html.*

5. John Zukowsky, ed., *Building for Air Travel* (Chicago, 1996), p. 129. This typeface was developed for the first Boeing postwar long-range aircraft, the 377 Stratocruiser.

6. See *http://www.boeing.com/news/releases/1997/news.release.970801.html.*

7. The Boeing Company, corporate brochure, 1997, p. 5.

8. See *http://www.boeing.com/news/releases/1997/histlogo.htm* for a history of the Boeing and the McDonnell Douglas logos.

9. Formerly Anspach Grossman Portugal, Enterprise IG is a wholly owned subsidiary of WPP Group plc, a marketing communications group.

10. See Lockheed Martin's web site at *www.lockheedmartin.com.*

11. See *http://www.enterpriseig.com/case/casepage/lockheed/lockh.html.*

12. Landor Associates is a wholly owned subsidiary of the global marketing communications group Y and R. See *http://www.landor.com.*

13. Netscape Communications was bought out by America Online in November 1998.

14. See *http://www.landor.com.*

15. The Saturn was not publicly announced as established until January 1985 and its identity was not launched until December 15, 1987. The time gap between formation and operation was caused by the new product development process, see *http://www.saturn.com.*

16. The Saturn Group, e-mail correspondence, Sept. 7, 1999.

17. Graphis, *Corporate Identity 2* (Zürich, 1994), p. 26.

18. See *http://www.interbrand.com.*

19. See Michio Kaku, *The Space Race* (Oxford, England, 1998).

20. The Saturn Group, e-mail correspondence.

21. For further reading, see U.S. Chamber of Commerce, *The National Importance of the Development of Space* (Washington, D.C., Mar. 16, 1999).

22. Reuters (Aug. 11, 1999). See *http://www.newscientist.com/ns/19940814/newsstory12.html.*

23. James C. Collins, *Built to Last: Successful Habits of Visionary Companies* (New York, 1997).

24. David W. Reed, ed., *Spirit of Enterprise: The 1990 Rolex Awards* (Bern, Switzerland, 1990).

25. Michio Kaku, *Visions: How Science Will Revolutionize the 21st Century* (New York, 1998), ch. entitled "Masters of Space and Time."

26. The logo was originally designed by Saul Bass in 1984.

27. The logo was originally designed by Wolf Olins, London, 1991; it was redesigned by Enterprise IG, London, 1999.

28. See *http://www.cnn.com/TECH/space/9906/07/shuttle.newser/index.html.*

29. See *The Electronic Telegraph* (Jan. 30, 1998), issue 953.

30. The process of commercial exploitation is currently encouraged by NASA. See "Technology Opportunities," press release, May 1998, NASA.

31. See NASA administrator Daniel S. Goldin's presentation before the Committee on Science, United States House of Representatives, Apr. 28, 1999, *ftp://ftp.hq.nasa.gov/pub/pao/Goldin/1999/April28oral.html.*

32. Lockheed Martin has accomplished this arguably through technology licensing. Tefal, with its exploitation of teflon technology, has led the way in benefiting from the space program. The Teflon material was developed in the 1930s, but the adhesive technology, which allowed the mass manufacturing of non-stick frying pans, was the direct result of the American space program.

33. Peter Gorb, *Design Management* (London, 1990).

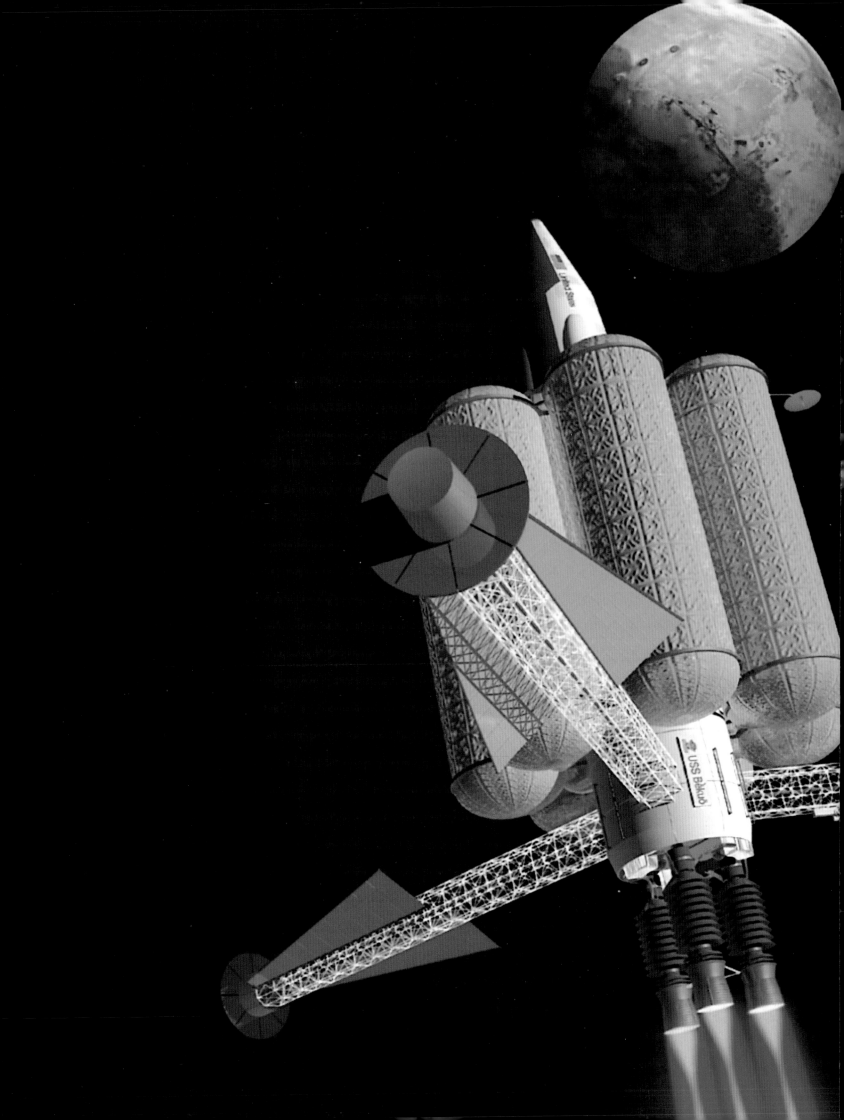

Exploration and Inhabitation
of the Wilderness

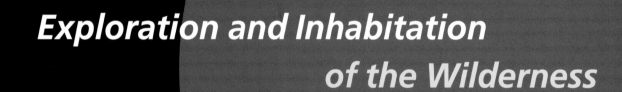

66
John Frassanito and Associates.
VASIMR plasma-powered
spacecraft entering Mars orbit.
ca. 1997–98. Computer-generated
rendering. ca.1997–98

67
Willy Ley. *Space Stations.* 1958

Rocket pioneer Willy Ley (1906–1969) left Germany for the United States in the 1930s. Here he developed a successful career as a freelance writer on scientific subjects and became a media celebrity for children through products ranging from books to hobby kits. The jacket design for his book *Space Stations* depicts a variant of the famous rotating wheel space station designed by Wernher von Braun that was popularized throughout the 1950s and early 1960s on lunch boxes, road maps to the stars, and other items. Also among such depictions are views of von Braun's three-stage rocket of the type that Ley and von Braun popularized in their *Collier's* magazine articles of 1952, many of which were accompanied by the striking renderings of Chesley Bonestell, Fred Freeman, and Rolf Klep. The extension of these images throughout popular culture attests to their significance within the space-conscious society of the 1950s and 1960s.

68
Monogram model kit for 1959
spacecraft designed by Willy Ley

69
Lunch box depicting a space station
and multi-stage spacecraft designed
by Wernher von Braun. 1958

70
The Amoco Map of Space
Mysteries. 1958

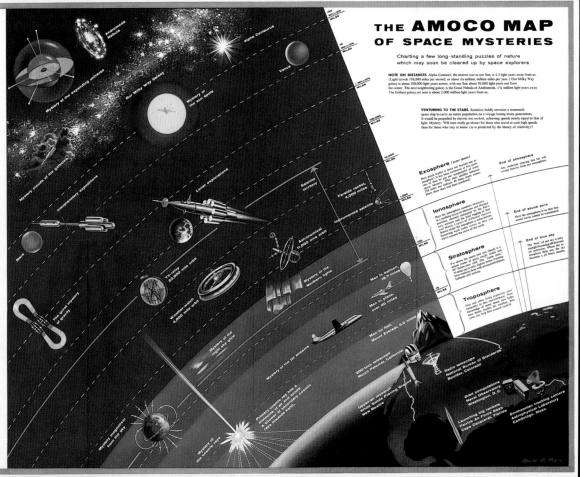

An epic drama of adventure and exploration

Space Station One: your first step in an Odyssey that will take you to the Moon, the planets and the distant stars.

2001: STANLEY KUBRICK'S **a space odyssey**

STARRING KEIR DULLEA · GARY LOCKWOOD SCREENPLAY BY STANLEY KUBRICK AND ARTHUR C. CLARKE PRODUCED AND DIRECTED BY STANLEY KUBRICK · IN SUPER PANAVISION® · METROCOLOR

G GENERAL AUDIENCES All Ages Admitted MGM United Artists A Transamerica Company

71
Robert McCall. Poster for *2001: A Space Odyssey.* 1968

2001: A Space Odyssey (1968) was a landmark science-fiction film directed by Stanley Kubrick and written by noted futurist Arthur C. Clarke, who also wrote the sequel, *2010* (1984). The film is important for a number of reasons, some of which relate to design for space exploration, in both science fiction and reality. *2001* was the first science-fiction film to elaborately portray the epic of space travel. Its realistic approach to visualizing space travel as an everyday occurrence was so convincing that Wernher von Braun himself was said to have encouraged the designers then working in Raymond Loewy's office on Skylab, America's first space station (launched in 1973), to see the film. Part of the credit for this approach to spacecraft interiors goes to Frederick I. Ordway III for his technical advice, to the production designers Ernest Archer, Harry Lange, and Anthony Masters, and to fashion designer Hardy Amies, who was the costume designer for the film. In *2001,* stewardesses overcome the lack of gravity in the Pan Am spaceliner as well as in the Aries Moonship by wearing Velcro slippers called Grip Shoes. The spacecraft interiors themselves are reminiscent of the modular-panel interiors of airliners from the 1960s, and so reinforce the realism of these scenes. Perhaps fueled by the compelling picture portrayed by the film, as well as by the *Apollo 8* orbital Moon flight of 1968, Pan Am began collecting names for a waiting list for a future commercial flight to the Moon; by July 1969, the list included more than 25,000 people.

72, 73
Stanley Kubrick, director. *2001:
A Space Odyssey*. 1968. Production
stills showing interiors of the
spacecraft *Discovery* (top) and
Aries 1B (bottom)

Along the way of **TWA** . . .

FABULOUS
Disneyland
© Disneyland Inc. 1955

TWA takes you comfortably, swiftly, to fabulous Disneyland. Enjoy all the wonders of Fantasyland, Frontierland, Adventureland and Tomorrowland...
take a ride in TWA's "Rocket to the Moon."

TWA is the Official Airline to Disneyland — Fly TWA to Los Angeles

TWA
TRANS WORLD AIRLINES
U.S.A. · EUROPE
AFRICA · ASIA

Use your camera — remember your trip with pictures.

74
Postcard of Tomorrowland in
Disneyland, showing the Rocket
to the Moon, designed by John
Hench with the advice of Wernher
von Braun and Willy Ley. 1955

Although there were space-travel and science-fiction displays at world's fairs in Chicago (1933–34), New York (1939), Brussels (1958), and Seattle (1962), to name a few, Disneyland was the first modern amusement park to feature an exhibition related to future space-flight. Rocket to the Moon Park in Disneyland was sponsored by Trans World Airlines, and, five years later, a large flying saucer at Freedomland in the Bronx was sponsored by Braniff Airlines. Since then, exhibitions of actual space artifacts, such as those installed in the 1990s by the firms BRC and Architectura at Space Center Houston and the Saturn V Pavilion at the Kennedy Space Center, respectively (see plate 33), have become more theatrical in their presentation, combining the excitement of the theme park with the educational value of the artifact. The Landmark Entertainment Group has specialized in the design of science-fiction theme parks throughout the world. Founded in 1980 by Tony Christopher and Gary Goddard, Landmark's design practice often actively incorporates visitors into the script. The most notable examples of their work include Caesar's Magical Empire and Forum Shopping Mall in Caesar's Palace, Las Vegas; Jurassic Park: The Ride, for Universal Studios in Hollywood; T2/3D (Terminator 2/3 Dimensions) in Universal Studios, Orlando, Florida; the Amazing Adventures of Spiderman at Universal's Islands of Adventure in Orlando; and Star Trek: The Experience in the Las Vegas Hilton. In the latter, visitors tour a Star Trek museum display, shop and dine in Quark's Bar, and are transported aboard the *Enterprise* during a crisis to interact with officers.

75
Landmark Entertainment Group.
Star Trek: The Experience, Las Vegas
Hilton, Las Vegas, Nevada. 1998

76
McDonnell Douglas DC-XA *Delta Clipper* making its first test liftoff. May 18, 1996

In 1996, three companies were engaged in a competition to develop the Space Shuttle's successor: McDonnell Douglas with its DC-X and small-scale prototype, *Delta Clipper*, which actually conducted vertical takeoffs and landings; Rockwell, the contractor for the Space Shuttle, with its next generation model; and Lockheed Martin, with its radical lifting body design that would take off and land like an airplane. NASA awarded the contract for developing the prototype X-33 to Lockheed Martin, and it is currently under construction at Lockheed's Palmdale, California, "Skunk Works" plant (plate 80). If successful, it will result in a larger space plane called VentureStar. But other proposals are in the works from a variety of private concerns looking for investors and spurred on, in part, by the burgeoning commercial satellite market as well as the X Prize, which was established 1996. The St. Louis-based X Prize Foundation has offered a ten-million-dollar award to the first team that builds a spacecraft to fly sixty-two miles into space two times within two weeks – in essence, a successful reusable launch vehicle (RLV). As of 1998, fifteen teams have registered to compete, including Kelly Space and Technology, Inc., and Kistler Aerospace Corp.

77
Computer-generated view of the
Kelly Space Eclipse Astroliner
deploying a satellite above Earth.
Image created in 1997

78
Computer-generated view of the
Kistler K-1 launch vehicle showing
ignition of the second stage, and
redeployment or return of the
first stage to Earth for reuse. Image
created in 1998

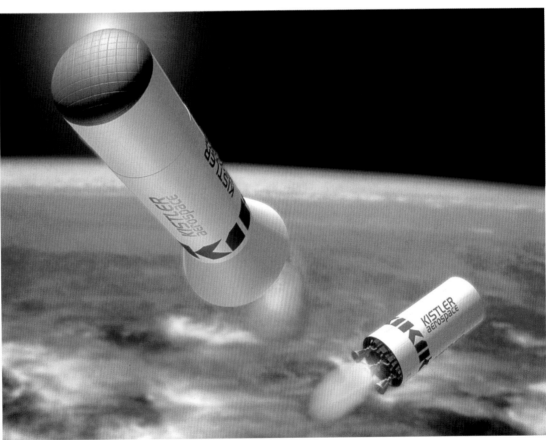

79
John Frassanito and Associates.
Computer-generated view of the
X-33 docked with the International
Space Station. The X-33 shown
here illustrates Lockheed Martin's
earlier model, which was derived
from a 1995 design patented by
Lockheed engineer David Urie, Jr.

80
John Frassanito and Associates.
Computer-generated view of the
X-33 in orbit

The X-33 will be an unmanned, half-scale prototype of the eventual replacement for the Space Shuttle. It is a lifting body, an aircraft whose shape provides the actual lift in the atmosphere instead of traditional wings. It draws on the pioneering research of earlier lifting bodies from the 1960s, particularly the Northrop HL-10 (1966–67) and Martin X-24A (1970). The X-33 and its planned full-size successor VentureStar are intended to operate from recycled airbases around the country, flying satellites into orbit and cargo to the International Space Station, and then returning to Earth in a powered descent, landing as an airplane would. The prototypical airfield was built in 1999 at Edwards Air Force Base by Sverdrup, an architectural design firm with long-standing experience in aerospace work. (One of Sverdrup's largest ongoing projects since it began work there forty years ago is the forty-thousand-acre Arnold Engineering Development Center for the U.S. Air Force in Tullahoma, Tennessee). The X-33 is designed so that its fuel tanks function as structural elements and its skin is covered with thin metallic thermal sheets that overlap each other like shingles on a roof. It will use a bank of "aerospike" engines whose individual combustion chambers provide greater and more accurately controlled thrust than current rocket nozzles. The X-33 also reuses existing moving parts, such as the nose gear of an F-16 fighter and the main landing gear of an F-15 fighter, in an effort to reduce costs. When finished, the X-33 will be sixty-nine feet long and weigh 273,000 pounds. VentureStar is designed to be 144 feet long and weigh 2.6 million pounds, with a payload capacity of 50,000 pounds. This is remarkable compared to today's Space Shuttle, which, with its boosters, weighs twice as much and is 184 feet long.

81
Boeing engineer Charles Pease with
mahogany and aluminum models
of a lifting-body space plane,
both products of early computer-
generated designs. 1964

82
B-52 mother-ship above an HL-10
lifting body of 1966–67

Industrial designer John Frassanito worked for Raymond Loewy's office in 1968, designing Skylab, America's first space

station (launched in 1973). Frassanito started his own design practice shortly thereafter, working on a variety of products,

including Datapoint computers. He has been a design consultant for NASA since the mid 1980s, when the agency began

exploring the creation of a large space station, which eventually metamorphosed into the design of the current International

Space Station. Over the past few years, Frassanito has actively participated in NASA's future mission planning, visualizing

the proposed missions in a series of computer-generated animations. The scenes illustrated here are part of a Mars mission

scenario where astronauts inflate their crew transfer vehicle (CTV), laboratory, and habitation modules as Frassanito

had proposed for lunar and other interplanetary missions. Other space architects, such as Constance Adams in Houston,

are working with NASA architects such as Kriss Kennedy to develop the interior architecture of such temporary structures.

Their latest work is an inflatable TransHab unit for the International Space Station (see McCurdy, fig. 9; Hall, fig. 5).

83–85
John Frassanito and Associates.
Scenes from a NASA computer-
generated animation of a proposed
manned mission to Mars. Images
created in 1997–2000

86
View of the connected *Zarya* and *Unity* modules, the first units of the International Space Station (ISS) put in orbit, 220 miles above Earth. December 4–15, 1998

87
Zarya (Sunrise) control module under construction. ca. 1997–98

88
Computer-generated view of
the International Space Station
(ISS). Image created ca. 1998

America's space station *Freedom* of 1984 was the forerunner of the current International Space Station (ISS). At the same time that the Soviet Union was creating its own space station, *Mir* (Peace), which was launched in 1986, NASA engineers and architects began collaborating with outside consultants such as John Frassanito and Associates and Sundberg Ferar, Inc., design firms that had previously worked on Skylab (see the essay by Rebecca Dalvesco in this volume), to develop a new space station. Unlike Skylab, which had an inside diameter of thirty-three feet and whose cylinder was boosted into orbit by an Apollo Saturn launcher, the ISS module could be no greater in diameter than thirteen feet three inches because it had to fit into the cargo bay of the Space Shuttle, which is about fifteen feet in diameter. Segments of the space station taken aloft in shuttle flights could be assembled in space; eighteen-foot-long units were considered the most practical. The disposition of the station's interior was determined in meetings between NASA designers and outside consultants, and a "four standoff" design was chosen. According to this scheme, the cylindrical tube is divided into four quadrants, essentially creating modular-panel walls inside each tube to house station functions. Another important design decision, made in 1986–87, was the creation of a station cupola – a viewing dome where the occupants could survey the exterior of the station for any signs of damage and structural problems. A variety of mock-ups of this cupola were created and tested, taking into consideration human factors analysis, and a polygonal viewing node remained part of the final station design. *Mir* has eleven modules and measures 107 by 90 feet; the ISS will have fifteen modules, giving it total dimensions of some 290 by 356 feet, and an approximate weight of 1.05 million pounds – more than four times that of *Mir.* The ISS is to have a crew of seven. The first modules of the ISS, *Zarya* and *Unity,* were launched in late 1998, and a Russian service-unit module called *Zvezda* (Star) was added in summer 2000. The entire station is scheduled for completion in 2004–5 and will carry a final price tag of more than $50 billion – something that has made it a controversial project to a cost-conscious public and U.S. Congress.

89
Shimizu Corporation. Rendering of
proposed orbiting hotel. 1989

Space tourism became a buzzword in the 1990s. Since the end of the cold war, companies have been looking forward to capitalizing on the public's desire to experience space travel firsthand. Zero-gravity flights are now being marketed, as are in-depth tours of the Yuri Gagarin training center in Star City, east of Moscow, and high-altitude, edge-of-space flights in Russian fighter planes. The Japanese construction company Shimizu, with its Space Systems Research Division, planned to build permanent structures, such as an orbiting hotel, as well as a Moon base made of lunar concrete. As first publicized in 1989, the orbital hotel would be something akin to a space station. Two-day trips for tourists were envisioned. Visitors would stay in sixty-four guest-room modules, each measuring about twenty-three by thirteen feet. These modular rooms were to be arranged in a circle with a radius of more than 275 feet, and would rotate to produce some level of artificial gravity for the occupants. Newer designs by Shimizu have extended this concept to include such amenities as a casino and microgravity recreational spaces in a larger enclosed core. With these dreams in mind, Kawasaki Heavy Industries proposed in 1994–95 a tourist spaceship that would be launched from Kansai airport in Japan. The spacecraft, about seventy-one feet high and fifty-eight feet in diameter, would be centrally planned. Fifty travelers would sit in two rows of seats facing the windows at the periphery. As in Shimizu's orbiting hotel, though at a smaller scale, there would be a microgravity amusement room for passengers.

90
Shimizu Corporation. Rendering
of proposed Moon base. 1989

91
Publicity brochure showing
Kawasaki's proposed *Kankoh Maru*
tourist spaceship and Shimizu's
proposed orbiting hotel. 1994–95

Space Ship
KANKOH-MARU

Hotel Concept by SHIMIZU Corporation
Earth View by NASA

Space stations in science-fiction films and television shows such as *Star Trek: Deep Space Nine* and *Babylon 5* are gigantic in scale, compared with the reality of what has been built in Salyut (1971), Skylab (1973), *Mir* (1986), and the International Space Station (begun 1998), and even what has been proposed by Shimizu (plates 89, 90). Although its normal permanent residency is supposed to be 300, *Deep Space Nine,* or *DS9,* is scaled to accommodate seven thousand people. By comparison, the *Babylon 5,* or *B5*, space station was even more enormous, at approximately five miles long and able to hold 250,000 inhabitants. The size of these stations has been influenced by publications such as Gerard K. O'Neill's *The High Frontier* (1977), which proposed the establishment of massive "human colonies in space," a phrase that is also the book's subtitle. In fact, the cylindrical model and drawing of O'Neill's "Island One" relates to the elongated station design shown in the computer-generated images of the *Babylon 5,* whereas the station in *Deep Space Nine* seems more akin to a three-dimensional version of rotating wheel designs that date back to Wernher von Braun's proposals of the early 1950s published in *Collier's* magazine.

92
Herman Zimmerman, production designer. Computer-generated exterior view of space station *Deep Space Nine,* from *Star Trek: Deep Space Nine.* 1992

93
John Iacovelli, production designer. Computer-generated view of space station and *Star Fury* spacecraft, from *Babylon 5.* ca. 1992–93

94
John Frassanito and Associates.
Computer-generated rendering of
a laser-assisted Bussard intersellar
ramjet. ca. 1997–99

NASA designers have been planning future missions to the far reaches of space. Traveling these distances

via traditional chemically based propulsion systems, however, would take too long and require too much

fuel. A conventional liquid- or solid-fueled, rocket-powered human journey to Mars would last about seven

months each way. NASA mission planners and aerospace engineers are experimenting with propulsion systems

that would cut this time to 100 days, or just over three months. One such prototypical engine being devel-

oped at NASA in Houston is the VASIMR or Variable Specific Impulse Magnetoplasma Rocket. In it, electrical

energy, like that of a microwave oven, heats the plasma propellant, the fuel itself being the result of an ion-

ization between positive and negative atoms. The heated plasma is then expelled through a nozzle that

provides high-power, continuous acceleration with minimal energy consumption compared to today's rocket

engines. With engines such as these, NASA mission planners have proposed Mars missions that are realistic

in terms of time (see plate 66). Moreover, they are continuing to think about future propulsion systems, from

fusion engines to matter-antimatter interstellar rockets.

Challenging the Conventions of Science Fiction:

HOWARD E. McCURDY

The Design of the International Space Station

In few areas of space architecture have expectations departed so significantly from actual design as in the International Space Station (ISS), planning for which began under the leadership of the National Aeronautics and Space Administration (NASA) in 1982. In theory, stations that float in space are free to assume any form their designers choose to give them. Unaffected by the constraints of gravity or atmospheric drag, such objects can take the shape of spheres, tubes, towers, or forms inspired by children's toys. Despite this freedom, prior to the construction of any real space station, a single form came to dominate public conceptions of such facilities. In the popular mind, space stations would be round. "If you ask the public at large," said John Hodge, leader of the NASA task force that won approval for the ISS, they would tell you that a space station looks like "a very large rotating wheel" (fig. 1; see plate 67). So would "quite possibly most of the people within NASA," Hodge added.[1] The actual shape of NASA's space station, however, is not round. It does not resemble a large rotating wheel. With its jumbled mass of modules and trusses, it was criticized for looking like something a child might create out of tinker toys (fig. 2; see plate 88). In other words, its architecture departs radically from the conceptions that dominated thinking about space stations in the century that preceded their actual construction.

The most impressive image of a space station released prior to actual construction appeared in 1968, one year before humans landed on the Moon, in Stanley Kubrick's film *2001: A Space Odyssey* (see plate 71). The sequence depicting modern times opens with an image of a very large space station rotating slowly in an orbit two hundred miles above the surface of the globe. The station consists of two gracefully thin wheels, nine hundred feet in diameter, each linked by four spokes to a central hub. The hub serves as a portal for arriving and departing spacecraft. In the movie, one of the two wheels is finished, while workers in space suits labor to complete

the other one. Inside the finished wheel, the facility resembles a modern hotel, albeit one with a spectacular view. A sign above the registration desk announces that visitors will reside in quarters provided by the Hilton corporation. The rotating station is a transfer point; it provides lodging for scientists and bureaucrats as they pass to and from permanent bases on the Moon. In order to facilitate the transition, Kubrick's nine-hundred-foot-wide wheel rotates at a rate of one revolution per minute, precisely calculated to replicate the gravity felt on the lunar surface.

Kubrick and screenplay writer Arthur C. Clarke derived the concept of a very large space station serving lunar bases from NASA's plans for the post-Apollo space program. NASA executives wanted to build a large space station, which they viewed as a laboratory for scientific research and an operational base for expeditions beyond. A 1969 White House report, issued one year after the release of Kubrick's film, called for construction of a one-hundred-person space station, a winged space shuttle, a nuclear-powered spaceship that could carry passengers to the Moon, and expeditions beyond.[2]

The shape of Kubrick's space station was based largely upon a proposal made by Wernher von Braun in an issue of *Collier's* magazine sixteen years earlier. Von Braun worked for NASA and headed the team of German rocketeers who, with their American counterparts, developed the giant Saturn V rocket that took the first astronauts to the Moon. Von Braun's concept dominated both popular culture and practical design. The March 22, 1952, cover of *Collier's* magazine greeted readers with a painting of a winged shuttle rising into orbit and the words "Man Will Conquer Space Soon." Inside, a series of articles presented von Braun's proposal for an Earth-orbiting space station accompanied by a two-page panorama painted by space artist Chesley Bonestell. In addition to the winged space shuttle and a co-orbiting telescope, the painting depicted a large wheel floating one thousand miles above Central America (see Ordway, fig. 2). Bonestell's

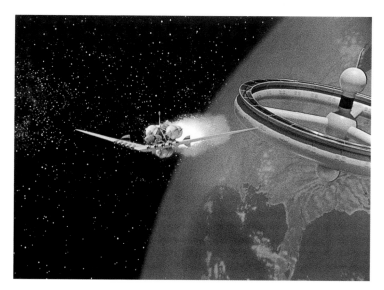

Fig. 1
Byron Haskin, director. *Conquest of Space*. 1955. This film featured a space station based on designs by Wernher von Braun and sets by Chesley Bonestell

Fig. 2
U.S. International Cooperation Phase III, Space Shuttle docked to the International Space Station. 1995. Computer-generated rendering

painting of von Braun's rotating wheel became one of the most widely-reproduced works of twentieth-century space art.[3]

Although other designs were proposed, none was as influential as the rotating wheel. Willy Ley, the German-born writer of popular science books for adults and children, also commonly portrayed the space station as a rotating wheel (see plate 67).[4] In addition to Kubrick's adoption of the wheel for his science-fiction classic, Walt Disney adopted von Braun's wheel for a 1955 television program on the conquest of space that Disney studios produced. The Disney corporation built a revolving platform called Space Station X-1 for the Disneyland theme park that opened that year in Anaheim, California. Lindberg toys also sold an "authentic scale plastic model construction kit" of a U.S. space station based exactly on the von Braun design (fig. 3). When engineers at NASA's Langley Research Center in Virginia received permission to begin space station design studies, they built a 24-foot-diameter scale model in the shape of a wheel.

A number of factors, both practical and conceptual, encouraged the wheel-shaped design. Paramount among them were the physics of rocketry and centrifugal force. Science-fiction writers could imagine space travel using moonbeams or antigravity devices, but rocket scientists had to contend with much less efficient means. "Landing on the moon is beyond the borderline of what chemical fuels can do," observed Ley.[5] Early designs for practical rocketships relied upon fuels that could not propel passengers much beyond low-Earth orbit. The three-stage rocketship that boosted von Braun's winged shuttle employed hydrazine, a fuel so inefficient that von Braun had planned

to install fifty-one motors on the rocket's first stage. To reach the Moon and planets, pioneers needed an Earth-orbital station from which they could dispatch spacecraft specifically designed for expeditions into outer space.

Designers recognized that space stations would have to perform many functions in order to justify their enormous cost. In early conceptions, however, such stations served primarily as operational bases for moving humans and material deeper into space. When President John F. Kennedy challenged Americans to reach the Moon, von Braun and his fellow rocketeers insisted that a space station or at least Earth-orbit rendezvous techniques be used to assemble an adequate flotilla to complete the voyage. Rocketships under development at that time could lift material into Earth's orbit, and even send a small spacecraft on a voyage around the Moon, but they could not dispatch sufficient mass to land on the lunar surface and return.

For a station to serve as an operational base, one of the primary design requirements was the comfort of the crew. Prolonged exposure to weightlessness was thought to be uncomfortable at best and potentially fatal at worst. By spinning a space station, and placing the crew on the inner edge of the outer rim, designers could create a sense of "pseudogravity" that overcame the problem of weightlessness. Engineers easily calculated the centrifugal force produced by rotation and converted that into units of gravity. The primary purpose of early stations was space operations, for example, trips to the Moon. Research assumed a secondary purpose, and to fulfill that purpose, engineers proposed co-orbiting platforms that would not

Fig. 3
Lindberg Space Base Star Probe,
toy model kit. 1976

rotate and would not have people on board. To placate scientists who wanted to conduct experiments in space, station designers proposed the construction of platforms orbiting in formation with the space station; from them research and observations could be carried out.

Of course, a space station need not be round in order to produce artificial gravity. One of the earliest scientists to contemplate station architecture created artificial gravity with ballistic-shaped components and wire. In 1923, scientist Hermann Oberth published *Die Rakete zu den Planetenraumen* (*Rockets in Planetary Space*), a pioneering work in what was then an embryonic field. Oberth suggested that large rockets placed in permanent orbits around Earth could function like small moons. "If ill effects result from experiencing weightlessness over long periods of time," Oberth said (though he doubted they would), "two such rockets could be connected with a cable and caused to rotate about each other.[6]

Another influential proposal created artificial gravity through a pinwheel design. The one-hundred-person space base that NASA planners proposed for the post-Apollo space program produced artificial gravity without the advantages of a rotating wheel. The facility was constructed out of cylinders, some as large as thirty-three feet wide, fixed by hollow rods to a central spindle. In one design, engineers extended the spindle and attached a nuclear electric-power generating plant at a safe distance from the crew (fig. 4). Crew members standing on the decks of the cylinders would experience a sensation akin to gravity when the spindle was turned.

Surprisingly, in 1869, the American novelist Edward Everett Hale, best known for his classic short story, "The Man Without a Country," presented plans for an artificial-gravity space station in the shape of a sphere. In Hale's novel *The Brick Moon,* engineers accidentally launch a populated sphere that has its own gravity, atmosphere, crops, and rainfall. Hale never explained how his two-hundred-foot

sphere would accumulate sufficient mass to produce gravity, a freedom accorded fiction writers. In 1929, an Austrian army captain using the pseudonym Hermann Noordung presented plans for a gravity-producing space station in the shape of a cup and saucer. The "cup" focused solar energy on a boiler so as to generate electricity; the "saucer" contained living quarters in its outer rim to provide artificial gravity when rotated.

None of these earlier designs was as aesthetically pleasing as von Braun's wheel. The aesthetics of von Braun's design depended considerably upon another requirement influencing early space station design, its military function. In opening his *Collier's* article, von Braun suggested that his space station would serve as "the greatest force for peace ever devised, or one of the most terrible weapons of war." Among its many functions, von Braun planned to use his space station as a military reconnaissance post, from which "nothing will go unobserved," and as a potential platform for launching nuclear missiles.[7] Elsewhere in the March 22 issue, editors at *Collier's* suggested that the nation that first built a space station would control the world. "A ruthless foe established on a space station could actually subjugate the peoples of the world," the editors warned in urging the U.S. to begin work on one immediately.[8] Advocates of exploration cleverly exploited anxiety about nuclear bombs and the outcome of the cold war to promote the conquest of space.

As a weapon of defense and an operational base for expeditions beyond, the space station also assumed functions easily recognizable to people in a nation transfixed by the memory of their western frontier. Space stations would serve as fortresses or way stations on the new frontier, a concept that did not require much elaboration in what one commentator called "the most internally fortified territory in the world."[9] To prove its worth as a modern fortress, a space station had to appear formidable or at least fortlike. Two spacecraft

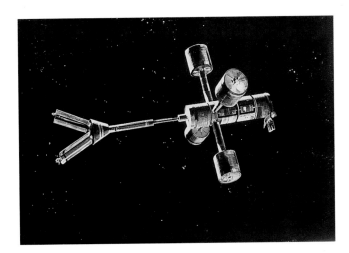

Fig. 4
Artist's rendering of a large Earth-
orbiting space base. 1970

Fig. 5
David Afton Willment. Rendering
of a six-sided space station. 1962

spinning at the ends of a tether hardly looked menacing; neither did a cup of tea. Von Braun's wheel, with defenders on the outer edge and core functions within, assumed a more appropriate form. Early NASA designs, which broke the wheel into a six-sided ring, were even more fortlike in appearance (fig. 5).[10] Space planning inside the wheel also emphasized military analogies. A cutaway view of von Braun's wheel painted by Fred Freeman for *Collier's* magazine drew on submarine designs (fig. 6). Low ceilings in a three-deck structure, small compartments, and pump rooms all suggested the cramped quarters of a naval vessel.[11] This theme was repeated in the 1955 movie *Conquest of Space,* in which the station's all-male crew are portrayed as rowdy, sex-starved sailors at sea.

Having established the aesthetic significance of a wheel, engineers faced the practical difficulties of creating a workable construction plan. Von Braun's wheel measured 250 feet from rim to rim. No rock-etship could launch any object that wide. To minimize construction difficulties, von Braun developed an ingenious solution. He proposed a space station made out of fabric that could be compressed on the ground and inflated once in orbit. "After the 'wheel' has been put together and sealed," von Braun explained, "it will then be inflated like an automobile tire."[12] In this manner, technology encouraged wheel-shaped designs.

During the 1960s, when design work on von Braun's wheel took place, tire and rubber company executives strove to join the ranks of aerospace firms. Executives from the Goodyear Aircraft Company met with NASA officials to promote their "inflatable torus" design (fig. 7). Goodyear prepared advertisements touting their inflatable design and proclaiming that the company was "in a unique position to put this new technology to work at once."[13]

Shortly after the founding of the U.S. civil space program, NASA engineers began to prepare space-station designs.[14] Practical difficul-

ties plagued the wheel-shaped design from the beginning. Engineers worried about the effects of meteorites on large, inflatable struc-tures and the commensurate difficulties of repairing a flat tire in space. Astronauts worried about the dangers of extravehicular activity, discouraging the construction of metal rings such as those shown in *2001,* in which astronauts assemble the station using girders and metal plating. Engineers soon gravitated to designs based on modules that could be docked in space. Not only did this simplify construction, but it also fit government spending habits. Modular designs could be incremental, a substantial advantage in a system where program funding occurs in spurts. Engineers could launch a single module and build up to larger designs as more money became available.

By 1970, modular designs dominated practical space-station plan-ning in both the United States and the Soviet Union. In 1971, the Soviet Union launched the *Salyut 1* module, beginning their slow march toward the *Mir* space station (fig. 8). In 1973, the United States launched the 22-foot-wide Skylab module (see the essay by Rebecca Dalvesco in this volume). Both were considered orbital workshops, the precursors to real space stations, which by definition must have the capacity for permanent habitability. When NASA planners decided to use the U.S. Space Shuttle as the nation's primary launch vehicle, they reduced the size of modular components in order to fit within an approximately 15-foot-wide space inside the shuttle's cargo bay. NASA officials still wanted to build a large space station, and one with the capability for producing artificial gravity, but they did not assemble space station modules in the shape of a wheel. Contracts with the McDonnell Douglas Corporation and North American Rockwell produced pinwheel-shaped designs.

As station planners moved further into the architecture of modu-lar design, they also moved away from artificial gravity. While mak-ing plans for project Apollo, aerospace engineers discovered that

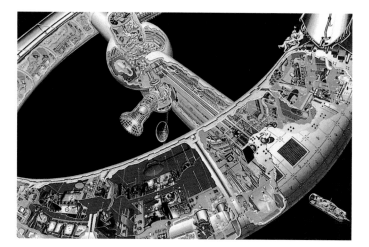

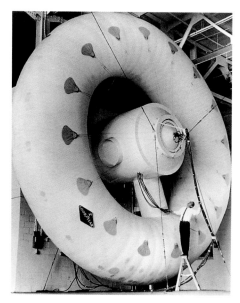

Fig. 6
Frederick Freeman. Rendering of
space station interior for *Collier's*.
March 22, 1952

Fig. 7
Model of proposed Goodyear
inflatable space station. 1961

they did not need space stations or Earth-orbit rendezvous to reach places like the Moon. This was largely due to the development of rocket engines that burned liquid hydrogen, a more powerful fuel than that which propelled the visionary vehicles of earlier pioneers. As the need for transfer points declined, the value of stations as research laboratories increased. Space travelers needed artificial gravity; space scientists wanted none at all. Furthermore, the most promising activities to be conducted on orbiting research stations – from protein crystal growth to the development of new metal alloys – required that gravity forces be minimized. The commercial potential for microgravity manufacturing was a major consideration in President Ronald Reagan's 1983 decision to start work on what became the International Space Station. Station advocates did not have sufficient support to win White House approval for the undertaking by appealing to a special space group within the National Security Council. Instead, they won Reagan's endorsement by shifting the issue to the Cabinet Council on Commerce and Trade, where commercial interests prevailed.

During the battle to win White House approval for the ISS, NASA officials suspended official space-station design. Task force leader Hodge would not let task force members draw configurations. In part, he did this because he wanted the government to define station requirements before engaging in design efforts. He also recognized that modular, microgravity designs departed significantly from the wheel image that most people held in their minds.

Nearly thirty months passed before NASA officials announced the "baseline configuration" for what became the ISS. A "skunk works" team at the Johnson Space Center produced a reference configuration during the summer following White House approval. Their graceful "power tower" design, which resembled a tall broadcast antenna, revealed the importance that trusses would play in any large, microgravity space station. NASA officials released their "baseline

configuration" two years later. Founded on a dual-keel design, the configuration featured a large H-shaped truss 361 feet tall, stabilized with a 503-foot horizontal boom that extended beyond the sides of the H. The demand for large quantities of electric power, a result of commercial research and production requirements, was a major factor driving the truss-based design. Trusses served as mounts for stellar and solar observatories, Earth-observation equipment, canisters housing scientific experiments, small factories, satellite-servicing bays, and a mobile crane, as well as solar collectors and photovoltaic arrays needed to generate the station's electric power. To generate electricity on his wheel-shaped design, von Braun attached a metal trough to the circumference of the wheel. The trough focused solar energy on a pipe filled with liquid mercury. Hot mercury vapor drove a turbogenerator and produced – by von Braun's estimation – 500 kilowatts of electricity. To produce about half that much power, designers of the dual keel had to install four large solar arrays and solar collectors someplace on the station structure. Arrays and collectors had to be placed so as not to obstruct experiments, satellite operations, or the vision of the crew.

On a rotating space station, crew members live and work inside the outer ring. On a microgravity station, they reside in the central core. Engineers who proposed the "power tower" configuration made a serious error when they placed station modules at the base of their antennalike structure. A large space station generates its own gravity. To reduce the force of gravity to the lowest possible level, work modules must be placed as close to the center of gravity as possible. In all space-station designs beginning with the dual keel configuration, engineers placed laboratory and habitat modules at the center of the facility. And in all of them, they placed solar arrays and collectors at the ends of the boom.

Engineers drawing plans for the aesthetically challenged International Space Station labored to present its form in a manner that

Fig. 8
Mir. After 1986

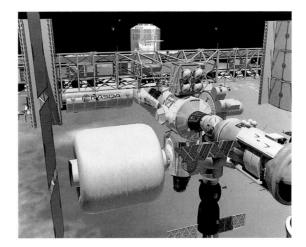

Fig. 9
Computer-generated rendering of
the International Space Station
with TransHab, an inflatable space
habitat designed by William
Schneider, Horacio de la Fuente,
and Kriss Kennedy at the Johnson
Space Center. 1997–99. Rendering
by John Frassanito and Associates

appealed to a public accustomed to graceful wheels. In one effort, engineers superimposed a computer-generated image of the dual-keel design across the face of the U.S. Capitol to emphasize its size. (In all major versions, the breadth of the ISS exceeded the diameter of von Braun's design.) To place at the front of the report of the National Commission on Space, members commissioned a repainting of Bonestell's famous station panorama, inserting the dual keel for von Braun's wheel. This proposal, however, did not satisfy critics at all. Mitchell Waldrop, writing for *Science 83* magazine, complained that the station looked like "something a child would build with an Erector set." *Science* magazine editors headlined their cover with the words *"2001* it's not."[15]

The U.S. space station effort faced many difficulties along the road from conception through design. Cost overruns, frequent redesigns, missed deadlines, and close votes on Capitol Hill have marked the history of the International Space Station. The practical difficulties of creating a large structure in space were compounded by the fact that the actual facility departed from conventional expectations by such a large degree. It was hard to sell the fulfillment of a dream when the fulfillment looked so strange. In response, architects and engineers are proposing new materials that would revive old designs, including the use of inflatable structures such as those proposed by von Braun (fig. 9). Space architect Constance Adams describes this endoskeletal space habitat made of woven Kevlar (an aramid-fiber material used today in bullet-proof vests) as: "A major breakthrough both in technology and in tectonics: capable of tight packaging at light weight for efficient launch, the vehicle can then be inflated to its full size on orbit via its own inflation tanks."[16] Inevitably, as scientists, engineers, and architects develop new plans for space habitation, they will confront the gap created between practical realities and the prototypical schemes popularized by people writing for the general public.

1. House Science and Technology Committee, Subcommittee on Space Science and Applications, *NASA's Space Station Activities,* 98th Cong., 1st sess., 1983, p. 4.
2. Space Task Group, *The Post-Apollo Space Program,* report to the President (Washington, D.C., 1969).
3. Wernher von Braun, "Crossing the Last Frontier," *Collier's* (Mar. 22, 1952), pp. 24–25.
4. Willy Ley, *Space Stations* (Poughkeepsie, N.Y., 1958).
5. Willy Ley, *Rockets and Space Travel: The Future of Flight Beyond the Stratosphere* (New York, 1948), p. 284.
6. Hermann Oberth, *Rockets in Planetary Space,* NASA TT F-9227 (Washington, D.C., 1964), p. 94.
7. Von Braun, "Crossing the Last Frontier," p. 25.
8. "Man Will Conquer Space Soon: What Are We Waiting For?" *Collier's* (Mar. 22, 1952), p. 23.
9. Robert B. Roberts, *Encyclopedia of Historic Forts* (New York, 1988), p. xii.
10. See the cover of *Astronautics: A Publication of the American Rocket Society* (Sept. 1962).
11. Willy Ley, "Station in Space," *Collier's* (Mar. 22, 1952), pp. 30–31.
12. Von Braun, "Crossing the Last Frontier," p. 29.
13. Advertisement, *U.S. Naval Institute Proceedings* (Feb. 1961), p. 9.
14. See W. Ray Hook, "Historical Review," *Transactions of the ASME* 106 (Nov. 1984), pp. 276–86.
15. Mitchell Waldrop, "Space City: 2001 It's Not," *Science 83* (Oct. 1983).
16. From an unpublished, unpaginated text provided by Constance Adams and NASA, Feb. 11, 2000.

Spaceships of the Imagination

in *Collier's* and *2001*

FREDERICK I. ORDWAY III

I. Setting the Stage for Space Travel

For centuries, imagination dictated the design and architecture of what are sometimes referred to as "spaceships of the mind." The shining, apparently nearby Moon captured the earliest attention. Around A.D. 165, the Syrian satirist and sophist Lucian of Samosata composed his *True History,* the first authenticated work of space fiction, complete with a trip to another world, the Moon; a landing thereon; descriptions of adventures in an alien environment; and a return to Earth. Although no contemporary image exists of Lucian's lunar voyage, Gustave Doré's 1883 wood engraving depicts a scene from Lucian of Samosata's *Verae Historiae* of a sailing ship with Greek athletes aboard being lofted by a violent whirlwind. By the seventeenth century, bird power had become the preferred method of lunar travel, typified by Bishop Francis Godwin's *The Man in the Moone; or, A Discourse of a Voyage thither, by Domingo Gonsales* (1638).

The most famous historical spacecraft design appeared more than two centuries later in the form of Jules Verne's cannon-propelled spaceship, as described in his novels *From the Earth to the Moon Direct in Ninety-Seven Hours and Twenty Minutes* (1865) and *Round the Moon* (1870). Verne's success set the stage for a legion of followers. One of them, Robert Cromie, chose a spherical, gravity-insulated spaceship aimed at Mars in his 1890 novel, *A Plunge into Space.* Four years later, in *Journey to Other Worlds,* John Jacob Astor offered the same propulsion scheme for his spaceship *Callisto.* Early in this century, science-fiction pioneer Hugo Gernsback described a spaceship in *Ralph 124C41+,* which was serialized in 1911–12 and published as a full novel in 1925.

From the tail end of the nineteenth century and on into the twentieth, four scientifically trained individuals from four different countries ushered in the modern space flight revolution: Konstantin E. Tsiolkovsky in Russia; Robert H. Goddard in the United States; Hermann Oberth from a German-speaking enclave in Transylvania,

part of the former Austro-Hungarian Empire; and Robert Esnault-Pelterie of France. Their writings encouraged not only more realistic spaceship designs but also the publication of a growing number of popular books and articles on rocketry and space travel during the 1930s. At the same time, experimental rocket societies emerged, especially in Germany, the Soviet Union, and the United States. Of the four pioneers, Goddard alone devoted most of his energies to the practical development of the rocket, which all four of them realized was the key to space travel. Building on the work of prewar amateur experimenters, the combatants in World War II – most notably the Germans – developed rockets for military purposes. Their V-2 soon became the prototype of the postwar rocket, missile, and eventually space-vehicle design.

In 1945, captured V-2 structures, motors, and other components were brought from Germany to the United States; others ended up in the Soviet Union and, to a lesser extent, in France and the United Kingdom. In the U.S., V-2s were reassembled, refurbished, and instrumented for upper atmospheric research and other peaceful purposes. Over a period of about six years, more than seventy were launched from the U.S. Army's White Sands Proving Ground (today, the White Sands Missile Range) in New Mexico. Wernher von Braun, the leader of the German team hired by the army, recognized the converted V-2 as the precursor to space travel. Indeed, when first flown successfully at Peenemünde, Germany, in October 1942, it had arched briefly into space along its ballistic trajectory. After the war, V-2s fired from White Sands sometimes attained altitudes in excess of a hundred miles. During a flight on August 22, 1951, one reached a record 130 miles altitude. When mated with a small American-made WAC-Corporal upper stage in the "Bumper" Project, the combination soared 244 miles into space on February 24, 1949. These science and engineering advances ushered in a whole new realm of possibilities for increasingly detailed concepts of space travel.

156

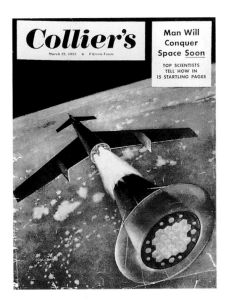

Fig. 1
Chesley Bonestell. "Man Will Conquer Space Soon." *Collier's* cover, March 22, 1952

II. Space Design and Architecture: Courtesy *Collier's*

In November 1951, Gordon Manning, managing editor of *Collier's* magazine, noticed an announcement of a symposium in San Antonio, Texas, on the physics and medicine of the upper atmosphere. Curious about this unusual investigation of space, Manning sent his associate editor Cornelius Ryan to find out what was brewing. At the conference, Ryan met von Braun, Harvard University astronomer Fred L. Whipple, and UCLA physicist Joseph Kaplan. Together, they convinced Ryan that space flight was not an idle dream, that it could occur in the relatively near future. As a result of this encounter, *Collier's* devoted a series of eight articles to space travel. Ryan carefully edited essays by von Braun, Whipple, Kaplan, and other experts, and illustrated them with contributions by three leading illustrators of the day, Chesley Bonestell, Fred Freeman, and Rolf Klep, to maximize their public appeal.

At the time, *Collier's* was one of the big four mass-circulation, large-format, illustrated weeklies – the others being *Life, Look,* and the *Saturday Evening Post.* With a circulation of more than three million and an estimated readership of twelve to fifteen million, the magazine's features on space travel were bound to cause a stir. *Collier's* first space issue was published on March 22, 1952, enticing readers with the promise, "Man Will Conquer Space Soon." The introduction declared "On the following pages *Collier's* presents what may be one of the most important scientific symposiums ever published by a national magazine. It is the story of the inevitability of man's conquest of space. What you will read here is not science fiction. It is serious fact."[1] The issue featured presentations by von Braun, Whipple, and Kaplan, as well as science writer Willy Ley, space medical expert Heinz Haber, and United Nations lawyer Oscar Schachter. Its handsome cover by Bonestell showed the separation of the upper two stages of a huge three-stage launch vehicle (fig. 1).

Step One: The Launch Vehicle

Von Braun began the series with a description of a launch vehicle that would later be recognized as the precursor to the Saturn V rocket of the Apollo era. The proposed launch vehicle was 265 feet tall – about the height of a 25-story building – with a base diameter of 65 feet. Its multiple engines operated on nitric acid and hydrazine propellants. The startling architecture envisaged by von Braun and artist Klep called for, in its first stage, 51 engines generating a total of 28 million pounds of thrust; in its second stage, 34 engines generating 3½ million pounds of thrust; and in its third stage, four engines plus a cruise motor, creating 440,000 pounds of thrust. The third or upper stage was winged and designed to be recoverable and reusable, much like the modern Space Shuttle. Von Braun suggested possible launch sites: Johnson Island in the Pacific or the Air Force Proving Ground near Cocoa, Florida, and described the dramatic lift-off:

At the launching area, the heavy rocket ship is assembled on a great platform. Then the platform is wheeled into place over a tunnel-like "jet deflector" which drains off the fiery gases of the first stage's rocket motors. Finally, with a mighty roar . . . the rocket ship slowly takes off – so slowly, in fact, that in the first second it travels less than 15 feet. Gradually, however, it begins to pick up speed, and 20 seconds later it has disappeared into the clouds.[2]

Step Two: The Space Station

Next, von Braun called for the construction of a doughnut-shaped, 250-foot-diameter space station circling the Earth every two hours at a height of 1,075 miles. Components to assemble the station were to be lofted by the giant rocket, which was to deliver about thirty-six tons of cargo each trip. The station would rotate every twenty-two seconds to provide its crew of eighty with the sensation of one-third "gravity" at the rim, less toward the center. Bonestell's

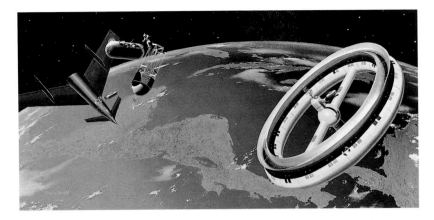

Fig. 2
Chesley Bonestell. Rendering of
a space station on Earth's orbit.
Collier's, March 22, 1952

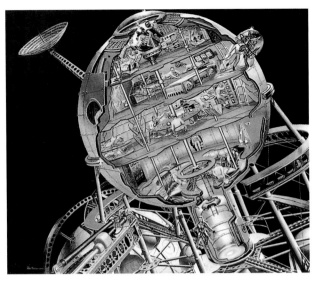

Fig. 3
Fred Freeman. Rendering of
the interior of the lunar spaceship's
passenger sphere. *Collier's,*
October 18, 1952

painting showed not only the completed space station but also a reusable, winged, third-stage at left, a nearby space telescope, and three little "space taxis" busy at work (two at left and one near the station's core) (fig. 2). Compared to the World War II Manhattan atomic bomb project's $2 billion, von Braun estimated that the space station could be ready by 1967 at a cost of $4 billion.

Step Three: Expedition to the Moon

Once the space station had been constructed, von Braun and his colleagues designed a full-scale, multiship expedition to the Moon, to be assembled near the space station. Von Braun estimated its cost at about $500 million and that even though "such a trip takes a great deal of planning . . . the project could be completed within the next 25 years" – that is, by 1977.[3] The journey called for two passenger craft, each with twenty men aboard, and a single cargo ship with a ten-man crew. All three ships are 160 feet long and 110 feet wide, powered by thirty hydrazine-nitric acid–propellant rocket engines, and fitted with passenger spheres at top.

The architectural design of the spheres, illustrated by Freeman, called for an upper control deck where an engineer would check various gauges while the radio operator would keep in touch with the space station and the other two ships (fig. 3). Directly below, a deck devoted primarily to navigation also contains a sponge-bath stall and bunks. The attitude of the ship is determined by readings from an artificial horizon mechanism in the astrodome at the extreme right. The living quarters, occupying the largest deck, contain bunks, an automatic dining unit with a table, a short-wave heater, a dishwasher, and, at right, a snack dispenser. Below the living quarters – the fourth level down – is an area for stowage, the electrical switch-

board, and a washroom. The bottom-most level houses the engineering deck, which is lined with water tanks, yellow oxygen tanks, an air blower pump, as well as tanks containing water that has been recovered from the spaceship's constantly recycled atmosphere.

Once components for the passenger and cargo ships have been delivered to orbit by the giant rocket, space-suited workers begin assembly. Personal minirocket motors allow them to move small items from position to position, while pressurized, rocket-powered "space taxis" maneuver larger elements into place.

As soon as the Moonships are ready, the trip can begin. "The takeoff itself," predicted von Braun, "will be watched by millions. Television cameras on the space station will transmit the scene to receivers all over the world. And people on the earth's dark side will be able to turn from their screens to catch a fleeting glimpse of light – high in the heavens – the combined flash of 90 rocket motors."[4]

Toward the end of the five-day voyage through space, the three ships' descent motors are fired preparatory to touchdown on *Sinus Roris,* or Dewy Bay, on the northern branch of *Oceanus Procellarum,* or Stormy Ocean. The site is approximately 650 miles from the lunar North Pole. Von Braun narrated the descent onto the lunar surface, and Bonestell drew it (fig. 4): "The broad round shoe of the telescopic landing leg digs into the soft volcanic ground. . . . For a few seconds, we balance on the single leg. Then the four outrigger legs slide out, and are locked into position. The whirring of machinery dies away. There is absolute silence. We have reached the Moon."[5]

Once there, the crew sets about unloading supplies needed for the planned six-week stay on the lunar surface. Large cranes, folded against the cargo vehicle's framework, swing out to unload 285 tons of supplies (Earth weight; about 50 tons on the low-gravity Moon).

Fig. 4
Chesley Bonestell, rendered by Ron
Miller (original lost). Moon landing.
Collier's cover, October 18, 1952

Fig. 5
Chesley Bonestell. Rendering of an
expedition to Mars. *Collier's* cover,
April 30, 1954

A 75-foot-long, 36-foot-wide cylindrical, silo-shaped structure detaches from its framework and is lowered in sections by winch-driven cables hanging from the cranes. Placed on tractor-hauled trailers, they will soon become, in von Braun's words, "two ready-to-use Quonset huts."

The overland, ten-day expedition requires two tractors, each hauling three trailers loaded with supplies, scientific equipment, and a total complement of ten. The destination, *Harpalus* crater, believed to be meteoritic in origin, spans 24 miles. Its surrounding ridges rise over 3,000 feet, creating a depth from peak to base of almost 11,000 feet. Although the crater would be only 195 miles away if one could fly there directly, it is actually about 250 miles by ground traverse. En route to and at the target site, a wide variety of experiments are to be undertaken and automatic recording devices will be left behind before the expedition heads back toward the lunar base. As the exploration of the Moon comes to an end, preparations are made for the return voyage to Earth – or rather, for the rendezvous with the space station, the facility from which the trip began six weeks earlier.

Step Four: The Supreme Challenge – Mars
By the time von Braun and his colleagues had described the opening phases of their space program, readers were clamoring for information as to how crews would be selected, what kinds of training would they undergo, how they would cope with potential disasters, and what might be the effects on the human body of long-term exposure to space flight. In response, *Collier's* called upon an array of experts, who, in four sequential issues published between February and June 1953, attempted to shed light on these and related matters.

The magazine completed its space series on April 30, 1954, with

an issue devoted to Mars. The spectacular Bonestell cover (fig. 5) portrays a fleet of ten 4,000-ton spaceships traversing interplanetary space en route to the red planet. Von Braun described his ships as "bulky bundles of girders, with propellant tanks hung on the outside and great passenger cabins perched on top."[6] Von Braun stressed at the start of his presentation that, "The first men who set out for Mars had better make sure they leave everything at home in apple-pie order. They won't get back to earth for more than two and a half years." That included a full fifteen months on the Martian surface. And when might such a voyage occur? Speculated von Braun: "It will be a century or more before [mankind is] ready."[7]

The seventy-man expedition assembles first in Earth's orbit, and after the fleet has traversed interplanetary space for eight months, reassembles in a 600-mile orbit around the red planet. Once in Martian orbit, three of the ten spaceships are prepared for landing. These specially designed, torpedo-shaped craft incorporate landing skids and folded wings that, at the appropriate time, are deployed for glide-descent onto the Martian surface (back in 1954, the atmosphere was believed to be ten times denser than we now know it to be). After fifteen months of intense study of the geography, geology, and environment of Mars, the explorers prepare to return to Earth. They remove the wings and landing gear of the two equatorial landers and erect the core return rockets that will carry them to the seven spaceships circling 600 miles above.

III. 2001: My Space Odyssey
Less than two years after the *Collier's* space series came to an end, I joined the von Braun rocket team at the Army Ballistic Missile Agency, Redstone Arsenal in Huntsville, Alabama. In this role, I continued to

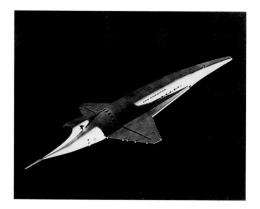

Fig. 6
Model of the *Orion III* craft made for Kubrick's film *2001: A Space Odyssey.* 1968

Fig. 7
Model of the *Aries IB* spacecraft made for *2001.* 1968

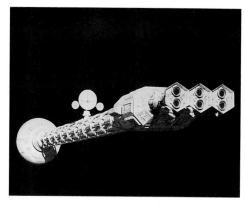

Fig. 8
One of two models used for filming *2001.* 1968

be influenced and mesmerized by the plans, programs, and advanced design concepts put forward by von Braun's innovative and highly motivated group. In the decade that followed, the manned Mercury and Gemini satellite programs captured the attention of the American public, President John F. Kennedy announced the Apollo lunar landing challenge, and preliminary studies called for manned expeditions to Mars as early as the mid 1980s. Indeed, one series begun in 1962 examined the feasibility of manned fly-by missions to both Mars and Venus in the 1970–72 time frame.

These programs were very much in my mind when my Huntsville-based colleague Harry Lange and I were invited to New York to join the preliminary planning team for Stanley Kubrick's Polaris Production. I readily accepted our task to examine the technical and scientific aspects of what would become the classic film *2001: A Space Odyssey,* based on the novel by Arthur C. Clarke and directed by Kubrick. Not surprisingly, the epic scale of von Braun's vision exerted a strong influence on the unfolding drama.

Following six months of preproduction work in New York, our small but growing team left for London in the summer of 1965 and set up shop with Kubrick's production organization, Hawk Films Ltd., at the M-G-M British Studios in the suburb of Borehamwood. With us was the American illustrator Richard McKenna, who, with Lange and Roy Carnon, was assigned the task of creating design concepts that met Kubrick's and Clarke's exacting standards. It was my responsibility to ensure that these designs passed scientific and technological muster.

Following von Braun's paradigm, as described in the *Collier's* space series, our sequences called for a number of sophisticated space vehicles: a recoverable Earth-to-orbit craft named *Orion III* (which today we would describe as a shuttle); a large, doughnut-shaped space station; a virtual hotel in space; an Earth-orbit-to-lunar-surface

spacecraft, *Aries IB;* a rocket, or lunar, "bus" created to transport passengers and cargo from one place to another on the Moon; and finally, the huge *Discovery* interplanetary spaceship. The *Discovery,* in turn, housed several small "space pods," the descendants of what von Braun called "space taxis" back in the *Collier's* days.

The detailed model of *Orion III* reveals an elegantly designed, jet airliner-inspired configuration capable of providing shuttle service to and from Cape Canaveral and low Earth orbit (fig. 6). All exterior filming relied on models, while a full-scale interior was constructed for sequences involving the actors. Clearly, *Orion III* was an aesthetic improvement over von Braun's winged recoverable third stage from the *Collier's* era. The model shows the cockpit viewport at the front, observation windows, and the propulsion system at the rear. The craft housed an automated kitchen, communications, docking, and other equipment, as well as accommodations for a two-man crew, a couple of stewardesses, and some thirty passengers (see Hall, fig. 4).

The orbiting space station, which was never named per se, was referred to as Space Station I by Arthur C. Clarke in the novel version of *2001.* In planning for the film, however, we predicted that by the year 2001 there would be more than one such craft in orbit. So for us Space Station I became Space Station V. How optimistic we were in those days! The doughnut shape was reminiscent of what had been projected in *Collier's,* though we did depart from the earlier architecture by offering a twin-wheel design. Our Space Station V orbited at 200 miles, considerably lower than the altitude von Braun anticipated.

As with *Orion III,* a model of the *2001* station was constructed for filming exterior sequences, while a portion of the interior was built at full scale. Only one of the two wheels, designated A and B, was assumed to be completed by the year 2001. On opposite sides of the station's core we placed the Orion III docking port and that for *Aries IB.* Passing from these ports to the outer, permanently inhab-

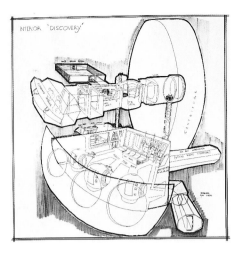

Fig. 9
Interior layout of the interplanetary spaceship *Discovery*, made for
2001. 1968

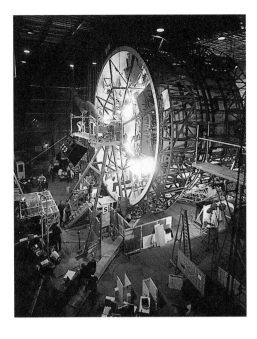

Fig. 10
Exterior of *Discovery*'s centrifuge as it appeared during
filming of *2001*

ited rim, arriving visitors would first be cleared through a voice-print identification booth. Then an elevator would take them to the rim, where they were greeted by a Hilton Hotel, a snack-bar, a Bell System "visionphone," Olivier Mourgue furnishings, and other elements designed to make them feel at home.

A three-foot model of *Aries IB* reveals many clearly visible details, including soiled areas introduced purposely to enhance realism (fig. 7). The spacecraft was, in fact, another shuttle, designed to travel not from Earth to orbit but to and from the space station and *Clavius Base* on the Moon. Its landing legs are retracted in this image. Blast deflec-tors surround the small steering rocket motors. Near the top are the passenger deck and observation windows. *Aries IB*'s crew consisted of a pilot, a copilot, and two stewardesses who attend to some twenty passengers during routine flights. Like *Orion III,* it contained the facilities one would expect aboard a sophisticated jetliner on Earth (see Hall, fig. 3; plate 73).

The lunar or rocket bus, also unnamed, was designed for passen-ger and light cargo transport and for undertaking selenological surveys, rescue operations, and other missions. It would fly five to ten miles above the surface over a range of a thousand miles or more.

The magnificent spaceship *Discovery* was imagined to be capable of navigating the interplanetary depths from Earth orbit to Jupiter orbit. Two models were used for filming, one fifteen and the other fifty-four feet long (fig. 8). The slender craft would have measured up to seven hundred feet long if it were ever built. A "Cavradyne" gaseous-core nuclear propulsion system at the rear is separated from the inhabited spherical structure at the opposite end by hundreds of feet of tankage and structure, much of which is used for storage (see plate 72). The communications and telemetry antennas occupy a prominent midship position. The large spherical structure at the head of the ship houses a centrifuge, where the crew spend most of

their time, a command module containing the ship's flight controls, a bay to garage three small repair and inspection craft, a "ware-house" for spare parts, an airlock, and the notorious HAL 9000 logic complex, the talking computer that controlled virtually all of *Discovery*'s functions (figs. 9, 10).

Even though the elaborate architecture of space travel seen in *2001* has yet to be built, von Braun's epic vision expressed in the *Collier's* series has been partially fulfilled. The huge Saturn V launch rocket, the Apollo spacecraft, and the Space Shuttle all came into being within a few decades of being proposed, as did his short-lived Skylab space station. The huge, permanent International Space Station now under construction may be ready by 2005, a half cen-tury or so after von Braun proposed his particular design. Large-scale lunar operations remain to be realized, a fact that would have disappointed von Braun. Meanwhile, manned expeditions to Mars elude us and probably will for at least a couple more decades. That challenge still remains for a generation to come.

1. "Man Will Conquer Space Soon: What Are We Waiting For?" *Collier's* (Mar. 22, 1952), p. 23.
2. Wernher von Braun, "Crossing the Last Frontier," *Collier's* (Mar. 22, 1952), p. 28.
3. Wernher von Braun, "Man on the Moon: The Journey," *Collier's* (Oct. 18, 1952), p. 53.
4. Ibid., p. 56.
5. Ibid., p. 60.
6. Wernher von Braun, "Can We Get to Mars?" *Collier's* (Apr. 30, 1954), p. 28.
7. Ibid., p. 23.

Architecture in Motion:
The Interior Design of Skylab

REBECCA DALVESCO

In October 1957, after the satellite *Sputnik 1* had been launched by the Soviets, *Life* magazine ran a cover story declaring that it was necessary for the United States to regain its leadership in space (see Hales, fig. 2). Almost a year later, the Space Act of 1958 created the National Aeronautics and Space Administration (NASA) to propel America toward space exploration and promote the United States' leading role in technology.[1] To these ends, in the mid 1960s, NASA created the Apollo Applications Program, which produced America's first space station, Skylab (fig. 1).

Over the years, numerous metaphors have been used to describe Skylab. It has been deemed a house, a classroom, a hotel, a test tube, and an apartment; it has also been referred to as non-architecture. Functioning as all of these in one capacity or the other, Skylab was the first mission in space involving an extended stay "in a house with all its rooms and corridors."[2] In addition to biomedical and other scientific studies, part of NASA's mission was to assess the habitability of the space station by studying the astronauts' efficiency in moving or handling things. To do so, the astronauts' daily schedules were dictated and monitored by Mission Control in Houston. Thus, different from the Apollo mission to the Moon, the Skylab voyage investigated daily living experiences over an extended period of time.

Unlike the Soviet manned satellite *Salyut 1,* first launched on April 19, 1971 (and its successor, fig. 2), Skylab was created from an empty rocket stage, twenty-two feet wide and fifty-eight feet long.[3] At the time, it was to be the biggest structure put into Earth's orbit, four times heavier and considerably larger than *Salyut 1.* There were three three-manned missions to Skylab, following its unmanned launch on May 14, 1973. Robert R. Gilruth, the director of the Manned Spacecraft Center in Houston, wanted a space station that would enhance the United States' manned space-flight development, as the Mercury and Apollo missions did. He advocated a modular, multi-unit structure for Skylab. These goals, however, may not have been realistic for a space station such as Skylab, which was constructed from used parts, could contain only a few crew members, and, most significantly, had a limited lifetime in space.

NASA engineers and scientists, and a few NASA officials – in particular, Dr. George Mueller, the associate administrator for manned space flight – thought that the initial design of Skylab revealed a lack of sensitivity to human needs. In 1967, NASA hired the industrial and interior designer Raymond Loewy through the Martin Marietta Corporation to act as the habitability consultant. Loewy's firm, Raymond Loewy/ William Snaith, Inc., was asked "to develop conceptual designs, drawings, and to build small models and mock-ups" as well as recommend "a variety of concepts from which a selection may be made by NASA."[4]

Raymond Loewy (1893–1986) came to America from France in 1919, after World War I. Working in New York as a fashion illustrator, Loewy began designing department store displays. Eventually he turned to industrial design, taking a job with the mimeograph company Gestetner, which in 1929 asked Loewy to improve the design of its duplicating machine. Thus began a long career in the field of industrial design, during which Loewy developed products for Coca Cola, Ford, Frigidaire, Formica, IBM, Chrysler, BMW, Jaguar, and Studebaker. His interest in space design began in 1939, when he created a model of a rocket-launching spacecraft installation for Chrysler to promote the corporation as a visionary of technological advancement (see Brodherson, fig. 5).

Loewy/Snaith was responsible for studies in the Skylab habitability program that would consider issues of psycho-physiological safety and efficiency during missions in space and on the return to Earth. Loewy and his team, comprising approximately twelve staff members from his New York office, had little knowledge about living in space and the effects of weightlessness on the astronauts' normal bodily functions. At the time, there were no designers to emulate in the field of space design, only the engineers and scientists working at NASA laboratories on the Skylab design. In order to transform the rocket tank into a quasi-home and laboratory, Loewy's team broke away

Fig. 1
Skylab viewed from the command
and service module on the
day the station was abandoned.
February 8, 1974

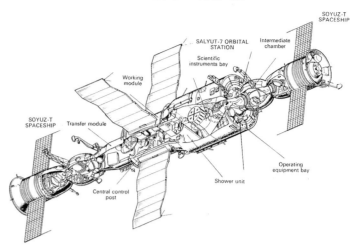

Fig. 2
Drawing of Salyut 7/Soyuz Piloted
Orbital Complex. ca. 1982–85

from traditional design methods used for products in an environment with gravity. They relied instead "upon logic and educated intuition."[5]

In designing Skylab, Loewy and his team confronted a number of questions: How should the astronauts' living environment be equipped when in space there is no firm distinction between up and down? Exactly what controls, sensors, and instruments are needed? How and where will the astronauts sit or stand when working or eating? How will they bathe or shave, use a toilet or clean their teeth in a weightless environment? How will they traverse smoothly and quickly to their destinations while on board Skylab? How will the astronauts clean the space station of any floating debris? With such lack of data regarding living in deep space for long periods of time, Loewy, having trained only briefly before the war as an electrical engineer, relied upon his years of practice in the field of industrial design.

Loewy and his colleagues created numerous drawings, reports, and mock-ups for the Skylab project. Among these were a crew member's stateroom, separate sleep stations for the astronauts, a fecal collector and waste management compartment, a sleep/chair station, color selections for the interior, a table for the wardroom (where food preparation and eating took place), a food tray, a porthole window, a flight suit, and a floor plan. Loewy also recommended that each astronaut be allowed eight hours a day to himself, that they should eat meals facing each other, and that all surfaces be smooth for easy clean-up if space sickness should occur. Loewy claimed that at the beginning of his research, many of NASA's engineers and astronauts disagreed with him concerning his design philosophy of the space station. To Loewy, "what followed was a redesign so complete that only the shape of the rocket stage left the impression that it was the same space station."[6]

Although Loewy's team proposed a profusion of designs and recommendations for Skylab, only a few were actually accepted and implemented into the final design. Caldwell Johnson, chief of the Houston Spacecraft Design Office, filed two reports dated July 1970 and August 1971 listing a number of projects that Loewy's team had completed, of which only four were used in Skylab: the designs for the flight suit, the garment-storage modules, the porthole in the wardroom, and the colors used in the interior. Nonetheless, in his report of 1970, Johnson stated that "Loewy, Inc., has been especially useful by helping us to reduce the harsh appearance of some of our design concepts while maintaining their functionality."[7] Though not mentioned in Caldwell's reports, Loewy's circular floor plan, which flowed with the shape of the rocket, was also chosen over NASA's original design for a square plan for the crew's living quarters.

The five major assemblies that made up the Skylab cluster resembled a string of cylindrically shaped parts joined with wing-shaped solar panels that jutted out from the sides of the largest cylinder (fig. 3). Another cylindrical device extended perpendicularly from the center cylinder, to the end of which windmill-like rectangular, solar-winged devices were attached. These solar panels provided the astronauts with electric power.[8] The astronauts would proceed from the command-and-service module through a seventeen-foot-long, tunnellike white room, through a hatch into a small airlock module, then through another hatch into a tunnel and into the largest space, the workshop (fig. 4). The space of the workshop was divided into an upper and a lower deck. The upper deck contained the water supply, storage, and the food freezer; the lower deck, about the height of the average man, contained the wardroom, sleep stations, and waste containment facility.

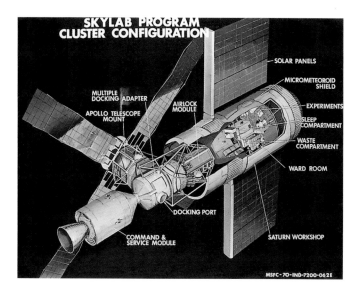

Fig. 3
Artist's rendering of Skylab cluster
configuration. 1970

Although the astronauts enjoyed the upper deck of the work-shop to alleviate any problems with claustrophobia, they felt most comfortable in the space of the lower deck. It was easier to move around, as well as more secure, in the shallow space of the wedge-shape rooms, than the upper deck area. The lower deck also housed the experiment work area, where biomedical and other experiments were performed. The forward compartment was used primarily for experiments requiring large areas or those designed to use one of the two airlocks put in for external viewing. One of the airlocks was directed toward the Sun, the other faced in the opposite direction. In the two compartments there were also storage containers for food, water, and clothing. Handles, grips, and foot restraints were placed at various points throughout the two compartments to aid in the astronauts' movement in a weightless environment. These handrails were painted blue for easy identification. Tools, supplies, repair kits, films, tapes, clamps, scissors, thermometers, photographic lights, and movie and still cameras were also included on board. Attached to the workshop was a manned solar observatory that was used to study the ultraviolet light and x-rays that did not reach the Earth's surface.[9]

At the forward end of the workshop was the airlock module that allowed the astronauts to enter and exit the workshop without depressurizing it. Circular hatches were installed at both ends of the airlock module and a rectangular hatch on the side, each sealed air-tight against the vacuum of space. The circular hatch at one end of the airlock module allowed entry to the multiple-docking adapter, which led to the command-and-service module, while the other cir-cular hatch provided access to the workshop. The side hatch, known as the extravehicular activities hatch (EVA), permitted the astronauts to make excursions outside the space station. The Gemini spacecraft used this same type of hatch, and it was tested on *Gemini 4* when astronaut Edward White used it to become the first American astro-naut to walk in space. Following their philosophy "to use, as much

as possible, equipment that had proven itself in the environment of space,"[10] NASA engineers felt that the hatch was sufficiently tested to be included in the Skylab design.

Loewy chose a triangular form for the table (fig. 5) in the ward-room because he "was opposed to preferential hierarchical treat-ment for crew members during long missions."[11] However, all of the astronauts thought the table was too low. They suggested that a more suitable one should be considerably higher and have a slanted top, similar to a drafting table. Despite this complaint, the table suc-cessfully approximated Earth-style dining, and served for such activi-ties as writing and playing games.

The astronauts' aluminum food trays (fig. 6) were designed to fit into the top of the table for heating. NASA slightly changed Loewy's food compartment design in both the size of the food stor-age holes and their location. For the duration of the flight each astronaut had his own food tray along with a spoon, fork, and knife. Magnets were dispersed at various points on the food tray in order to attract the utensils. These magnets did not always work, however, and the astronauts found themselves using rubber bands to secure their utensils. The experience of eating on Skylab differed consider-ably from that on the Apollo missions, where astronauts had to eat their food from packets using tubes. During Skylab's missions, most of the astronauts complained that many of the food cans were too small for the holes they were placed in: they often had to catch them as they floated out and wedge them back into place. One astronaut from Skylab's last mission, Gerald P. Carr, suggested that future space stations should have dispensers for food.[12] The astro-nauts also noted that the food was often tepid because the heating element in the food trays did not work as well as it should have.

Thigh restraints, composed of a round bar with two crossbars, were attached to the lower portion of the table for the astronauts' legs. To use these restraints, the astronauts had to straddle the main bar, with their legs placed between the crossbars. But doing so was

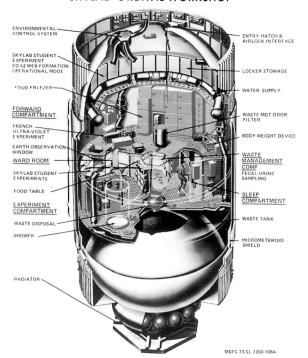

SKYLAB ORBITAL WORKSHOP

ENVIRONMENTAL
CONTROL SYSTEM

SKYLAB STUDENT
EXPERIMENT
ED-52 WEB FORMATION
OPERATIONAL MODE

FOOD FREEZER

FORWARD
COMPARTMENT

FRENCH
ULTRA-VIOLET
EXPERIMENT

EARTH OBSERVATION
WINDOW

WARD ROOM

SKYLAB STUDENT
EXPERIMENTS

FOOD TABLE

EXPERIMENT
COMPARTMENT

WASTE DISPOSAL

SHOWER

RADIATOR

ENTRY HATCH &
AIRLOCK INTERFACE

LOCKER STOWAGE

WATER SUPPLY

WASTE MGT ODOR
FILTER

BODY WEIGHT DEVICE

WASTE
MANAGEMENT
COMP
FECAL-URINE
SAMPLING

SLEEP
COMPARTMENT

WASTE TANK

MICROMETEROID
SHIELD

MSFC-73-SL-7200-108A

Fig. 4
Cutaway view of Skylab Orbital
Workshop. 1973

not always comfortable, and the normal sitting position was not always the best position for someone eating in space. Instead, most of the astronauts preferred to latch their shoe restraints to the floor: they did not wish to find themselves upside down before eating.[13]

Since the structure of the space station was to be enclosed completely from the exterior world of space, Loewy suggested that a porthole window be placed within the wardroom. This idea met with some resistance, but two astronauts, Jack Lousma and Paul Weitz, convinced NASA officials to include it in the final design. The inclusion of a porthole was of utmost importance to Loewy, and he believed that it "played such a large part in the mission."[14] Stargazing and Earthgazing were part of the astronauts' everyday routine. From this porthole they photographed and filmed various atmospheric conditions occurring around Earth. Charles Conrad, Jr., who was on the first manned mission, exclaimed during his voyage: "You can see the whole Bahama chain and all the shallow water and all the deep water in one big picture. It's really fantastic."[15]

Two colors were chosen for the cabinets that lined the walls of the wardroom: brown and off-white. Alan L. Bean, a navy captain, found the colors attractive. Astronaut Edward G. Gibson, however, thought that NASA should have selected a brighter color, such as light blue or light green. Owen K. Garriott, an astronaut on the second manned mission, objected even more strongly. He reported to Houston base from the space station: "It seems to me that the color arrangement that we've got in here might very well have been designed by a navy supply department or something, with about as little imagination as anybody I can imagine. All we've got in here

are about two tones of brown, and that's it for the whole blinking spacecraft interior."[16] The civilian scientist-astronauts were thus more discriminating than the military-astronauts concerning the architectural space and colors used within.

The showering station was a cylindrical, cloth enclosure, located in the experiment and work area of the workshop (fig. 7). It could be flattened when not in use. The device's bottom ring was fastened to the floor and contained foot restraints; the shower head and hose were connected to the upper ring. To use the shower, a pressurized portable bottle filled with heated water was attached to the ceiling, and a hand-held shower head was connected to the water bottle by a flexible hose. This design had some flaws: the water usually squirted all over, the suction in the drains did not always work, and it made a gurgling sound similar to that in airplane lavatories. Several astronauts suggested improving the showering station by having an enclosed space that they could put their hands entirely into so that they could be squirted safely, and a sandblasting device so that they would not have to use water.

Each crew member had his own private sleep station. A sleeping bag hung on a frame against the compartment wall served as the astronaut's bed. To prepare for sleep, the astronaut zipped open the bag and placed blankets around his body, attached a body strap and closed the zipper, thus creating a "pillowed sleeping bag." Sleep restraints prevented the astronaut from floating freely about the cabin while he slept.[17] Sometimes a crew member would sleep outside his restraining device and would assume a fetal position (or the "G-neutral position," as the Houston base referred to it). Those who did so, however, would constantly bump into objects on board and be awakened throughout the sleep session.

This design was not so different from Loewy's sleep-restraint design for the crew member's stateroom, in which the astronaut reclined on a hinged hammock that featured a desk and credenza mounted off to the side. A seat was mounted onto the credenza.

Fig. 5
Skylab wardroom during a training
exercise. 1972

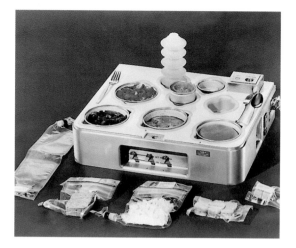

Fig. 6
Skylab space food tray. 1972

Underneath the bed area was storage space, while above was a locker for the astronaut's flight suit. This composition was much more luxurious than the final design created by NASA engineers, in which each crew member had limited space for his stateroom. Another design that Loewy proposed – though it was not incorporated into the final scheme – was a sleep/chair station for the astronaut. NASA's final design for the sleep quarters called for an extremely limited space, similar to the size of a walk-in closet, and divided into three separate modules. Each module contained a bed, a locker, and a privacy curtain, and each crew member had his own adjustable air vent. Although Skylab was never damaged by a meteorite, the astronauts suggested that future space stations place the sleep stations closer to the command module, because it was their only means of escape in case of emergency.

The waste containment area functioned according to a weightless environment, and therefore did not resemble conventional bathroom toilets. The system included a fecal-urine collector, collection and sample bags, sampling equipment, odor control filters, and a fan. The collector was mounted on the wall at 180 degrees, as Loewy's design recommended, rather than on the floor, as NASA's original plans dictated. However, the final version of the formal and mechanical functioning of the collector was different from Loewy's proposal. Similar to a folding telephone-booth door, the bathroom door was rectangular rather than round (as were doorways in other areas of Skylab). The waste containment area itself was a rather small compartment, with a floor made from sheet metal for easy cleaning. Many of the astronauts complained about the size of this room, which resembled the bathroom in most commercial airplanes; they also claimed that they would ricochet off the sides of the room with the slightest movement. Astronaut Joseph Kerwin praised the design of the fecal-urine collector. "We owe our greatest appreciation to the people who designed it. It has worked much better than anticipated, and it has been essentially trouble free and not terribly time-consuming."[18]

Although the astronauts on Skylab seemed to find fault with many of Loewy's designs, overall they thought it functioned like a home in an environment very different from Earth. In a place where up and down are relative, where floors and ceiling are open metal grids, and where voices carry only a few feet, the space station served its purpose: it accomplished its mission to stay in space for an extended length of time, which, before Skylab, had not been accomplished.

Most of the interior and product designs were, finally, the work of NASA engineers and scientists. For instance, NASA's engineers designed the aluminum astrogrid that composed the walls and floors of Skylab. The astrogrid had small hooks placed at intervals for the attachment of various items brought on board by the astronauts. The astrogrid prototype had been developed to hold the weight of large crowds, but the version that was used in Skylab had a weight stress requirement that was considerably lower. NASA also used this prototype as an educational tool in teaching children about the requirements for living in space.[19]

Loewy thus influenced several important design decisions, to the benefit of the astronauts. He had previously executed designs for the government, including the interiors of warships. In a 1974 letter to Loewy, Mueller claimed that the Skylab mission would have been impossible without the design considerations offered by Loewy/Snaith, which enabled the astronauts to live comfortably, efficiently, and in high spirits. Loewy and his team brought an understanding of psychology and other human factors to their interior and product designs, and this ultimately improved many of NASA's final designs.[20]

The structure of Skylab was conceived and designed to be an architecture that was in constant motion, traversing the universe; yet it also was intended to be abandoned in space – left to die. Because there was no way to refuel the station in space or to renew its oxygen, nitrogen, and water supplies after the end of the third mission, Skylab was abandoned, though still usable, on February 8, 1974. An astronaut from the third mission regretted that no life would be

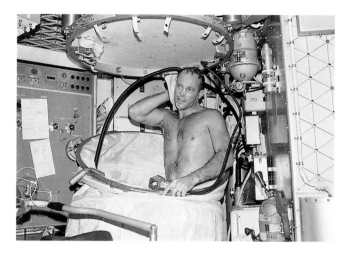

Fig. 7
Skylab astronaut Jack R. Lousma
taking a hot shower in the crew
quarters of the workshop. 1973

inside it again, floating weightless in its rooms, working on experiments, and looking out the window for hours as they had done when they arrived on November 16, 1973. Almost five years later, on July 11, 1979, Skylab fell to Earth and landed in the Indian Ocean.

Only nine astronauts had the experience of being on board the space station. As Americans viewed crewmen in their environment, they could watch the fantasies of the space cartoons and movies they had grown up with come to life. The surreal, almost ideal space became more real. It was a fragmented space, however, brought into our homes via satellite television, videos, and photographic images, most of these hazy and distorted. Most of us are left to wonder what it is like to travel into and live in space, and we can only experience the Skylab project through these incomplete images. Skylab became in many ways a theatrical event. Today Americans can log-on to their computers and view a broad array of space voyage photographs, from the Skylab missions to the recent *Mars Pathfinder* and the launch of the most recent addition to the International Space Station in summer 2000. Like a Hollywood film, NASA's self-consciously styled images allow us to become the spectators of an adventure, to share astronauts' experiences during their voyages.

When Skylab was launched, it seemed to be another example of Manifest Destiny – Americans conquering the only landscape left, the final frontier in which to plant the American flag. But Skylab also offered a last hope for humanity. Skylab presented itself as a new chance for humankind to find something unspoiled. British rock singer David Bowie released his album *Life on Mars* in June 1973, questioning the existence of another species that might be better than our own. It may be that we have lost faith in our "Spaceship Earth," as the architect and inventor R. Buckminster Fuller called our planet in the late 1960s. Perhaps viewing the images of Skylab in photographs, models, and film footage brings the mystery and hope back into our lives.

I wish to thank Maynard Dalton for reviewing this manuscript.

1. Alan Ladwig and Sally K. Ride, "Blueprint for Leadership," in Frederick I. Ordway III and Randy Libermann, eds., *Blueprint for Space: Science Fiction to Science Fact* (Washington, D.C., 1992), pp. 179–88.
2. Henry S. F. Cooper, Jr., *A House in Space* (New York, 1976), p. 6.
3. Similar to Skylab, Salyut had a three-man crew, but the first attempt to board its crew members failed due to docking problems. Although they did succeed in the second attempt to board, Salyut crew members met a tragic ending when a valve in the spacecraft, which equalized internal and external pressures, opened while the craft was descending through the atmosphere. The crew members, not wearing space suits, perished. The third attempt to board Salyut was successful, and the mission finally became the first successful "space station." Humans lived on it for twenty-three days, and it was taken out of orbit 175 days after its launch.
4. Don J. Green, *Awards Study Contract to Loewy/Snaith* (Houston, 1972).
5. Raymond Loewy, *Industrial Design, Raymond Loewy* (Woodstock, N.Y., 1979), p. 205.
6. Dave Dooling, "Industrial Design in Space," *Spaceflight* 23 (June 1981), pp. 169–71.
7. Quoted in Loewy, *Industrial Design*, p. 208.
8. George C. Marshall, *Skylab: Classroom in Space*, ed. Lee B. Summerlin (Washington, D.C., 1977), p. 9.
9. George Marshall, *Skylab: A Guidebook*, ed. Leland F. Belew and Ernst Stuhlinger (Washington, D.C., 1973), p. 3.
10. Marshall, *Skylab: Classroom in Space*, p. 9.
11. Loewy, *Industrial Design*, p. 207.
12. Cooper, *A House in Space*, p. 43.
13. Ibid., p. 40. See also George C. Marshall, *Skylab: Our First Space Station*, ed. Leland F. Belew (Washington, D.C., 1977), p. 82.
14. Loewy, *Industrial Design*, p. 207.
15. Marshall, *Skylab: Our First Space Station*, p. 80.
16. Quoted in Cooper, *A House in Space*, p. 39.
17. Marshall, *Skylab: Our First Space Station*, p. 82.
18. Quoted in ibid., p. 80.
19. Telephone interview with John Frassanito, Sept. 1999.
20. Loewy, *Industrial Design*, p. 205.

Gravity, Space, and Architecture

THEODORE W. HALL

I am not in favor of compact designs which give an impression of solidity and recall heavy earthly buildings. Other laws prevail in space and there is no reason why the old architectural rules should be followed.

—Hermann Oberth, *Man into Space*

Introduction

The history of architecture is, to a large extent, the history of a struggle with gravity. In the ziggurats and pyramids of Babylon, Egypt, and Mesoamerica; in the posts and beams of the Parthenon and Stonehenge; in Roman arches and Gothic flying buttresses; in Bedouin tents and tensile structures; in the domes of igloos and Olympic stadiums – architecture is shaped by gravity. The shape may or may not be intentional, because unintentional shapes often result from structural failure. With recent advances in space exploration, questions about what happens to architecture if gravity is increased, decreased, or removed altogether have taken on new importance. For instance, scientists ponder what happens if natural gravity is replaced with an artificial substitute, such as centripetal acceleration (rotation). This essay surveys how designs for both science and science fiction have explored the range of gravitational states – partial gravity, microgravity, and artificial gravity – to varying degrees of success.

Gravity and Architectural Design Theory

The force of gravity on architecture and architects is not only physical but also psychological. Familiarity with gravity is not innate, but is learned in infancy. At four months, infants begin to realize that a rolling ball cannot pass through an obstacle, but they are not yet aware that an unsupported ball will fall. At five months, they discriminate between upward and downward motion. At seven months, they show sensitivity to gravity and the natural acceleration of a ball rolling upward or downward. By adulthood, people expect falling objects to accelerate naturally on a parabolic path. These judgments arise not from mathematical reasoning but rather from visual experience. When asked to reason abstractly about such motion, many adults are prone to error.[1]

Gravity imparts a notion of *principal directions,* which imbue space with an inherent structure. Six directions on three axes are innately perceptible: up-down (height), left-right (breadth), and front-back (depth). The up-down axis is tied to the force of gravity – the plumb line; the other axes are free to rotate around it. The up-down axis is called "vertical," while all possible left-right and front-back axes are called "horizontal." The anisotropic character of this space is judged by the effort required to move in any given direction: up and down are distinct irreversible poles; left, right, front, and back are interchangeable simply by turning around. Thus, gravitationally, there are three principal directions – up, down, and horizontal – and three basic architectural elements – ceiling (or roof), floor, and wall. These common-sense ideas, rooted in the experience of terrestrial gravity, permeate architectural theory. Thomas Thiis-Evensen built his entire architectural grammar around the three elements of floor, wall, and roof.[2]

People construct environments for themselves according to their symbols of reality.[3] Architectural design for a gravitational environment that is distinctly different from Earth's requires a fundamental reexamination of basic design principles. The characterizations of the directions and boundaries of space must be reevaluated – if not refuted – in extraterrestrial environments.

Architecture in Partial Gravity

Gravity is a vector that varies in magnitude as well as direction. Nevertheless, architecture for the Moon as well as Mars and other planets has been inconsistent in its accommodation of gravities other than Earth's. Some designers have made deliberate efforts to

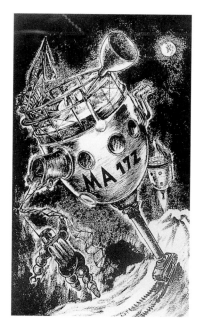

Fig. 1
Hermann Oberth. Frontispiece from
The Moon Car. 1959

Fig. 2
Topps Chewing Gum, "Space Cards,"
"Gymnastics on Moon." 1958

adapt to partial gravity and even take advantage of the opportunities it offers, while others have apparently given little thought to the local gravitational environment. After careful consideration of the rugged, airless, low-gravity environment, scientist Hermann Oberth envisioned his "Moon car" as a combination gyroscope, mobile home, pogo stick, and bulldozer (fig. 1). A whirling mass above the habitat provides the momentum to keep the stack vertical. Just below, inhabitants survey their surroundings from their perch atop the pole. The foot of the vehicle treads across the trackless landscape. When it comes to an otherwise impassable crevasse, the vehicle leaps across on its retractable column, like some mechanical decathlete.[4]

Popular media have also fantasized about life in partial gravity. For instance, Topps Chewing Gum's 1958 series of "Space Cards" introduced images of space exploration and habitation to the adolescent masses, based on recent history as well as future projections.[5] A card labeled "Gymnastics on Moon" shows a young man jumping easily ten feet into the air, while behind him a weight lifter hoists a massive barbell with a single hand (fig. 2). The gymnasium ceiling is high enough to accommodate unrestrained exercise in the low-gravity environment of the Moon. Lunar athletes such as these will, by necessity, learn the difference between weight and mass. A 100-kilogram mass, which weighs 220 pounds on Earth, weighs only about thirty-six pounds on the Moon. Yet it retains its full 100 kilograms of mass and inertia, and is six times as difficult to accelerate as a thirty-six-pound weight on Earth. Unsuspecting lunar jocks who attempt to clean-and-jerk such a mass may be in for a rude surprise. Weight lifting on the Moon will be a slow-motion exercise compared to lifting comparable weights on Earth.

As for lunar basketball, the height of the net should be reconsidered. One approach (not necessarily the best one) is to consider the height of a jump necessary to touch the rim, measured from the initial squatting posture where the work begins. In the Moon's one-sixth gravity, a jump with equal energy will achieve six times the height. This implies that, as a first estimate, the rim should be raised by five times the Earth-jump height to match Earth-normal exertion. If on Earth a person could touch a ten-foot rim with a three-foot jump, then on the Moon the rim should be raised by fifteen feet, to a height of twenty-five feet. Unfortunately, most current designs for early lunar bases are spatially constrained to small, rigid, prefabricated modules that can be launched from Earth. High ceilings are a low priority. The recreation module might accommodate weight training, but lunar basketball will have to await more generous quarters.

Designs for different gravities have captured the imagination of many, including filmmaker Stanley Kubrick and science-fiction writer Arthur C. Clarke, who collaborated on *2001: A Space Odyssey.* The 1968 film paints an all-or-nothing picture of gravity. The conference room at the lunar base appears to be a typical terrestrial design; the photographer scurries around as if on Earth, unfettered by reduced floor traction (proportional to weight) and unconcerned with bumping his head.

Even as this film was being produced, Apollo astronauts were practicing basic mobility using lunar-gravity simulators. Still, they needed actual experience on the lunar surface to develop their technique. Most of them favored a loping stride in which they alternated feet, pushing off with each step and floating forward before planting the other foot. Stopping and changing direction required some

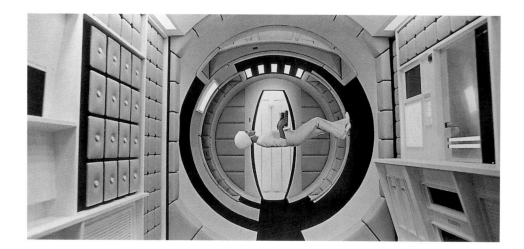

Fig. 3
Interior view of the cislunar transfer vehicle *Aries IB* featured in Stanley Kubrick's *2001: A Space Odyssey.* 1968

extra attention: partial gravity reduces weight and traction, but not mass or momentum. The Moon's one-sixth gravity doesn't accommodate an Earth-normal stride. In the Apollo expeditions, the massive Moon suits and backpacks partially compensated for the gravity deficit. That will not be the case, however, in a larger lunar base intended to provide a shirtsleeve environment for extended stays.

Architecture in Microgravity

As in the tale of Icarus, Earth-dwellers have always dreamt of soaring like birds to the heavens. Unfortunately, Icarus's waxen wings melted when he flew too close to the Sun, and he fell into the sea. Ironically, it is the falling, not the flight, that is the best analog to space travel. Orbit is simply free-fall, with a forward velocity so fast that the curvature of the fall matches the curvature of the Earth (or whatever celestial body one is orbiting). Architects, in their exuberance for the novelty of space flight, have conceived it to be like swimming or floating. In a rush to free themselves from the shackles of gravity, they have overlooked the downside of free-fall and its attendant disorientation, and happily abandoned the notion of principal directions. For example, in September 1967, the architectural firm of Warner Burns Toan and Lunde (WBTL) began to collaborate with Grumman Aerospace to develop design concepts for a zero-gravity space station. Working with a stack of cylindrical modules, they explored several schemes for subdividing the volume, sometimes varying the up-down orientation from one chamber to another. *Progressive Architecture* magazine commended its creative approach: "Its clear expression of the properties of space, of life in space, of the body freedom, are appealing to the imagination. Where is the fun, after all, if the Earth environment is too closely duplicated? Taken to extremes, it could mean lace curtains and French provincial in light-weight plastic."[6]

Meanwhile, Kubrick and Clarke had fun with the notion of zero-gravity body freedom, particularly in the cislunar transfer vehicle

and the Pan Am spaceplane (figs. 3, 4). A stewardess, equipped with special gripper shoes, steps "head up" into the galley, removes a tray of food from the oven, then trundles her way around a circular portal, up the wall and onto the ceiling, to emerge "head down" into the passenger cabin. This maneuver, and the odd interior design that demands it, serves no obvious purpose other than to entertain the audience. (In fact, since the craft must eventually land in the Moon's non-zero gravity, the design may be seriously flawed.) After observing this action for a few seconds, the camera follows the stewardess's lead and rolls 180 degrees to achieve a more comfortable orientation with respect to its new surroundings.

Unlike fictional designs, where creative license could overlook inconsistencies in dealing with gravity, the 1973 Skylab offered the first real experience with significant freedom of movement in microgravity. Astronaut Edward G. Gibson reported: "Being upside down in the wardroom made it look like a different room than what we were used to. When I started to rotate back and go approximately 45 degrees or so off the attitude which we normally call 'up,' the attitude in which we had trained, there was a very sharp transition in my mind from a room that was sort of familiar to one which was intimately familiar."[7] The wardroom furnishings provided the astronauts with an important vertical reference for internal activities. Nevertheless, when looking out the window, they switched to an Earth-down reference, even if this meant floating sideways or upside down relative to the furnishings. In contrast to the wardroom, the workshop did not provide any particular vertical. The Skylab astronauts found it a bit disorienting and preferred smaller but more familiar living quarters.[8]

Microgravitational space may be amorphous and isotropic, but the human body is not. Based in part on the Skylab experience, current designs for microgravity habitats shun the disorientation of earlier architectural fantasies and present the inhabitants with a consistent up-down axis. This is evident, for example, in the TransHab inflatable

Fig. 4
Interior view of the passenger cabin
of the Pan Am spaceplane, *Orion III*,
in *2001: A Space Odyssey*

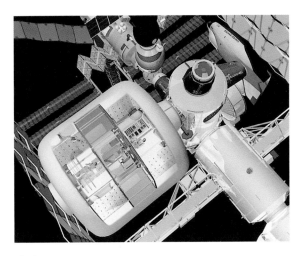

Fig. 5
Computer rendering and cutaway
view of TransHab, an endoskeletal
space habitat designed by William
Schneider, Horacio de la Fuente, and
Kriss Kennedy, of the NASA Johnson
Space Center, and Constance
Adams, of Lockheed Martin Space
Operations Co. 1999–2000

module – initially conceived at NASA Johnson Space Center as an Earth-to-Mars transit habitat and later proposed for the International Space Station (ISS) (fig. 5). One of the "important design objectives" of TransHab is "to maintain a local vertical configuration."[9] The orientation of the internal vertical axis with respect to external space is somewhat arbitrary. What is important is that the habitat is at least internally consistent with respect to vertical orientation.

Another aspect of microgravity habitation that real designs, unlike fiction, cannot ignore is the physiological adaptation to weightlessness. It is not the euphoric experience that many people imagine – at least not during the first few days, during which about half of all space travelers suffer symptoms of motion sickness. People adapt, and the overt sickness subsides. But as bodily fluids shift from the lower extremities toward the torso and head, more insidious adaptations settle in: fluid loss, muscle loss, bone loss, weakened immunity, flatulence, and nasal congestion, to name a few.[10] Housekeeping in a microgravity space hotel will also be a major task; every surface of the chamber must be designed with this in mind.

Architecture in Artificial Gravity

Isaac Newton's *Mathematical Principles of Natural Philosophy,* published in 1687, contains everything necessary to explain the relationships of force, mass, acceleration, orbit, weightlessness, and artificial gravity. Decades before *Sputnik 1* achieved orbit, the early visionaries of space habitation foresaw problems with weightlessness and questioned whether people could long survive in such a state. Designers continue to propose artificial gravity as a panacea for all of the ills

associated with prolonged weightlessness. Engineers have devoted extensive study to the artifact (structure, stability, propulsion, and so on), but relatively little to the environment from the point of view of someone living and moving within it. Authors have implied that artificial gravity should permit the adoption of essentially terrestrial designs. They have downplayed the *artificiality* of the gravity. But saccharin is not sucrose, and centripetal acceleration is not gravity as we know it.

Off-axis motion in a spinning space station involves transient forces that distort the apparent gravity in proportion to the relative speed. A person in linear motion perpendicular to the axis (radial or tangential) encounters Coriolis force, which is perpendicular to both the station's axis and the person's relative motion. Similarly, a person in rotational motion that is not aligned with the station's spin – such as when turning side-to-side around a vertical "spoke" while that spoke spins around the station's horizontal "axle" – encounters torque that is perpendicular to both the station's spin and the person's own rotation. Such non-aligned rotations are said to be cross-coupled. These cross-coupled rotations give rise to unusual torques in the vestibular organs of the inner ear, leading to dizziness and illusions of rotation around a perpendicular axis.

As a result, in artificial gravity, there are at least five, not three, principal directions: up (toward the axis), down (away from the axis), east (prograde), west (retrograde), and axial. Architectural design for artificial gravity has barely begun to address its peculiarities. The goal is not to mimic Earth but rather to help the inhabitants adapt to the realities of their rotating environment.

Fig. 6
"Stanford Torus." 1975. From Richard D. Johnson and Charles Holbrow, eds., *Space Settlements: A Design Study.* 1977

Artificial gravity dominated the early space station concepts. Only after substantial experience with weightlessness did microgravity concepts come to the fore. Since the Salyut and Skylab missions of the 1970s, access to microgravity has been one of the main motivations for space flight. Ironically, while extended stays in weightlessness have revealed its dangers, they have also shown that it is survivable; several cosmonauts have survived microgravity missions of a year or more. Such missions are milestones of human endurance; they are not models for space settlement. Artificial gravity is both the past and future of long-duration space-habitat design.

As early as 1903, Konstantin Eduardovich Tsiolkovsky published plans for orbital outposts incorporating artificial gravity.[11] Twenty years later, Oberth independently developed similar ideas; he was followed by Hermann Noordung, Wernher von Braun, and others.[12] By the 1950s, the image of the space station as a rotating torus was firmly established. Much of the credit (or blame) for this must go to von Braun, who brought his vision to the masses through the media of *Collier's* magazine and Walt Disney films.[13] The torus is a powerful gestalt. People expect that it is the form a space station should have, even if they don't understand why. For example, another card issued by Topps, entitled "Space Supply Depot," depicted the station as a pair of tori surrounding a roughly conical core. An astronaut stands on the outer skin of the structure, aligned with the axis. If this station rotated, as the wheel shape suggests it should, the artificial gravity would be at right angles to what the artist seems to expect: the windows would be in the floor and the astronaut would be flung from his precarious perch.

Before Sputnik, space-station design was a pursuit of comic book artists, fantasy film producers, and engineers with perhaps too much time on their hands. After Sputnik, it became a national priority. With the dawn of manned space flight in the 1960s, teams of engineers began a concerted effort to realize the visions of their forebears. Some of the biggest problems were packaging, launch, and deployment in orbit. In particular, they looked for ways to pack a rotating space station into the right circular cylinders of rocket payload fairings. NASA Langley Research Center and North American Aviation developed plans for an "automatically erectable modular torus" (AEMT). They conceived a hexagonal arrangement of cylindrical modules joined by hinges at the vertices. The station would be constructed entirely on the ground, folded for launch, and unfolded in orbit. Because spin-induced artificial gravity is centripetal, a "level" floor must be circular in the plane of rotation. A six-sided torus would feel as lumpy as a six-sided wheel. To avoid that, the designers arranged the finished floor as a series of concentric arcs stepping up and down across the length of each module (see the essay by Howard E. McCurdy in this volume).[14]

The Lockheed Aircraft Corporation avoided the problem by stepping away from the torus paradigm and turning their modules parallel to the axis of rotation. This configuration has the added advantage of reducing the crew's encounters with Coriolis acceleration, which is zero for motion parallel to the axis.[15] Nearly forty years later, working at a substantially grander scale, designers at the Shimizu Corporation have assumed a similar strategy in their proposal for a space hotel (see plate 89). Echoing the relatively modest Lockheed proposal, they foresee assembling their structure from cylindrical modules arranged parallel to the rotation axis. Unlike the Lockheed design, however, the prevailing form here is still the torus.[16]

Grander still are the enormous space colonies championed by physicist Gerard K. O'Neill, such as the Stanford Torus, the Bernal Sphere, and various models of cylindrical "islands" as much as four miles in diameter (fig. 6).[17] Descriptions of life in these places are rife with the incongruity of trying to transplant middle-class America

Fig. 7
Lewis Gilbert, director. *Moonraker.*
1979. Interior view of the space
station

into the concave environment of a self-contained spinning cylinder. O'Neill imagined a settlement wrapped around the inside surface of the shape: "It would be like urban living in this country, with the difference that instead of looking into the windows of another apartment one would be looking out onto farmland. One could imagine having a promenade of shops, cinemas, restaurants, markets, and libraries, extending all the way around the cylinder."[18] Space colony architecture such as this is often conceived as an idealization of Earth rather than a departure from it.

Perhaps the most famous portrayal of artificial gravity appears in *2001: A Space Odyssey* (see plate 71). The gracefully spinning space station waltzing its way around the Earth, and the rotating ring in the spaceship *Discovery* on its journey to Jupiter, are endearing images for many modern space enthusiasts. They are also among the most technically correct, with their upward curving toroidal floors and spin-despin interfaces. Nevertheless, certain details, though not necessarily wrong, leave room for improvement. For example, as the Earth shuttle approaches the station, it begins to match the station's spin. While this looks poetic on film, it may be impracticable. Until they mate, the shuttle and station follow slightly different orbital tracks. Orbital adjustments required for docking may be exceedingly difficult to execute once the shuttle has started rolling. As another example, the ladder in *Discovery*'s rotating section is mounted in the side wall, parallel to the plane of rotation. In this arrangement, Coriolis accelerations would tend to pull the astronauts sideways off the ladder, especially near the top, where centripetal acceleration is small. It would be better to turn the ladder out of the wall, perpendicular to the plane, so that Coriolis accelerations work with the astronauts rather than against them.

By comparison, more recent portrayals of artificial gravity have been dismal failures. In *Moonraker* (1979), the space station is an oddly asymmetric jumble of tubes (fig. 7). Though it supposedly rotates to simulate gravity, the designers evidently had no idea how artificial gravity works. The film shows shuttles docked with the station, aligned variously on their roll, pitch, or yaw axes, as if relying on trial and error to get the proper orientation with respect to the station's spin. In contrast, the 1998 film *Armageddon* is at least consistent, though consistently wrong. Determined to do everything the hard way, the director sets the station spinning just as the shuttles arrive, turning what should be a routine docking maneuver into a navigational nightmare. The shuttles are now forced to perform the virtually impossible task of simultaneous tangential docking to the end points of rotating spokes. The spokes would be vertical shafts with respect to the artificial gravity, but the film portrays them as horizontal corridors. Producers and movie fans may view such criticisms as nit-picking, but architects ought to know, at a minimum, which way is up.

Notably absent from this essay so far is any mention of *Star Trek, Star Wars,* or several other popular space-theme adventures. The gravity they portray is without explanation, with no basis in known physics. These productions are essentially fantasies, mostly unrelated to the reality of space travel, with few pretensions in that regard.

It used to be said that pictures never lie, but in this age of virtual reality and sophisticated special effects, the old adage no longer applies. Convincing visions of space habitation have progressed rather faster than reality, and not always in ways that reality can accommodate. Nevertheless, space-station designers have always gleaned at least some of their inspiration from science fiction and fantasy. It should be interesting to see how the vision and reality of space habitation evolve in the coming decades.

1. See Bruce Bower, "Infants Signal the Birth of Knowledge," *Science News* 142 (Nov. 14, 1992), p. 325; In Kyeong Kim and Elizabeth S. Spelke, "Infants' Sensitivity to Effects of Gravity on Visible Object Motion," *Journal of Experimental Psychology: Human Perception and Performance* 18 (May 1992), pp. 385–93; Timothy L. Hubbard, "Cognitive Representation of Linear Motion: Possible Direction and Gravity Effects in Judged Displacement," *Memory and Cognition* 18 (May 1990), pp. 299–309.

2. See Christian Norberg-Schulz, *Genius Loci: Towards a Phenomenology of Architecture* (New York, 1980), p. 169; Thomas Thiis-Evensen, *Archetypes in Architecture* (Oslo, Norway, and Cambridge, Mass., 1987).

3. Vincent Scully, *Architecture: The Natural and the Manmade* (New York, 1991), p. 1.

4. Hermann Oberth, *The Moon Car,* trans. Willy Ley (New York, 1959).

5. Topps issued two identical series of cards under the titles "Space Cards" and "Target: Moon."

6. Alis D. Runge, "Spaces in Space," *Progressive Architecture* 50 (Nov. 1969), pp. 132–44.

7. Quoted in Mary M. Connors, Albert A. Harrison, and Faren R. Akins, *Living Aloft: Human Requirements for Extended Spaceflight,* Special Publication 483, NASA Scientific and Technical Information Branch (Washington, D.C., 1985), p. 38.

8. James E. Oberg and Alcestis R. Oberg, *Pioneering Space: Living on the Next Frontier* (New York, 1986), pp. 12, 186, 196.

9. Kriss J. Kennedy, "ISS TransHab: Architecture Description," paper no. 1999-01-2143, in Society of Automotive Engineers, *Proceedings of the 29th International Conference on Environmental Systems* (ICES), July 12–15, 1999 (Denver, Col., 1999).

10. See Connors, Harrison, and Akins, *Living Aloft;* Oberg and Oberg, *Pioneering Space;* Daniel Woodard and Alcestis R. Oberg, "The Medical Aspects of a Flight to Mars," paper no. AAS 81-239, in American Astronautical Society, *The Case for Mars,* ed. Penelope J. Boston (Washington, D.C., 1984), pp. 173–80; Phil Gunby, "Space Medicine Faces Massive Task as Humans Venture Farther from Earth," *Journal of the American Medical Association* 256 (Oct. 17, 1986), p. 2009; Terra Ziporyn, "Aerospace Medicine: The First 200 Years," *Journal of the American Medical Association* 256, p. 2010; Charles Marwick, "Physicians Called Upon to Help Chart Future Space Effort," *Journal of the American Medical Association* 256, pp. 2015ff; Phil Gunby, "Soviet Space Medical Data Grow, Other Nations Joining In," *Journal of the American Medical Association* 256, pp. 2026ff; Chris Anne Raymond, "Physicians Trade White Coats for Space Suits," *Journal of the American Medical Association* 256, pp. 2033ff; Beverly Merz, "The Body Pays a Penalty for Defying the Law of Gravity," *Journal of the American Medical Association* 256, pp. 2040ff; Marsha F. Goldsmith, "How Will Humans Act as Science Fiction Becomes Fact?" *Journal of the American Medical Association* 256, pp. 2048ff; Ingrid Wickelgren, "Muscles in Space Forfeit More Than Fibers," *Science News* 134 (Oct. 29, 1988), p. 277; and Stanley R. Mohler, "Aging and Space Travel," *Aerospace Medicine* 33 (May 1962), pp. 594–97.

11. Konstantin Eduardovich Tsiolkovsky, *Beyond the Planet Earth,* trans. Kenneth Syers (New York, 1960). The main text was originally published in the Soviet Union by the Kaluga Society for Natural History and Local Studies in 1920. See also John M. Logsdon and George Butler, "Space Station and Space Platform Concepts: A Historical Review," *Space Stations and Space Platforms: Concepts, Design, Infrastructure, and Uses,* ed. Ivan Bekey and Daniel Herman (New York, 1985), pp. 203–63. Logsdon and Butler provide a Tsiolkovsky illustration from 1903. Though they do not name the original source, this is the year that Tsiolkovsky published his article "The Exploration of Space by Means of Jet Devices" in the Russian journal *Nauchnoye Obozreniye.*

12. See Oberth, *The Moon Car;* Hermann Oberth, *Man into Space,* trans. G. P. H. De Freville (New York, 1957); Willy Ley, *Rockets, Missiles, and Space Travel,* rev. ed. (New York, 1957); Wernher von Braun, Frederick I. Ordway, and Dave Dooling, *Space Travel: A History* (New York, 1985); the latter is the fourth edition of a book previously published under the title *History of Rocketry and Space Travel.*

13. Wernher von Braun, "Crossing the Last Frontier," *Collier's* 129 (Mar. 22, 1952), pp. 24ff; Willy Ley, "A Station in Space," *Collier's* 129, pp. 30–31. Ley's article accompanies a detailed rendering by Fred Freeman. In "The Future as It Was," *Final Frontier* 2 (Aug. 1989), pp. 20ff, Les Dorr summarizes several related *Collier's* articles and Walt Disney films from the 1950s; von Braun is the common thread. This article includes full-color reproductions of some of the original artwork created for *Collier's* and Disney.

14. Paul R. Hill and Emanuel Schnitzer, "Rotating Manned Space Stations," *Astronautics* 7 (Sept. 1962), pp. 14–18; Rene A. Berglund, "AEMT Space-Station Design," *Astronautics* 7 (Sept. 1962), pp. 19–24; Peter R. Kurzhals and James J. Adams, "Dynamics and Stabilization of the Rotating Space Station," *Astronautics* 7 (Sept. 1962), pp. 25–29.

15. Saunders B. Kramer and Richard A. Byers, "A Modular Concept for a Multi-Manned Space Station," *Proceedings of the Manned Space Stations Symposium,* Apr. 20–22, 1960 (New York, 1960), pp. 36–72.

16. The Shimizu Corporation "space hotel" is illustrated in a brochure for the International Symposium on Space Tourism, Bremen, Germany, Mar. 20–22, 1997.

17. See NASA Scientific and Technical Information Office, Special Publication 413, *Space Settlements: A Design Study,* ed. Richard D. Johnson and Charles Holbrow (1977); Gerard K. O'Neill, *The High Frontier: Human Colonies in Space* (New York, 1977).

18. Gerard K. O'Neill, "The Colonization of Space," in American Institute of Aeronautics and Astronautics, *Space Manufacturing Facilities (Space Colonies): Proceedings of the Princeton / AIAA / NASA Conference, May 7–9, 1975,* ed. Jerry Grey (Reston, Va., 1977), pp. A5–11. Appendix A consists of the Proceedings of the May 1974 Princeton Conference on Space Colonization.

The Future of Space Tourism

RACHEL ARMSTRONG

Living in space is a utopian ideal but not a fantasy. A great deal of evidence suggests that within the next thirty years, people will be able to spend time in orbit. Recently, a report published by NASA and the Washington-based Space Transportation Association drew fresh attention to the radical changes taking place in the space industry by predicting that tourism will be the only promising new market in the space industry.[1] Many in the industry hope that space tourism will be just as lucrative as tourism on Earth. According to Patrick Collins, vice president of Spacetopia ("Japan's First Space Travel Company"), space tourism is the largest, fastest growing industry in the world economy, turning over several trillion dollars every year, and employing approximately 10 percent of the world's working population.[2]

For the architectural community, this is certainly an exciting opportunity. The Earth's orbit has no conventional architectural features, so pioneers have the freedom to examine new design principles that will embrace the latest materials and newest technologies. As the world shifts toward international cooperation and the globalization of culture, space travel and space habitation pose more than an architectural challenge: they constitute a political and social issue embodying the cultural aspirations of the human race. With effective international cooperation, it is possible that in the near future people will travel into orbit to go on holiday and, perhaps later, settle there. The way in which these social spaces are constructed will shape the future of the human race physically and mentally.

In the absence of the "natural" world, space architecture will become the source of selective pressures acting on the human body. According to Darwinian theory, these forces will gradually cause extraterrestrial humans to evolve in a way different from that of their relatives on Earth. Orbital architecture will therefore need to embrace, support, and even extend the physiological principles on which the human body functions. In the hostile orbital environment, astronauts and tourists will completely depend on their space suits

and spacecraft for survival. Experimentation in space-suit design occurred even before advanced space flight technology was developed; pioneering pilot Wiley Post, for instance, who was the first to fly solo around Earth, participated in pressurized-suit experiments as early as 1935 (fig. 1). The space travelers' bodies are actually part of the "unnatural" materials to which they are umbilically attached. The immediate surroundings, such as gravitational settings, light intensity, humidity, and oxygen concentration, will influence their comfort, health, and safety just as the amniotic fluid in a mother's uterus nurtures a developing baby. Outside these fabricated structures the human body quickly dies.

Artificial environments are most likely to be designed to normalize or reproduce the conditions on Earth and stabilize the environmental pressures on the human body. The process of creating Earthlike situations in an extraterrestrial location is known as "terraforming" and is believed to naturalize the human body by reducing the degree of adaptation needed to function normally and by reducing stress. The best architecture designs will protect the body from the extreme conditions of orbit so that extraterrestrial habitats will become as stress-free as possible. Poor design has already been shown to seriously affect the health of the inhabitants. NASA astronauts installing equipment on the International Space Station have suffered from headaches, nausea, and burning eyes after a docking. Their symptoms cannot be entirely attributed to the condition known as "space adaptation syndrome." Poor air quality may be partly to blame because of a high build-up of carbon dioxide, or because of the release of volatile chemicals from adhesive materials used to assemble the craft.

Although convention dictates that we should establish as normal an environment as possible for the human body under extreme conditions, some architects may challenge this convention and take advantage of the new way in which the weightless environment confers superhuman strength on the body. Human nature seeks

Fig. 1
Wiley Post and a colleague in
pressure-suit experimentation.
February 23, 1935

novelty and danger as well as security, and it is therefore likely that space walks or extravehicular activity (EVA), although risky, will be a popular pursuit. NASA is currently investigating the fundamental design of space suits, as it appears that the current designs could be more finely tuned to the needs of the human body (compare figs. 2, 3). Designer Brand Griffin, for instance, has developed a space-suit prototype for a future mission to Mars featuring a rigid upper torso and helmet to house advanced avionics, including on-board computers and visual displays (fig. 4).

Stelarc, an Australian performance artist, has already performed some pioneering work with robotics engineers and communications systems to upgrade his abilities so that he can function differently from other unmodified humans in orbit. His aim is to make his body architecture harder, dryer, and more machinelike so that he will eventually achieve the freedom to explore the extravehicular environments without a spacesuit: "In the extended space-time of extra-terrestrial environments, the body must become immortal to adapt. Utopian dreams become post-evolutionary imperatives. This is no mere Faustian option nor should there be any Frankensteinian fear in tampering with the body."[3] Stelarc couples his body to robotic appendages that are driven by the tiny electrical impulses generated by his muscular contractions (fig. 5). As he moves, these minute currents are measured, interpreted, and amplified by the electronic circuitry and used to orchestrate computer, audio, and video sequences as part of an automatic interaction between man and machine. Stelarc in turn responds to these new sensations and choreographs his extended body to respond to the artificial sensory stimuli. The electronic circuitry that links his body and the machines is called the SIMBOD interface. Third parties can influence the signals to Stelarc's body depending on how it is wired up to receive these extra signals. It is possible that in the future, ground control would be able to guide the limbs of an astronaut during EVA and remotely direct the explorer to safety. Stelarc's current activity investigates

the possibly of creating an "extended artificial neural network" to supply the muscles of space adventurers to come.

Free floating in orbit is still a long way from becoming a standard holiday adventure despite the fact that the first human, Yuri Gagarin, was sent into orbit forty years ago, in 1961. Arguably, the biggest obstacle to private ventures beyond the Earth's atmosphere has been the cost of the flights. Each flight to and from space currently runs into the hundreds of millions of dollars, but should travel to and from orbit become cheap enough, individuals, private companies, and organizations will begin to explore the commercial possibilities of relatively low orbits – trips to what is called "near space." Buzz Aldrin, chairman of the National Space Society, has advocated the earliest possible investment in a program to develop reusable space vehicles and set up the infrastructure that will drastically reduce launch costs and encourage private investors to respond to the market opportunity of space tourism.[4] Aldrin believes that the first commercially operated vehicles will be reusable rocket-powered systems that will evolve to provide a virtually limitless future for both commercial and government activities in near space.

At present, there are only two vehicles to choose from in the quest to reach the low, medium, and high Earth orbits – the U.S. Space Shuttle and the Russian Soyuz (see plates 32, 48) – and only the Soyuz is available for commercial hire. For this reason the X Prize Foundation has recently offered $10 million to the winning team out of a group of fifteen registered finalists that designs a commercial space vehicle capable of traveling repeatedly to an altitude of 100 kilometers. Although this contest is an attractive, media-friendly incentive, the successful vehicle will not, according to Anders Hansson, founding director of the European Institute of Quantum Computing, set a gold standard for future commercial vehicles. Hansson has pointed out that, in the same way that the Wright brothers' original flying machines bear only a slight resemblance to modern passenger airlines, the X Prize vehicle winner will

Fig. 2
Space-suit prototype.
October 25, 1958

have little influence on the final look or design of future commercial orbital passenger planes.

Although serious development of the reusable orbital vehicles is necessary before the space tourism industry can be launched, most of the technologies necessary to establish a human base in orbit already exist. Architects considered the development of cities in the sky even before flight on the Earth was thought possible. Jonathan Swift's description of the "island of Laputa" in *Gulliver's Travels* portrayed a futuristic city, inhabited by scientists, that floated in the sky, as if by antigravity, as early as 1726. The first true science-fiction writer, Jules Verne, prophesied that no planetary environments would be out of bounds to the relentless inquisitiveness of humankind. His *Journey to the Center of the Earth* (1864) opened up the possibility of subterranean environments, and in *From the Earth to the Moon* (1865) Verne considered the consequences of people being fired to the Moon from Florida. A mad scientist orbits the Earth atmospherically in Verne's short story "Robur the Conqueror," and cities fly in "Propeller Island."

It would be a mistake, however, to think that orbital buildings remain the ambition of science-fiction writers when actual work has already begun. The Japanese Rocket Society and Shimizu Corporation have been working on the development of orbital hotels for almost a decade (see plate 89). Similarly, architect Howard J. Wolff, of Wimberly Allison Tong and Goo, has designed a space hotel, with a rotating outer ring to simulate gravity (fig. 6). David Ashcroft, managing director of Bristol Spaceplanes, Ltd., predicts that regular passenger flights into space could start by 2005. Alan Bond, managing director of Reaction Engines, Ltd., speculates that his company's first flight in 2013 will enable space tourism to start in 2016. The infrastructure to develop these projects into profitable commercial ventures, however, needs to be established. One of the biggest obstacles to recruiting pioneers and collaborators into the exciting new industry is a lack of faith that space tourism can be realized. Technological revolution is a powerful force for social change, yet serious commercial investors will need more than enthusiasm from NASA before they will invest the billions of dollars necessary to set up this new industry.

In *The High Frontier* (1977), Gerard K. O'Neill suggested that thousands of people would be living in orbital colonies within the lifetime of his readership, and that the reasons for doing so embraced a diverse range of commercial options, from solving the energy crisis to controlling population size.[5] But these highly practical suggestions on the utilization of extraterrestrial real estate were far less media-friendly than the globally broadcast lunar landing, because of which the image of the strange and fragile blue planet became a cultural icon of unity that spellbound millions of viewers over the whole of the Earth. During those moments, and with Buzz Aldrin's exclamation, "Beautiful! Beautiful! Magnificent desolation," as he walked on the Moon, space travel instantly was transformed into a mystical experience. Ironically, it seems almost at the same time to have been dismissed as a serious commercial venture by any potential blue-chip investors.

Although corporate investors may remain cynical about the possibilities of space tourism, the public's love affair with space has grown. The Japanese Space Agency, for example, estimates that 70 percent of people want to become space tourists, even if the costs for such a trip amount to one year's salary. Meanwhile, the American company Celestis, which manages Encounter 2001, has developed a registry of submissions for people to send their DNA to outer space. Hansson has noted that there is increasing demand for a growing industry in high adventure and exotic experiences. Even before the first reusable commercial orbital vehicles can escape the pull of Earth's gravity, the legal, geographical, and regulatory infrastructure for the prospective space tourism industry needs to be established. The registration, regulation, and policing of privately funded space vehicles need to be jointly handled by governments, air traffic controllers, and legal departments, and they will most likely oper-

Fig. 3
Astronaut Jerry L. Ross during a
space walk. This NASA image was
recorded by James H. Newman as he
perched on the end of *Endeavor*'s
remote manipulator system (RMS)
arm. December 1998

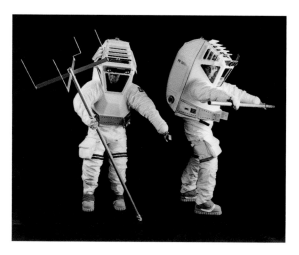

Fig. 4
Brand Griffin. Space-suit prototype,
1992–93, as shown in *Aviation Week,*
April 12, 1993

ate on a system very similar to current aviation law. Due to the expected large number of participants and the complications involved in regulatory oversight, the final legislation is not likely to be passed for a long time.

Yet, once the orbital highways are secure, the first destinations for tourists will quickly be opened. The first accommodations in orbit available to the public are likely to offer only the most basic facilities. The Shimizu Corporation's blueprints suggest that the hotels will likely be rooms in pre-fabricated cylindrical modules (see plate 88), perhaps recycled from discarded space shuttle fuel tanks that are connected together. Naturally, as the traffic increases, the degree of luxury and range of choices will grow, accommodations will become more affordable, and guests will stay longer.

From an architectural perspective, the possibilities in orbital design and construction are potentially limitless. Although we have the capacity to establish replicas of conventional cities in orbit, it is not necessary to copy what has gone before. The Association of Autonomous Astronauts is an organization that encourages private individuals to create their own vehicles that will transport them into orbit, where they will establish alternative ways of living and forms of social organization. It is likely that the first communities will be rather conventional but will make innovative use of recognized architectural techniques. Recycling material will play an important part in the upkeep of orbital environments to reduce the costs of building. It is likely that an orbital market for second-hand accommodation facilities will develop. Organic products and vital resources will be processed by the orbital hotel, and the environment will function as an artificial ecosystem that will involve the safe recycling of human waste materials, air, and water.

Another promising variable from an architectural-design perspective is that in weightlessness almost any three-dimensional shape is possible, providing it is strong enough to support an internal pressure of one atmosphere. Nonetheless, the unit currently favored by space architects is the

cylinder, because it is the simplest and cheapest structure to launch and assemble. These cylindrical units can be given specific, individual applications and be arranged around larger, centrally placed social spaces. The use of simple modular structures is likely to form the framework of the overall orbital hotel design, allowing the habitat to be updated, extended, and dismantled to accommodate the individual tastes of the residents. Hotels could even be so flexible in design and use that they could quite possibly vary their facilities with each new intake of tourists.

The different space tourism societies may provide shuttles to nearby satellite theme parks. Solar "yachts" with large wings made of double-sided solar panels to power them could prove a popular form of intersatellite transport and may even become a space sport as single-manned craft are raced between orbital locations. Sport stadiums are also likely to be very popular. The novelty of the effects of antigravity and partial weightlessness would be great social spectacles, and the space tourism societies could even sponsor various competitions, a space equivalent to the Olympic Games, in zero gravity.

Many of the orbital hotels will offer areas of artificial gravity for tourists so that they can reacclimatize to "normal" bodily functions, and will become spinning habitats in order to produce the necessary centripetal acceleration to achieve this. In his *Cities in Flight* trilogy (1955–62), James Blish described a civilization where cities acquire antigravity by a mechanism called the "spindizzy." The axis of each rotating city maintains a fixed direction relative to the distant stars and from which colonists launch their spacecraft. Research still needs to be carried out on the effects of clockwise or counterclockwise rotation of orbital habitats on human subjects in all planes to determine whether the body responds better to a particular direction

Fig. 5
Stelarc with involuntary arm, third
hand, and laser eyes, at the
Melbourne International Festival.
1990

Fig. 6
Howard J. Wolff, of Wimberly
Allison Tong and Goo. Proposed
space hotel. 1997–98

and at a particular level of g force. One peculiarity of orbital hotels is that they will need periodically to be boosted in their orbits, since even at an altitude of several hundred kilometers their orbits will gradually fall. This destabilizing process caused by minimal air resistance will require measuring and controlling the center of mass of a hotel as it grows, since its orbital position and stability will be affected.

Arguably, the most vital component of an orbital hotel will be the communications link to Earth, which will allow a terrestrial audience to experience orbital living through the technology of virtual reality. Images relayed directly from the orbital hotels will not only allow digital postcards to be sent to loved ones at home but will also encourage a voyeuristic, thrill-seeking audience to sign up for the "real" adventure. Some people are already extremely eager for international governments to give permission for the space tourism industry to grow before they experience the novelty for themselves. The organization Space Tours already offers zero-gravity experiences, flight simulator training, and residencies at their Space Camp in Belgium as a temporary stopgap to orbital tourism while the real-world orbital travel industry is being established.

Although many of these projects are rather advanced in their designs and ambitions for orbital architecture, none of the extraterrestrial projects is inevitable. Disbelief and apathy could destroy the aspirations of these pioneers, so skeptics play an important role in the development of space tourism. Their cynicism reminds us that every one of us needs to lobby or become involved in the endorsement of this exciting challenge if this, potentially the greatest of human adventures, is ever going to happen. Performance artist and, arguably, space travel advocate Rachel Rosenthal investigates the interconnectedness of all things, whether human, transhuman,

planetary, or cosmic. In a current performance that deals with the fantasy and reality of space travel, Rosenthal is portrayed as a human scapegoat who is sent into space in a strange organic capsule to embody and exorcise the "Ur-Boor," the global personification of our incivility, grossness, and lack of manners. Halfway through the performance, a sneeze releases a chip from her nose, revealing that her space adventure has been but an illusion and that she is really in a dirty backyard in Brooklyn, full of garbage and rotting cars. Gradually things begin to grow, and the capsule transforms into a gazebo covered in vines. Perhaps Rosenthal's adventure reminds us of the need for good housekeeping on Earth before we turn our attention to extraterrestrial ambitions. At the same time, it reveals how we can be trapped in our own squalor if we do not aspire to greater endeavors.[6]

1. Daniel O'Neil, compiler, "General Public Space Travel and Tourism," NASA Report no. NP-1998-03-11-MSFC.
2. See www.spacetopia.com.
3. Quoted from the personal manifesto of Stelarc, as presented on his web site, http://www.stelarc.va.com.au.
4. Starcraft Boosters, Inc., "A Cargo Aircraft for Space," paper prepared for AIAA/ASME/SAE Joint Propulsion Specialists' conference, June 22, 1999, Los Angeles, Calif.
5. Gerard K. O'Neill, The High Frontier: Human Colonies in Space (New York, 1977).
6. For further reading, see http://www.spacefuture.com/tourism/tourism.shtml, and the "Space Architecture" issue of Architectural Design 70 (Mar. 2000).

A Biographical Glossary of Architects, Aerospace Engineers, and Designers
Thomas Foltz

Adams, Constance

Constance Adams was born in 1964 in Boston and raised in Dallas. She earned her bachelor of arts degree from Harvard University-Radcliffe College in 1987 and her master's in architecture from Yale University in 1990. She worked for a variety of well-known architectural offices around the world between the late 1980s and the mid 1990s, including those of Cesar Pelli and Associates in New Haven, Connecticut, Josef Paul Kleihues in Berlin, and Kenzo Tange in Tokyo. Since 1997, she has been employed by Lockheed Martin Space Operations in Houston to work with NASA architects to design and develop the habitation module for BIO-Plex, a test facility for the Mars surface habitat, and TransHab structures, inflatable habitations for future space missions. She teaches studios in space architecture and design at Yale, Rhode Island School of Design, and the Technical University in Munich.

Armstrong, Harris

Harris Armstrong was born in 1899. He studied architecture at Washington University and Ohio State University, and designed smaller functionalist homes and offices in the 1930s. His career blossomed in the postwar era, when he became one of St. Louis's leading architects, designing structures such as the 1952 Cancer Research Building at Washington University as well as projects farther afield, such as the American consulate in Basra, Iraq, in 1957. Because of his prominence in St. Louis, he received several commissions from the McDonnell Aircraft Company in the 1950s, including the design of their new technical center, with its attractively landscaped park setting and basement bomb shelters that could protect seven thousand employees in case of nuclear attack. Armstrong retired from architectural practice in 1993 and died two years later.

Barmin, Vladimir Pavlovich

Born 1909 in Moscow, Vladimir Barmin graduated in 1930 from Bauman Technical University and was employed thereafter by the Kompressor Plant and an offshoot design bureau that created the famous Katyusha rockets used by the Red Army in World War II. After the war, he traveled to Germany to study captured rocket equipment and facilities, and he subsequently designed and built all major Soviet launch facilities, most notably the Baikonur Cosmodrome,

begun in 1950. Barmin expanded upon Sergei Korolev's and Vasily Mishin's initial ideas about horizontal assembly and transport of rockets to their launch sites and incorporated that principle into the design of his launch facilities. He also assisted in the design of machinery used for interplanetary soil sampling missions. He died in 1993.

Bonestell, Chesley

Born in San Francisco in 1888, the artist Chesley Bonestell is best known for his space paintings and illustrations. His training as an architect at Columbia University and his subsequent experience in Willis Polk's architectural office in San Francisco from 1911 to 1919, and several firms in New York afterwards, gave him the opportunity to work on major structures of the 1920s and 1930s, such as the Chrysler Building in New York and the Golden Gate Bridge in San Francisco. At the age of 50, he changed careers and began working in Hollywood as a special-effects artist. His movie credits include science-fiction classics such as *War of the Worlds, When Worlds Collide,* and *Destination Moon.* In the 1940s, he also started illustrating articles by Willy Ley, Wernher von Braun, and others in such magazines as *Life, Scientific American,* and *Collier's.* These articles and technically accurate illustrations helped fire the public imagination and brought space travel from the realm of science fiction to serious feasibility. Bonestell died in Carmel, California, in 1986.

Bossart, Karel J.

Commonly known as the "father of Atlas," Karel J. "Charlie" Bossart was born in Belgium in 1904. He earned a degree in mining engineering from the University of Brussels in 1925, then came to the United States and enrolled at the Massachusetts Institute of Technology. There he studied aeronautics and specialized in aeronautical structures. He went to work for Convair (which later became General Dynamics) and led the group that designed the Atlas missile. Among his revolutionary ideas for this rocket were the concepts of a pressurized fuel tank, which functioned like a large, metal balloon as part of the rocket's structure, and the ability to steer the rocket by turning or gimbaling the entire rocket engine. These achievements earned him the U.S. Exceptional Civilian Service Award in 1958 and led NASA to choose the Atlas rocket as the vehicle that would

carry America's first Mercury astronauts into orbit. Bossart retired from General Dynamics in 1967 and died in 1975.

Clarke, Arthur C.

Arthur C. Clarke is generally regarded as one of the foremost science-fiction authors and space visionaries of the twentieth century. He was born in Minehead, Somerset, England, on December 16, 1917, and joined the British Interplanetary Society in 1936, where he wrote the BIS *Bulletin* and began writing science fiction. In 1954, Clarke wrote a letter to Dr. Harry Wexler, the chief of the Scientific Services Division of the U. S. Weather Bureau, in which he proposed the idea of using space satellites as a meteorological tool. Ten years later, in 1964, he began work with Stanley Kubrick on the film *2001: A Space Odyssey,* which realistically portrayed moon bases, space shuttles, and a rotating space station. Clarke currently lives in Colombo, Sri Lanka, where he continues to write science fiction.

Connell, Maurice H.

Maurice Connell was born in 1894 in Greenwich, Connecticut, and earned a degree in mechanical engineering at the University of Pennsylvania in 1914. After service in the Signal Corps and the Air Corps in World War I, he returned to Connecticut to establish his own engineering practice. In 1925, he relocated his firm, Connell, Pierce, Garland and Fridman, to Miami, Florida, where they designed the mechanical aspects of a number of buildings. These include such local landmarks as the Dade County Courthouse, the Miami Post Office, and the Miami Biltmore Hotel, the launch gantries and service structures at Cape Canaveral, as well as similar projects at the Redstone missile arsenal in Huntsville, Alabama. Connell died in December 1967 in Hendersonville, North Carolina.

Dornberger, Walter Robert

A pioneer in the developing field of rocket technology, Walter Dornberger was born in Giessen, Germany, on September 6, 1895. He enlisted in the German army in 1914, and was commissioned a year later. In 1925, the army sent him to the School of Technology in Charlottenberg, where he specialized in ballistics and earned his master's degree in 1930. After graduation, he was assigned to help with the development of new rocket-powered weapons, which were

not banned by the Treaty of Versailles. Dornberger rose through the ranks and in 1932 was placed in charge of the Research Station West at Kummersdorf. Working as part of his team was the young scientist Wernher von Braun. The research group moved to Peenemünde in 1937 and began to develop the A-4 rocket (known to the Allies as the V-2). After the war ended, Lieutenant General Dornberger was held as a British prisoner of war for two years, but was released and came to the United States in 1947. He served as an advisor to the air force in the area of guided missiles, and helped with the development of the X-20 Dyna-Soar project before it was canceled. In 1965 he retired, and he died in Baden-Württemburg, Germany, on June 27, 1980.

Ehricke, Krafft Arnold

Krafft Ehricke was born on March 24, 1917. In 1942, he received his degree in aeronautical engineering from Berlin's Technical University. Because of the war, his talents were immediately put to use as part of the Peenemünde rocket development team, where he specialized in propulsion systems for the A-4 rocket. After the war, he came to the United States and continued his work on ballistic missiles and space vehicles working for the U.S. Army Ordinance Department. After leaving the army, he went to work with Convair General Dynamics and helped develop the Atlas rocket. In 1959, he became a vice president of the company and headed up the team that built the Centaur upper stage. This vehicle was the first hydrogen-fueled upper stage and was used almost exclusively to boost NASA's space probes to the planets. In 1974, he became the chief scientist at North American Rockwell's Space Systems Division, where he was free to pursue his ideas of using space resources peacefully for the benefit of all people. Ehricke died in 1984, and a year later the Krafft A. Ehricke Institute for Space Development was founded in his honor.

Esnault-Pelterie, Robert

Robert Esnault-Pelterie, sometimes known as REP, was born in Paris on November 8, 1881. He graduated with a degree in science (which encompassed botany, chemistry, and physics) from the Sorbonne College of Science and Letters of the University of Paris in 1902. In that same year, he received his first of many patents. As news of the Wright brothers' accomplishments reached France, Esnault-Pelterie knew that he wanted to build and fly airplanes. He did not like the crude control methods employed by the Wrights, however, so he improved the design, inventing the control stick and the aileron in the process. He completed his first successful monoplane in 1906, an all-metal design powered by a seven-cylinder, air-cooled radial engine, which he also designed. This engine was so successful that variations of it powered planes for the next thirty years. Soon, though, Esnault-Pelterie's interest turned to space flight. His studies were interrupted by World War I, but after the war he sued France, England, the United States, and Germany for patent infringement for their use of the control stick in their airplanes. He won his case, and every company that used a control stick in their airplanes had to pay him royalties. In 1920, he resumed his theoretical rocket research and began lecturing on rocket design. A year later, in association with banker André Hirsch, he instituted the REP-Hirsch International Astronautics Prize for the most influential original scientific work in astronautics. The first award was presented to Hermann Oberth. From 1926 to 1930, Esnault-Pelterie was engaged in writing *L'Astronautique,* an encyclopedia of everything that was known about rocketry and space travel. He continued his experiments and in 1931 lost four left-hand fingers when a rocket engine he had been working on exploded. He switched his research to the somewhat safer propellants – liquid oxygen and liquid hydrogen – and demonstrated an engine powered by these propellants in 1937. With the onset of World War II, however, he collected and destroyed all of his unpublished research to keep it from the Nazis. He retired to Switzerland and presented his last rocketry lecture in 1947. Esnault-Pelterie died on December 6, 1957, two months after the Soviet launch of *Sputnik 2.*

Faget, Maxime Allen

Max Faget was born in 1921 in British Honduras and studied engineering and aeronautical design at Louisiana State University. After graduation, he entered the U.S. Navy and served on submarines during World War II. When the war ended, he returned to his interest in aeronautics and went to work for Dr. Robert Gilruth designing high-speed and high-altitude aircraft for the Department of Defense. His projects included the Scout and Little Joe research rockets, the Polaris missile, and the X-15 rocket plane. With the launch of Sputnik,

national attention turned to space, and Faget followed Gilruth to the newly formed National Aeronautics and Space Administration. There, he championed the idea of a blunt capsule for manned missions, rather than the popular notion of a streamlined, winged spacecraft. His arguments eventually convinced NASA, and he went on to design the Mercury spacecraft, and helped with the Gemini, Apollo, and shuttle programs. After retiring from NASA, he founded his own company, Space Industries, Inc. Faget lives in Houston.

Fender, Donna L.

Born in 1965 in Decatur, Alabama, Donna Fender earned a bachelor of science degree in aerospace and aeronautical engineering from the University of Alabama in 1988. Since then, she has worked for NASA in a variety of positions related to test systems and space simulation. She presented a paper entitled "Manned Testing in a Simulated Space Environment" at the 1993 European Space Agency conference in the Netherlands on space simulation. She is currently the project manager for TransHab, coordinating the work of architects and engineers creating inflatable space habitats. Fender specializes in building and integrating systems for testing, particularly in space-simulation chambers.

Frassanito, John

John Frassanito was born in 1941 and raised in New York. He studied industrial design at the Art Center in Los Angeles (now Art Center College of Design in Pasadena), and graduated in 1968. He then joined Raymond Loewy's firm, Raymond Loewy/William Snaith, Inc., as part of the team that worked on the design of Skylab, NASA's first space station. Frassanito left Loewy's office shortly thereafter to take a job with the Computer Terminal Corporation, where he designed, among other early computers, the Datapoint 2000 (patented July 25, 1972). It was considered by *Invention and Technology* magazine (Fall 1994) to be the "direct lineal ancestor to the PC." Frassanito started his own design firm in 1975, where he continued to design Datapoint computers as well as products for Sani-Fresh, Scott Paper, and EMI Corporation. In 1983, he set up his practice in Houston so that he could collaborate again with NASA, which was beginning to plan the space station that resulted in the International Space Station. In the 1980s, Frassanito worked with NASA architects and engineers as part of one of the teams that developed concepts for the space station. His firm has continued to work for NASA on a contract basis in developing com-

puter-generated animations of their planned missions.

Glushko, Valentin Petrovich

Born in 1908 in Odessa, Russia, Valentin Glushko graduated in 1929 from Leningrad University. A few years later, while working at the Gas Dynamics Laboratory, he developed early Soviet rocket propulsion systems. It was in that job that he first met Sergei Korolev, who would serve as chief designer of the Soviet space program in the 1950s and 1960s. In fact, Glushko designed a rocket engine that was used in 1937 to propel one of Korolev's glider designs. As was Korolev, Glushko was arrested in a Stalinist purge and spent the war in a prison camp, where he continued to work on rocket design. Immediately after World War II, he studied captured German rocket launchers and was put in charge of the design bureau that eventually became NPO Energomash, the facility responsible for most of the Soviet Union's first-stage engines of their heavy launchers. Although Glushko disagreed with Korolev over the design of the latter's N-1 Moon Rocket (designed by Korolev favorite Vasily Pavlovich Mishin), his fortunes changed after Korolev's death in 1966. Glushko reorganized the design bureaus of the Soviet space program and has been credited with developing the massive Energia boosters, as well as Buran, the Soviet Union's answer to America's Space Shuttle. He died in Moscow in 1989.

Goddard, Robert Hutchings

Robert Goddard was born in Worcester, Massachusetts, on October 5, 1882. Although math was a difficult subject for him in high school, Goddard dreamed of building rockets and knew that math was critical. Through hard work and determination, he graduated at the top of his class. He entered Worcester Polytechnic Institute in 1904 and earned his bachelor's degree in physics. He then went on to earn his master's degree and doctorate at Clark University. After graduation, he began teaching physics. In 1912, Goddard was awarded a one-year research fellowship to Princeton, where he developed his basic theoretical rocket computations. His hard work and long hours, however, soon caught up with him. Near the end of his fellowship he had a breakdown and contracted tuberculosis. He was given two weeks to live, but managed to survive. He returned to Clark University as a part-time teacher, in order to dedicate more time to his research and experiments. In 1917, he began his long relationship with the Smithsonian Institution and received a $5,000 sponsor-

ship. A year later, he led the U.S. Army rocket research group. Goddard published his calculations and theoretical rocket models in 1919 in a paper entitled, "A Method of Reaching Extreme Altitudes." This study, however, earned Goddard nothing but skepticism and ridicule. He became more reclusive and secluded, but continued his research. He began developing liquid-fueled rockets, and on March 16, 1926, the world's first liquid-fueled rocket flew for 2.5 seconds and achieved an altitude of 184 feet. Goddard continued to improve his design, and in 1929 launched a rocket that contained a scientific payload, consisting of a thermometer, a barometer, and a camera to take a picture of the instruments at the top of the rocket's flight path. In 1930, Goddard received a $50,000 Guggenheim grant and moved to Roswell, New Mexico, where he built a new rocket research facility. He continued to improve his designs and achieved better stability by using gyroscopes, and in 1935 he launched a rocket to an altitude of over a mile on a perfectly stabilized flight. Following these successes, he published a second paper in 1936 titled, "Liquid-Propellant Rocket Development," which included experimental data from all his rocket flights. With the onset of World War II, Goddard joined the Naval Engineering Experimental Station in Annapolis, Maryland. He continued working there until his death in 1945.

Griffin, Brand Norman

Born in 1947, Brand Griffin was raised in the Pacific Northwest and educated at Washington State University, where he earned a bachelor's degree in architecture in 1970. He earned a master of fine arts from the California Institute of the Arts in 1971, and a master's in architecture from Rice University in 1972. Although Griffin taught at Tulane, Rice, and the University of Washington, he is probably best known for his long-term work with Boeing, particularly for designs for the International Space Station in the 1980s. He has received numerous awards, including the Prix de Rome fellowship in architecture at the American Academy in Rome, and his design work for spacecraft has been featured in publications such as *Aviation Week and Space Technology* and in exhibitions in Huntsville, Alabama, Seattle, and New York. He currently heads his own firm, Griffin Design, in Huntsville.

Hedrick, Wyatt Cephas

Wyatt Hedrick was born in Chatham, Virginia, in 1888, and was educated at Roanoke College and Washington and Lee University, where he earned a bachelor's degree in architecture in 1910. He established a variety of firms during a more than fifty-year career, beginning with the W. C. Hedrick Construction Co. of 1914 and culminating in Wyatt C. Hedrick Architect and Associates, based in Fort Worth, from 1925 until his death in 1964. He received major industrial commissions in Texas and abroad, and his other important projects included bases for the army, navy, and air force, among them the U.S. Air Force base in Keflavik, Iceland, of 1952–57, and the Shamrock Hilton in Houston of 1946 (now demolished). For NASA he designed the Central Laboratory and Office Complex at the Marshall Space Flight Center in Huntsville, Alabama, in 1961.

Hilten, Heinz

Born in Berlin in 1909, Heinz Hilten studied architecture at the Technical University there, earning a master's degree under the well-known architect Heinrich Tessenow in 1934. From 1939 to 1942 he worked as an architect at Peenemünde, mostly on the construction of the housing projects for the facilities workers and scientists there. After serving in the German army from 1942 to 1944, he returned to work with Wernher von Braun's group at Peenemünde until the war's end, and from 1945 to 1954 he was employed in the municipal architect's office in Augsburg. It was then that Hannes Luehrsen (see below) brought him to Huntsville, Alabama, to work on the master planning of the Redstone missile arsenal, which occupied him until 1960. Between 1960 and his retirement in 1978, he was employed by NASA's Marshall Space Flight Center in Huntsville, Alabama. At Marshall, he prepared the master plans submitted annually to Congress for budgetary and expansion approval, and he participated in the design of various laboratories there, including those for structures, mechanics, guidance, and aerodynamics. Since retiring he has continued to live in Huntsville.

Jones, Rod

William R. "Rod" Jones II was born in 1958 in Charlottesville, Virginia. He earned his bachelor of architecture degree from the Virginia Polytechnic Institute in 1984. Even before finishing his degree, he worked as a draftsman for the Los Angeles architects Pulliam Mathews and Associates in 1979–80, and as a junior designer with the Chicago firm of Fujikawa, Conterato, Lohan, and Associates (later Lohan Associates), from 1981 to 1982. In the latter firm he contributed to the design of the demonstration kitchen and extensive high-tech audio-visual functions for McDonald's headquarters in Oak Brook, Illinois.

Since 1984, he has worked with NASA's Johnson Space Center in Houston. There, he participated in the design of the International Space Station as well as managed the development of Space Station Crew Equipment, including restraints, interior partitions, crew quarters, galley, food service areas, and personal hygiene facilities. At present he is responsible for the oversight of all U.S. flights to assemble, outfit, and resupply the International Space Station.

Kennedy, Kriss

Kriss Kennedy was born in Potsdam, New York, in 1960. He earned his bachelor's degree in professional studies in architecture from the University of Buffalo in 1984 and his master of architecture degree from the Sasakawa Center for Space Architecture at the University of Houston in 1988. He has worked for a variety of architectural firms, sometimes simultaneously. From 1987 to 1995, he was a consulting designer for Allan James, Inc., in Houston, and in 1990, he established his own architectural firm, called Techne Architects. In addition, since 1987 he has also been employed at NASA's Johnson Space Center in Houston in a variety of design positions, including those related to the inflatable module TransHab for the International Space Station, Surface Base Planning, and Lunar-Mars habitats. His latest work for NASA involves the development of inflatable structures for space habitation.

Korolev, Sergei Pavlovich

Sergei Korolev was born in the Ukraine in 1907. In 1928, he entered Bauman Technical University, where he specialized in aeronautical engineering. While there, he cofounded GIRD, an unofficial organization that carried out some of the first liquid-fueled rocket experiments in the Soviet Union. Unfortunately, his increasing technological skills brought him unwanted attention, and in 1938 he was arrested in a Stalinist purge and accused of "subversion in a new field of technology." He was sent to the Kolyma gold mines in Siberia, where the average life expectancy of a prisoner was six months. Soon, however, he was transferred to a special prison for scientists and engineers, where he resumed his rocket research. After World War II, Korolev was sent to Germany to study captured A-4 rockets. He was put to work designing ballistic missiles, but he also persisted with his own plans to send people into space by designing missiles large enough and powerful enough to launch manned capsules. He eventually became the chief designer of the Soviet space program. Under his leadership, the Soviet Union set a stunning number

of space records: the first artificial satellite, the first person in space, the first spacewalk, the first spacecraft to reach the Moon, the first (and only) probes to land on Venus, the first Mars flyby, and the first spy satellite. He also led the U.S.S.R.'s attempts to land a man on the Moon. Korolev, however, did not live to see the conclusion of the race. He died prematurely in January 1966.

Ley, Willy

Fascinated by science, Willy Ley was one of the driving forces behind the popularization of spaceflight. Ley was born in Berlin in 1906, and studied astronomy, zoology, physics, and paleontology at the University of Berlin and the University of Königsburg. He wrote his first book on the topic of space travel in 1926 and worked with the film director Fritz Lang on a few of his movies, including *Frau im Mond*. Inspired by the writings of Hermann Oberth, in 1927 he helped form the Society for Space Travel and later recruited the young Wernher von Braun into the society. His enthusiasm for spreading knowledge, specifically the latest developments in rocketry, however, led to trouble when the Nazi party came to power. He left Germany, moved to Great Britain, and then came to the United States. After the war, he continued to write books about rocketry and space travel, collaborating on some of them with von Braun, and he strongly advocated the idea of sending people to the Moon. His books helped fuel the public support that eventually led to the Apollo program. He died in June 1969, just one month before the first Moon landing.

Lippisch, Alexander Martin

Alexander Lippisch was born in Munich on November 2, 1894. He received his engineering doctorate from Heidelberg University. In 1918, after his service in World War I, he went to work for the Zeppelin Company. Soon, though, his interests turned to high-speed aircraft. He developed some of the earliest studies, experiments, and theoretical models of high-speed aircraft performance, and was intrigued by the idea of a tailless aircraft. His first successful tailless design was a glider he designed in 1921. Seven years later, he created a rocket-boosted glider and achieved the first rocket-powered flight in history. He pursued his research on delta wing, tailless, high-speed aircraft and in 1939 was hired by the Messerschmitt Company. There, he designed the Me 163, the world's first rocket-powered interceptor. In 1946, he immigrated to the United States and worked with the U.S. Air Force. He died on February 11, 1976.

Loewy, Raymond Fernand

Raymond Loewy became one of the most influential industrial designers in America. He was born in Paris on November 8, 1893, and attended the University of Paris from 1910 to 1912. He served with the French Army Corps of Engineers as liaison officer to the American Expeditionary Force between 1914 and 1918. After the war, he immigrated to the United States; he was naturalized in 1938. He started his career as a window-display artist and fashion illustrator, but soon opened his own industrial design firm, Raymond Loewy Associates, in 1929. He developed the acronym MAYA – Most Advanced, Yet Acceptable – to describe his design philosophy. He helped design all kinds and aspects of American products, including International Harvester tractors, a Sears, Roebuck, and Co. refrigerator, Studebaker automobiles, and the Exxon and Shell Oil Company logos. From 1967 to 1973, his influence extended beyond the atmosphere as he helped design the interior of the Skylab space station. He died on July 14, 1986, in Monte Carlo.

Luckman, Charles

Charles Luckman was born in Kansas City, Missouri, in 1909. He graduated magna cum laude in 1931 from the School of Architecture at the University of Illinois. His career began at the Colgate-Palmolive-Peet Company, where he worked as a draftsman. His business sense and attention to detail were quickly noticed, and in 1935, he was offered the position of sales manager at the Pepsodent Company, whose profits he promptly quadrupled. This feat earned him a place on the cover of *Time* magazine in 1937 and the label, "Boy Wonder of American Industry." In 1943, Pepsodent was acquired by Lever Brothers, but Luckman again rose to the top, and in 1946 he was named president of Lever Brothers. One of his first tasks there was to help create the new corporate headquarters, which became one of the first glass skyscrapers in Manhattan – the famous Lever House on Park Avenue designed by Skidmore, Owings and Merrill. He enjoyed the process so much that he left the company and started the Luckman Partnership architectural firm. It was with this firm that he made his contributions to the space program. He was responsible for creating the original master plans for Edwards Air Force Base, north of Los Angeles, the Kennedy Space Center at Cape Canaveral, Florida, and the Johnson Space Center in Houston. These accomplishments are even more impressive when the timelines are taken into account. Because of the rush to land men on the Moon by the end of the decade, Luckman was given only forty-eight days to design the entire Johnson Space Center, including all the laboratories, training facilities, and Mission Control. Luckman died in January 1999.

Luehrsen, Hannes

Hannes Luehrsen was born in Bargteheide, Germany, in 1907 and studied at the Technical Universities in Aachen and Berlin, earning his bachelor's degree in 1930 and his master's degree in 1934, both from Aachen. He ran his own architectural practice in Berlin from 1938 to 1941 and during World War II was one of the architects who worked on the design of the V-2 facilities at Peenemünde, where he designed the various emblems on the V-2s. In 1949, he was brought to Huntsville, Alabama, by Wernher von Braun to work as the master planner for the Redstone missile arsenal. In 1960, two years after NASA was established, Luehrsen became chief of the master planning office for the NASA campus in Huntsville; he held this position until 1969. He also consulted on other master planning efforts, such as that for the restoration of Heidelberg, Germany, sponsored by the Portland Cement Company, in 1969, and for Point Mallard Park in Decatur, Alabama, in 1967. Luehrsen died in 1986.

Mount, Frances E.

Frances Mount was born in 1936 and was raised in Pennsylvania. She traveled extensively throughout the United States while completing her college work. From the University of Houston, she earned a bachelor of science in mathematics in 1974; a bachelor of science in psychology in 1975; and a doctorate in psychology, specializing in human factors, in 1993. She worked as a consultant to NASA's Johnson Space Center for a decade beginning in 1974, and since 1985 she has been a staff member. At NASA, she has worked on a variety of habitability issues related to spaceflights of long duration, particularly those pertaining to the space station *Freedom* (the precursor of the International Space Station), developing the programs for ergonomics, workstation design, and human-computer interface issues. Her research also addresses general space habitability factors, from window placement to color use and noise level determination. She currently researches space human factors, such as procedures, crew interfaces, and conflict resolution, which help maintain effective and efficient crew performance during spaceflight missions.

Nixon, David A.

Born in 1947 in Ilkey, Yorkshire, England, David Nixon studied architecture at the Polytechnic of Central London. After graduation in 1971, he worked for a variety of high-tech architectural firms, including those of Lord Richard Rogers, Sir Hugh Casson, Sir Norman Foster, and Nicholas Grimshaw, as well as Chicago's Skidmore, Owings and Merrill. In 1977, Nixon and architect Jan Kaplicky formed a group in London called Future Systems; they worked together on a variety of design projects for more than a decade. Nixon moved to California in 1980 to teach architecture at the Southern California Institute of Architecture and the University of California, Los Angeles. Between 1985 and 1989, he worked for NASA on the design of the astronauts' habitation in the International Space Station. With the experience gained from that contract, he created the firm Altus Associates and expanded his scope to include aerospace architecture and design projects, most notably for the Rotary Rocket Company.

Oberth, Hermann Julius

Born in Transylvania on June 25, 1894, Hermann Oberth became interested in spaceflight and rocketry at an early age when he began reading the works of Jules Verne. In 1912, he entered the University of Munich to study medicine, and he worked in a medical unit during World War I. Deciding not to pursue a medical career, Oberth returned to school to study physics. He presented his doctoral thesis, entitled "Rockets into Interplanetary Space," in 1922, but it was rejected for being too utopian. He did not rewrite his thesis, but instead published it on his own, hoping to show that without a degree he was a better scientist than those who had rejected his work. His interest in rocketry continued, and in 1928 and 1929 he worked as a scientific consultant to Fritz Lang during the production of the film *Frau im Mond*. Also in 1929, Oberth fired his first liquid-fueled rocket, assisted by students of the Technical University of Berlin. One of these students was Wernher von Braun, who later used many of Oberth's design improvements in his own V-2 rocket engine. Oberth also assisted with the production of the V-2 during World War II, and after the war he moved to Switzerland to be an independent consultant and writer. Oberth then came to the United States and worked for von Braun in Huntsville, Alabama, during the late 1950s. He retired to Germany in 1962, where he continued his writing. Oberth died in Nuremburg in 1989, at the age of ninety-five.

Tedesko, Anton

Anton Tedesko was born in 1903 in Gruenberg, Germany. He earned engineering degrees from the Polytechnic Universities in Vienna in 1926 and Berlin in 1930, as well as a doctorate from Vienna in 1951. Although he designed structures in Vienna as well as Poland and Czechoslovakia before World War II, he is best remembered for his work with Chicago engineers Roberts and Schaefer from 1932 and after, particularly thin-shell concrete roofs. Some of Tedesko's most famous buildings include the Seaplane Hangars at North Island Naval Air Station in San Diego from 1940–41 and the roofs of the 1951–56 terminal at Lambert Field, St. Louis, designed in conjunction with architects Hellmuth, Yamasaki, and Leinweber. He and his firm consulted on other aerospace projects as well, most notably the facilities at Cape Canaveral from the early 1960s, including the Vertical Assembly Building. Tedesko died in Seattle in 1994.

Tsiolkovsky, Konstantin Eduardovich

Konstantin Tsiolkovsky, the father of Soviet rocketry, was born on September 17, 1857, in the village of Izherskoye, about two hundred kilometers from Moscow. At age nine, a case of scarlet fever caused him to lose most of his hearing. Ridiculed by other children, he turned to reading for entertainment. He taught himself physics and began inventing such vehicles as a steam-powered carriage and a hydrogen-fueled balloon. At age sixteen, he went to Moscow to continue his studies; he taught himself differential and integral calculus, analytical geometry, and spherical trigonometry. Tsiolkovsky was driven by the idea of travel into space and starved himself so that he could spend most of his money on books and chemicals for his experiments. In 1876, he returned home and three years later began his career as a schoolteacher. He continued his experimentation and theoretical studies and was particularly interested in airplanes, an all-metal dirigible, and interplanetary rockets. In 1890, he constructed the first wind tunnel in Russia to test his designs. He even tried his hand at writing science fiction. His 1895 story, "Dreams of Earth and Heaven," describes a space station orbiting two hundred miles above the Earth, an altitude that is remarkably accurate. In 1897, he derived the formula for a liquid-fueled rocket, which relates the rocket velocity to its exhaust velocity and amount of fuel remaining. He described this formula in his 1903 paper, "Investigating Space with Reaction Devices," which also proved that rockets could theoretically achieve orbital speeds and escape velocity. The paper contained as well practical instructions for building rocket components and concluded that single-stage rockets were not the best design for interplanetary flights. His ideas, however, were not well received. Most people refused to give credit to the work of a self-taught scientist with no formal college degree. Tsiolkovsky continued his research, and a revised version of "Investigating Space" was published in 1911. This version also included a new section on using nuclear power for rocket propulsion and proposed the idea of using electric fields to increase the exhaust velocity. He began gaining more credibility for his work and was inducted into the Russian Socialist Academy of Sciences in 1919. He continued writing papers on reentry, solar propulsion, multi-staged rockets, and jet airplanes. Tsiolkovsky died in Kaluga, Russia, in 1935, having published four times as many articles during his last seventeen years as he had in his previous sixty years of life.

Urbahn, Max O.

Born in 1912 in Burscheid, Germany, and educated in architecture at the University of Illinois and Yale University, Max Urbahn began his design career in 1938 in the office of John Russell Pope. There he worked as part of the team that designed the National Gallery of Art and the Jefferson Memorial. He worked in the New York office of Holabird and Root, a prominent Chicago firm, during World War II. Urbahn practiced architecture on his own in New York from 1946 to 1978. His firm, originally Resiner and Urbahn, exists today under the name Urbahn Associates and is headed by Martin Stein. The Urbahn office specialized in, and still concentrates on, architecture for the public sector, some of its notable work being hospitals, schools, and research institutes, particularly in the New York City area. His office was part of the architectural team that designed Fermilab in Batavia, Illinois. Urbahn's greatest accomplishment in building for space travel was heading a consortium that designed the Vehicle Assembly Building and launch-control complex at the Kennedy Space Center at Cape Canaveral, Florida, in the early 1960s. He served as president of the American Institute of Architects in 1972. Urbahn made his home in Stonington, Connecticut; he died there in 1995.

Verne, Jules Gabriel

Jules Verne was born on February 8, 1828, in Nantes, France, into a family of lawyers. He earned his law degree in Paris in 1849. Verne became increasingly enchanted with the city's literary circles, and he began writing plays, the first of which was performed in 1850.

Verne also began teaching himself geology, engineering, and astronomy in order to write more realistic and believable stories. His first novel, *Five Weeks in a Balloon,* was published in 1863. Many more novels followed, including *From the Earth to the Moon, Direct in Ninety-seven Hours Twenty Minutes* in 1866, and its sequel, *Around the Moon,* in 1869. These stories of interplanetary travel, which were remarkably accurate for their time, later inspired many scientists and engineers to make space travel a reality. Verne lived a long and colorful life, which included witnessing a revolution, serving in the coast guard during the Franco-Prussian War, working as a stockbroker, receiving a private audience with Pope Leo XII, and being shot by his nephew, which left him permanently lame. He died in Amiens in 1905.

Von Braun, Wernher

Wernher von Braun was born into an aristocratic family in Wirsitz, Germany, on March 23, 1912. Upon his confirmation into the Lutheran church, his mother presented him with a telescope, which fueled his desire for space travel. The family moved to Berlin in 1920, but young Wernher did not perform well in school, particularly in math and physics. In 1925, he obtained a copy of Hermann Oberth's thesis, "Rockets into Interplanetary Space," and became extremely frustrated when he could not understand the math involved. He began to study more diligently and eventually mastered the subject. While studying at the Berlin Institute of Technology in 1930, von Braun joined the Society for Space Travel, where he assisted Oberth with the testing of liquid-fueled rocket engines. In 1932, he earned his bachelor of science degree in mechanical engineering and started his graduate work at Berlin University. In that same year, the Society for Space Travel ran into financial problems and could not afford to continue its rocket tests. The group was soon contacted by Captain Walter Dornberger, who was in charge of developing solid-fueled rockets for the German army and offered them a chance to keep working at the Kummersdorf Army Proving Grounds outside of Berlin. Von Braun completed his schooling and earned his doctorate in physics in 1934. His thesis, "About Combustion Tests," bore a title that was purposely vague due to military security. In it, von Braun intricately described the test firings of two different types of liquid-fueled engines developed at Kummersdorf. While at Kummersdorf, von Braun and his team also developed the rocket that became known as the V-1 buzz bomb. Soon, however, it became apparent that more room was

needed for their tests, and in 1937 the team moved to a town on the Baltic Sea called Peenemünde. There von Braun and his colleagues created the A-4 rocket, which later was renamed the V-2. The first test flight of the A-4 occurred on October 3, 1942. During this flight, the rocket broke the sound barrier and climbed over sixty miles high, literally reaching the edge of space. Work continued, and on September 7, 1944, the first operational V-2 was launched. As the war neared its end, all turned their eyes towards von Braun. The United States and the Soviet Union both wanted the mastermind behind the V-2, but the German military police force had orders to kill the entire team to keep the information from falling into enemy hands. Von Braun and his fellow scientists decided that they would much rather surrender to the Americans, so they stole a train and headed for the American lines. They were brought to White Sands, New Mexico, along with hundreds of tons of captured V-2 hardware, and continued their rocket research, this time working for the U.S. Army.

In 1952, von Braun moved to Huntsville, Alabama, and took charge of the army's ballistic weapons program. Under his control, the army developed the Redstone, Jupiter-C, Juno, and Pershing missiles. During the 1950s, von Braun also wrote numerous articles and books popularizing the idea of space travel. He became a United States citizen in 1955. In 1958, after the Soviet launches of *Sputnik 1* and *2,* and the failed launch of the U.S. Vanguard program, von Braun and his team at Huntsville launched America's first satellite, *Explorer 1,* aboard a Jupiter-C missile. In that same year, the rocket team was transferred to the newly formed National Aeronautics and Space Administration (NASA). Von Braun became the director of NASA's George C. Marshall Space Flight Center in Huntsville and began work on the Saturn series of rockets, the first boosters designed specifically as space vehicles. Saturn rockets eventually launched every manned mission to the moon, as well as the Skylab space station and the American half of the joint U.S.-Soviet Apollo-Soyuz mission. In 1970, von Braun was transferred to NASA headquarters in Huntsville, where he served as the deputy administrator for planning. He left NASA in 1972 and took a position as vice president with the aerospace company Fairchild Industries, Inc. He founded the National Space Institute in 1975 to promote the peaceful use of space. Von Braun died in Alexandria, Virginia, in 1977.

Guide to Museums and Institutions with Space-Related Collections
Dennis Parks

The following selective guide features institutions that collect space-related artifacts or papers, manuscripts, audio, video, or pictorial records concerning space exploration and technology. It includes only those museums, collections, and archives where one may view space-related objects or access documentary collections pertaining to design for space. One of the difficulties in compiling such a list is the lack of comprehensive information about space-related collections or archives. I hope it will prove useful until a more comprehensive resource can be produced.

Not surprisingly, an increasing number of web sites around the world now not only post guides to particular collections but also grant access to full-text documents, photographs, and even video clips. I highly recommend NASA's home page, located at *http://www.nasa.gov.* The NASA web site offers a portal to an ever-increasing amount of information, documents, and images, both for current and historic information. I also recommend Mark Wade's *Encyclopedia Astronautica,* located at *http://solar.rtd.utk. edu/~mwade/spaceflt.htm.* This comprehensive site includes chronologies as well as information about astronauts, programs, rockets, and spacecraft, all categorized by type. Both sites offer links to many other space-related web pages.

Very few objects used in the various space programs are currently on public view. The National Air and Space Museum owns the vast majority of NASA's space-related objects, though some have been loaned to other institutions. The Soviets kept their artifacts and objects secret for many years until the end of the cold war, when they sold many of them on the open market to generate revenue. Few remain in Russia. The following list provides some other locations where Soviet-era space objects and artifacts may be viewed.

California Institute of Technology
Robert A. Millikan Memorial Library, 1201 East California Boulevard, Pasadena, Calif. 91125, (818) 356-6433
Jet Propulsion Laboratory
Papers: 9 linear feet. The archive includes general history, fiscal papers and documents, pictures, and blueprints regarding property, proposals, contracts, and related correspondence
Theodore von Karman Archive
Papers: 96 linear feet; ca. 1920–63.

Theodore von Karman (1881–1963) was a physicist and aeronautical engineer. The archive contains correspondence, documents, speeches, lectures and lecture notes, scientific manuscripts, calculations, reports, photographs, technical slides, an autobiographical sketch, school notebooks, and other papers.

Colorado Historical Society
1300 Broadway, Denver, Col. 80203, (303) 866-4602
Martin Marietta Corporation, Denver Division
Films and scripts: 18 items; 1960–63. Martin Marietta Corporation is a Baltimore-based aerospace industry with a manufacturing plant in Littleton, Colorado. Its collection contains film clips and scripts about the *Titan II* ICBM launch at Cape Canaveral and Vandenburg Air Force Base, and the role of the Titan booster in project Gemini; data on the Titan II, a space station washing machine, zero-gravity shoes, and a space-cabin simulator; and information about forming metals with explosive charges.

Encyclopedia Astronautica
http://solar.rtd.utk.edu/~mwade/spaceflt. htm
This comprehensive online source contains text, photographs, and drawings about the history of space exploration.

Exhibition of Economic Achievement
150 Prospect Mira, 129366 Moscow, Russia
Objects: Vostok rocket, Apollo-Soyuz test project vehicles.

Gorky Park
Moscow, Russia
Object: A static-test mock-up of the Buran Space Shuttle orbiter from the NPO Molniya Tushino plant has been moved to Gorky Park in Moscow. The Kosmos-Zemlya Company, formed by NPO Molniya, the park, and Kosmoflot, headed by Gherman Titov, has put this test vehicle to commercial use as the framework for a new restaurant with a space theme.

Grumman Corporation
Public Affairs Department, History Center, Bethpage, N.Y. 11714, (516) 575-2401
Photographs, historical documentation: 1,300 linear feet; 1930–present. The archive covers the Space-Orbiting Astronomical Observatory, Apollo Lunar Modules, shuttle concepts, and current work on the International Space Station.

John Frassanito and Associates
1331 Gemini, Suite 230, Houston, Tex. 77058, (281) 480-9911, *http://www.frassanito.com*
This web site shows recent designs for NASA projects and includes the X-33, X-34, International Space Station, and Mars Mission.

Johnson Space Center
National Aeronautics and Space Administration, History Office, Mail Code BY4, Houston, Tex. 77058, (713) 483-6715
Johnson Space Center Historian's Source Files
Papers, photographs, other materials: 1,539 linear feet; 1952–86.

Kennedy Space Center
Visitor Complex, Cape Canaveral, Fla. 32899, (321) 452-2121, *http://www.kennedyspacecenter.com*
Objects: With an actual 363-foot, 6.2-million-pound Saturn V Moon rocket, a dramatic re-creation of the first manned Apollo launch, and hands-on exhibits, the Apollo/Saturn V Center brings the U.S. space program to life. On display are the rockets that launched astronauts and machines into space, such as the Mercury Redstone, similar to the one that carried Alan Shepard into space, and the awe-inspiring Mercury Atlas, which is identical to the rocket that carried John Glenn into space for America's first orbit. Exhibits also include the real Mercury and Gemini spacecraft that orbited Earth and the actual spacesuits worn by astronauts on those early missions. At the International Space Station Center, visitors may walk through full-scale mock-ups of space-station modules and view actual space-station components being readied for flight. Guided tours include some of the structural icons of the space age, the Vertical Assembly Building, the shuttle crawler, and the shuttle launch tower.

Kennedy Space Center Library Archives
Kennedy Space Center, Cape Canaveral, Fla. 32899, (305) 867-2407
Historical Documents Collections
Papers, photographs: 112 cubic feet of papers; 21,000 photographs. This collection of nearly 500,000 pages and more than 21,000 photographs documents the Kennedy Center's growth and development, including Skylab, *Apollo 1–12* and *17,* Apollo-Soyuz test project Space Shuttles, the Kurt H. Debus personal photograph collection, V-2 rocket work at Peenemünde in World War II, Wernher von Braun's rocketry predictions of 1945, project Gemini, the Mercury program, Space Shuttle launch tower, NOVA, Saturn/Apollo launches, unmanned launches, Vanguard-Martin,

status reports, building reports, and speeches.

Library of Congress
First and East Capitol Streets, S.E., Washington, D.C. 20540, (202) 707-5000
Wernher von Braun Archive
Papers: 44,000 items; 1796–1970. Wernher von Braun (1912–77) was an engineer, rocket scientist, and administrator. The archive includes correspondence, speeches, writings, public relations materials, subject files, and scrapbooks (chiefly 1950–70) related to von Braun's career in rocketry and aerospace engineering from his early work on the V-2 in Germany to his work for the Department of Defense, the Redstone Arsenal, and the NASA George C. Marshall Space Flight Center.

Massachusetts Institute of Technology Museum
265 Massachusetts Avenue, Building N52, Cambridge, Mass. 02139, (617) 253-4440
Charles Stark Draper Laboratory
Papers: 60 linear feet. The holdings comprise correspondence, reports, drawings, and blueprints documenting the work of the Draper Laboratory in aerospace and marine vehicle control, Apollo spacecraft guidance systems, and other areas.
Historical Aerospace Materials
Papers: 300 items. Featured are historical, biographical, photographic and instrumentation samples that relate to MIT's Department of Aeronautics and Astronautics (including objects from MIT wind tunnels), the Center for Space Research (including astronomy satellite parts), and the Charles Stark Draper Laboratory.

Memorial Museum of Space Exploration
150 Prospect Mira, 129366 Moscow, Russia
The brainchild of Sergei Korolev (1907–66), the chief designer of Soviet spacecraft, the Memorial Museum of Space Exploration is located in the base of the great titanium monument, the Space Age Obelisk. The museum's collections number more than 50,000 individual items, including documents, films, photographic material, and other objects related to space exploration, as well as coins, stamps, and art work. Not far from the space monument, at the beginning of Pervaya Ostankinskaya Street, there is a branch of the Memorial Museum of Space Exploration, the Sergei Korolev Apartment Museum, where visitors may learn about this remarkable scholar, whose history is inseparably linked with the beginning of the space age.

Museum of Flight
9404 E. Marginal Way South, Seattle, Wash. 98108, (206) 764-5700,

http:// www.museumofflight.org
Objects: The collection includes engineering test models of a lunar roving vehicle, a space truck, and an Apollo command module, as well as Resur-500, a Russian space capsule.
Papers, photographs, drawings: Lunar roving vehicle, Apollo program, Apollo PLSS (Portable Life Support System).

NASA Marshall Space Flight Center
Huntsville, Ala. 35812, (256) 544-2121, *http://www1.msfc.nasa.gov*
Objects: This is the only place in the United States where visitors may actually see pieces of the International Space Station being built and tested.

Powerhouse Museum
500 Harris Street, Ultimo, Sydney NSW 2007 Australia, (612) 9217 0111, *http://www.phm.gov.au*
The museum features exhibitions on science, technology, communications, decorative arts, and design, as well as Australian social history. The museum also governs the Sydney Observatory.

Smithsonian Institution
National Air and Space Museum, National Air and Space Archives, MRC 322, Seventh Street and Independence Avenue, S.W., Washington, D.C. 20560, (202) 357-3133, *http://www.nasm.edu*
Objects: *Explorer 1,* Mercury spacecraft *Friendship 7, Gemini 4* spacecraft, *Apollo 11* command module *Columbia, Apollo 11* space suit, *Sputnik 1, Mariner 2, Pioneer 10, Viking* Mars lander, *Apollo 17,* Hubble Space Telescope test vehicle and support stand (full scale).
The National Air and Space Museum has a large collection of Russian space-related objects included in the permanent exhibition *The Space Race.* Most of the Soviet objects displayed here were purchased by the Perot Foundation of Dallas, Texas, in 1993. Before their purchase, some of these items had suffered from years of neglect and deterioration; others were in danger of being lost or destroyed. The Perot Foundation intends to hold these artifacts in trust for eventual return to the Russian people. Meanwhile they have been placed on loan to the Smithsonian Institution.
Robert Hutchings Goddard Archive
Photographs: ca. 100 items; 1926–45. Robert Hutchings Goddard (1882–1945) was an inventor and American rocket pioneer. The archive includes photographs (some color) covering Goddard's work from World War I to his experiments near Roswell, New Mexico, as well as portraits of Goddard and his wife.
Willy Ley Archive
Papers: 33 cubic feet. The archive contains personal files of space writer Willy

Ley (1906–69): business correspondence, book contracts, galley proofs, publicity concerning Ley and his activities, and inquiries and comments from Ley's *Galaxy* magazine readership. Reference files include a wide variety of subjects including astronomy, space travel, biology, natural parks, mythology, psychic phenomena, and UFOs.
Michael Collins Archive
Papers: 25 cubic feet; ca. 1955–89. Michael Collins is an American astronaut. Collection includes training notebooks for Collins's *Gemini 10* and *Apollo 11* flights; training manuals, documents, and other materials from the two missions; speeches; audiotapes; correspondence; notes and drafts for his books; medals and certificates; and other space-program artifacts.

Space Center
P.O. Box 533, Top of New Mexico Highway 200l, Alamogordo, N.M. 88311-0533, (505) 437-2840, *http://www.zianet.com/space*
Aerospace Research Collection
Papers, photographs: 16 file drawers; 1930–present. The collection consists of primary research materials including photographs, original films, and slides documenting the history of aerospace research in New Mexico.
Oral/Video History Collection
Interviews: 22 individuals; 1930s–present. This ongoing program features interviews with individuals involved in early aerospace research and development in New Mexico (for example, White Sands Missile Range, Holloman Air Force Base, and New Mexico State University Physical Science Laboratory) recorded on audio and video tapes. Transcripts are also available to researchers.

State Museum of the History of Cosmonautics
Kaluga, Korolev St. 2, Kaluga 248650, 8-08422-45-010
This was the first museum of the history of space exploration in the world. Kaluga is the birthplace of Konstantin Tsiolkovsky (1857–1935), the founder of theoretical cosmonautics. Tsiolkovsky proved mathematically the possibility of space flight, and wrote and published more than 500 works about space travel and related subjects. These included the design and construction of space rockets, steerable rocket engines, multistage boosters, space stations, and life in space.
Papers: Notebooks, manuscripts, drawings, and publications by Tsiolkovsky. Also on display are models based on his designs.

U.S. National Archives and Records Administration
http://www.nara.gov

Almost 120,000 cubic feet of NASA records are stored in eight NARA facilities. They include more than 5,000 cubic feet of historical material that is in NARA's legal custody and is open to the public. Records from NASA Headquarters and NACA are stored at the National Archives facility in College Park, Maryland. Records from the Johnson Space Center are stored at the NARA's Southwest facility in Fort Worth, Texas. Records from the Langley Research Center are stored at the NARA's Mid-Atlantic Center, 900 Market St., Philadelphia, Penn., (215) 597-3000. See Records of the National Aeronautics and Space Administration (Record Group 255), 5, 182 cubic feet, 1903–88, at *http://www.nara.gov/guide/rg255.html*. NARA, SW Region (Fort Worth), 501 West Felix St., Bldg. 1, Ft. Worth, Tex. 76115-3405, (817) 334-5515, fax (817) 334-5511, *http://www.archives@ftworth.nara.gov*

U.S. Space and Rocket Center
1 Tranquility Base, Huntsville, Ala. 35805, (256) 837-3400, *http://www.ussrc.com*
Objects: The U.S. Space and Rocket Center is the only place in the world where visitors can stand under a "full stack" – the Space Shuttle orbiter, the external tank, and two solid-rocket boosters. Exhibits include a full-scale replica of the living and working area of the Russian space station *Mir*. The Rocket Park features a 363-foot, three-stage *Saturn V*, which is a national historic landmark. It also includes dozens of rockets and missiles developed by the U.S. Army at Huntsville's Redstone Arsenal.
Space and Rocket Archives
Papers, manuscripts, audio and pictorial records; at least 105,000 pieces.

University of Alabama, Huntsville Library
Special Collections, Huntsville, Ala. 35899, (205) 895-6523
Rudolf Hermann Archive
Papers: 18 linear feet plus 10 file boxes; 1940s–70s. Rudolf Hermann was an aerospace engineer and professor. A portion of this collection includes NASA materials and reports of corporate contractors and university research facilities dealing with rocketry and space science; in English or German. A computer index is in the process of being privately compiled.
Gerhard H. R. Reisig Archive
Papers: 35 linear feet; 1940–79. Gerhard H. R. Reisig was a physicist and aeronautical engineer. The archive includes published professional papers and articles used by Reisig in his research. Subject matter ranges from acoustics to wind-shear, and includes material emanating from NASA, U.S. Army Missile Command, and private researchers worldwide. A local computer index is in the process of being compiled.

Saturn History Collection
Papers: 1,607 items; 1940–76. The collection documents the official history of the Saturn project, with materials ranging from working papers to published NASA reports, from early army missile development to the Apollo Moon landings, and arranged chronologically and indexed by categories. A local computer file is available.

University of Illinois at Urbana-Champaign
University Archives, Room 19, University Library, 1408 West Gregory Drive, Urbana, Ill. 61801, (217) 333-0798
Note: There are automated finding lists for most collections.
Carl L. Colwell Archives
Papers: 2 cubic feet; 1962–76. Carl L. Colwell worked as Managing Engineer of Flight Analysis Group, the Chrysler Corporation, and in the space division at the Marshall Space Flight Center. Papers include technical reports on the Saturn IB rocket, Skylab project, and Apollo-Soyuz project.

University of New Mexico
Technology Application Center, 2500 Central, S.E., Albuquerque, N.M. 87131, (505) 277-3622
Space Photographs
Photographs, records: 50,000 items: 1960–present. The archive includes Skylab, Gemini, Apollo, Apollo-Soyuz, and Space Shuttle photographic and remote sensing data as well as a collection of aerial mapping photographs of New Mexico and the surrounding areas.

University of South Carolina
South Caroliniana Library, Columbia, S.C. 29208, (803) 777-3131
Charles Moss Duke Archive
Papers: 667 items and one reel of microfilm; 1968–75. Charles Moss Duke is an American astronaut. The archive features congratulatory letters, press releases, NASA transcriptions of communications and commentaries, newspaper and magazine articles, clippings, and photographs, chiefly relating to Duke's participation in the *Apollo 16* mission to the Moon, April 19–23, 1972.

UPI / NASA-Related Papers
Papers, photographs: 41 linear feet; 1962–80. The archive contains press releases, air-to-ground transcripts, mission commentary, photographs, and telexes related to the space program. The most heavily covered areas are the Apollo-Soyuz test project, Skylab, and *Apollo 11, 12, 15, 16*, and *17*. The UPI material has a great deal of information about these flights both in terms of background (reference books, procedures manuals, etc.) and in the actual flights (air-to-ground transcripts, briefings, telexes). The collection also has many eight-by-ten color and black-and-white photographs of all aspects of the various space flights.

Virginia Polytechnic Institute and State University
Archives of American Aerospace Exploration, Special Collections Department, University Libraries, Blacksburg, Va. 24061-0434, (703) 231-9205
Christopher Columbus Kraft, Jr., Archive
Papers: 25 cubic feet; 1941–82. Aeronautical engineer and NASA administrator Christopher Columbus Kraft, Jr. joined the Langley Aeronautical Laboratory in 1945 and was named an original member of NASA's Space Task Group in 1958. Kraft served as flight director for all the Mercury and many of the Gemini missions. He directed the design of Mission Control at the Manned Spacecraft Center in Houston and was named deputy director of the MSC in 1970 and director in 1972, a position he held until 1982. Papers include correspondence, notes, and limited-circulation NACA and NASA documents; these range from his notes and calculations on the P-47 Thunderbolt aircraft in the 1940s and annotated copies of the "Mission Rules" for space missions in the 1950s and 1960s to his extensive notes from meetings and conversations in the 1970s and 1980s.
F. Edward McLean Archive
Papers: 0.6 cubic feet; 1950–85. Aerospace engineer F. Edward McLean specialized in supersonic aerodynamic design and analysis and high-speed management with NACA and NASA from 1948 to 1978, and authored *Supersonic Cruise Technology* (Washington, D.C.: NASA, 1985). Papers consist of his writings, news clippings, correspondence, patents, technical reports, photographs, awards, and citations.
Hartley A. Soule Archive Ms87-004
Papers: 2 cubic feet; 1950–67. Aeronautical engineer and NASA administrator Hartley A. Soule (1904–88) joined the Langley Aeronautical Laboratory in 1927; he served as Head of the Spin Tunnel Section, Chief of the Stability Research Division, and Assistant Director of the laboratory. Soule was instrumental in establishing the NASA High Speed Flight Research Center at Edwards Air Force Base and the Mercury Ground Tracking and Data Acquisition System. Papers include notes, memoranda, calculations, and drawings on the High-Speed Flight Research Station (1950–54); Research Airplane program (1953–57); Dyna-Soar program (1957–62); X-15 program (1958–62); projects Mercury and Gemini (1961–62); and history of the high-speed aircraft program (1963–67).

Marjorie Rhodes Townsend Archive
Papers: 2 cubic feet; 1966–80. Aerospace engineer and NASA project manager Marjorie Rhodes Townsend worked at the Naval Research Laboratory from 1951 to 1959 and the Goddard Space Flight Center from 1959 to 1980. She was project manager for Small Astronomy Satellites between 1966 and 1975 and for Applications Explorer Missions in 1975–76. Papers include correspondence, notes on staff meetings, and drafts of speeches, newspaper, and magazine articles.

White Sands Test Facility
(JSC/WSTF), NASA, P.O. Drawer MM, Las Cruces, N.M. 88004, (505) 524-5771
Historical Materials
Papers: 100 linear feet. Historical materials cover test activities for the Apollo through the Space Shuttle programs.

About the Contributors

John Zukowsky holds a doctorate in art and architectural history from the State University of New York at Binghamton. As Curator of Architecture at The Art Institute of Chicago for more than twenty years, he has organized many highly acclaimed, award-winning exhibitions and books, including *Chicago Architecture, 1872–1922* (1987), *Chicago Architecture and Design, 1923–1993* (1993), and *Building for Air Travel* (1996). In recent years, he has increasingly specialized in architecture and design for the aerospace industry, authoring an article in *Design Issues* on Charles Butler and Uwe Schneider and a book titled *Space Architecture,* about the work of John Frassanito (1999).

Rachel Armstrong is a television producer and freelance writer. Trained as a medical doctor at both Cambridge and Oxford universities, she is frequently interviewed on science and technology topics for various publications and programs, including spots on cable television's Sci-Fi Channel. She has authored articles for various magazines including *Wired, Architectural Design,* and *Women's Art,* and she is currently preparing a book on the future of human evolution. Her latest publication responsibilities include being guest editor of a forthcoming issue of *Architectural Design* devoted to space architecture. Dr. Armstrong lives in England.

David Brodherson is a freelance architectural historian who holds a doctoral degree in architectural and planning history from Cornell University. He specializes in aerospace architecture and has contributed essays on the history of airport architecture to *Preservation* magazine, *Chicago Architecture and Design, 1923–1993* (The Art Institute of Chicago, 1993), and *Building for Air Travel* (The Art Institute of Chicago, 1996), as well as presented papers on the subject at a variety of professional conferences.

Rebecca Dalvesco is a doctoral candidate in architectural history in the Department of Environmental Design and Planning at Arizona State University. She earned her master's degree in industrial design theory from the same university. She has authored articles on design theory in semiotics and was honored as a Woman of the Year by the American Biography Institute in 1996. Her dissertation is titled "Richard Buckminster Fuller: From Outcast to Cultural Icon."

Thomas Foltz is a biology student at Arizona State University. This will be his second bachelor's degree; his first one is in geology from Earlham College in Richmond, Indiana. Both academic experiences will assist him in obtaining an advanced degree in astrobiology. Before returning to school he worked as Outreach Coordinator for the Museum of Flight in Seattle, circulating aerospace programs to regional schools and running the museum's summer aerospace camp. Prior to that he spent several years as a counselor for Space Camp in Huntsville, Alabama.

Anne Collins Goodyear is a doctoral candidate in the Department of Art and Art History at the University of Texas at Austin. As a 1999 fellow at the National Air and Space Museum in Washington, D.C., she is completing her dissertation, entitled "American Art of the Second Machine Age: Sputnik, Space, and Technocracy, 1957–71." She presented papers related to her doctoral research at the 1998 National Aerospace Conference in Dayton, Ohio, and the 1999 National Council on Public History in Lowell, Massachusetts.

Peter Bacon Hales is director of the American Studies Institute, University of Illinois at Chicago, and a professor of art and architectural history there. He earned his master's and doctoral degrees in American civilization from the University of Texas at Austin. He has written numerous articles and books on the history of photography in relation to American culture, including an award-winning book entitled *Atomic Spaces: Living on the Manhattan Project* (1998).

Theodore W. Hall is a post-doctoral fellow and research officer in the Department of Architecture at the Chinese University of Hong Kong. He earned master's and doctoral degrees in architecture from the University of Michigan. He wrote his dissertation on artificial gravity environments for space habitations, and has presented that, as well as research on computer-aided engineering and design, in professional papers and articles since 1987.

Roy F. Houchin II is a former professor of air and space history at Maxwell Air Force Base and is Military Space Editor for *Quest: The History of Spaceflight Quarterly.* He is a lieutenant colonel in the U.S. Air Force, currently stationed in Korea as a squadron operations officer. Lt. Col. Houchin has a doctorate in the history of technology and military history from Auburn University. He has written numerous articles and professional papers on aerospace history for *Quest, Journal of the British Interplanetary Society,* and *Aerospace Historian,* and his book, *The Legacy of the Dyna-Soar,* is forthcoming.

Howard E. McCurdy is Professor of Public Affairs at American University. He is one of the nation's foremost historians of public policy working on space-related projects. He has written a number of articles as well as major books such as *Space and the American Imagination* (1997), *Space Flight and the Myth of Presidential Leadership* (1997), *Inside NASA: High Technology and Organizational Change in the U.S. Space Program* (1993), and *The Space Station Decision: Incremental Politics and Technological Choice* (1990).

Frederick I. Ordway III is a consultant to the Science Advisory Committee of the U.S. Space and Rocket Center in Huntsville, Alabama. He was trained in geosciences at Harvard University, and he holds an honorary doctorate from the University of Alabama, Huntsville. At Huntsville, he directed the Space Information Systems Office for NASA. Dr. Ordway has served as consultant on a variety of projects, including the legendary film *2001: A Space Odyssey.* He has also published numerous articles and books on spaceflight, some of the most important being *History of Rocketry and Space Travel* (1966 to 1985, 4 eds.), *Blueprint for Space* (1992), and *Wernher von Braun: Crusader for Space* (1996).

Scott Palmer is an assistant professor in the Department of History at Western Illinois University. He is a specialist in Soviet studies, particularly as regards aerospace history, and has received many honors and awards for his work. He has presented and published numerous papers and articles on the subject of Soviet aerospace and is currently preparing two books: *Red Wings on the Silver Screen: Aviation and Cinema in the Soviet Union, 1917–1991* and *From Winged Serfs to Flying Proletariat: A History of Russian Aeronautical Culture to 1939.*

Dennis Parks, Curator of Collections at the Museum of Flight, Seattle, was trained in library science at Indiana University. He has more than twenty-five years of experience as a science and aviation librarian, archivist, and curator. Before joining the Museum of Flight in 1996, he served as director of the library and archives of the Experimental Aircraft Association (EAA) for ten years. His extensive research and publishing experience include numerous papers presented at professional conferences and editorial and writing responsibilities for *Vintage Airplane* and *Sport Aviation.*

Leonard Rau is Head of Brand Strategy at Stocks Austin Sice in London. He is a design historian who earned his master's degree from the Royal College of Art. His main area of interest is the development of corporate imagery, particularly for airlines and related aviation companies. He contributed an essay on the corporate imagery of Pan American and British Airways in relation to deregulation in the airline industry to *Building for Air Travel* (The Art Institute of Chicago, 1996), and he has presented professional papers on related topics at the 1998 National Aerospace Conference in Dayton, Ohio, and the 1993 Design History Society Annual Conference in London.

Johann Schmidt is Professor of English and Media Studies at the University of Hamburg. He earned his doctorate from the University of Munich with a dissertation on the work of Jonathan Swift. He has written articles and books on literary subjects such as Swift, Alexander Pope, Charles Dickens, and D. H. Lawrence as well as filmmakers, including Alfred Hitchcock. However, two of his more recent books have been on architecture: *Wolkenkratzker* (1991), a survey of skyscrapers, and *William Van Alen: Das Chrysler Building* (1995).

Deane Simpson is an architect with Diller + Scofidio in New York. He earned his master's in architecture from Columbia University. He has participated in several of the firm's design projects, including the Brasserie restaurant in New York's Seagram Building and the installation of the exhibition *The American Lawn* at the Canadian Centre for Architecture in Montreal. His own research focuses on the structures and designs within the Soviet space program, and he has given lectures on that subject following his trips to study the Baikonur Cosmodrome, which were made possible by a Skidmore, Owings and Merrill fellowship.

Index

Page numbers in *italics* denote illustrations.

Photo credits

Zukowsky

fig. 1: courtesy Griffith Observatory, Austin-Cholk Collection; fig. 2: courtesy AURA/NOAO/National Science Foundation; fig. 3: courtesy Liberstudio; figs. 4, 9: courtesy John Zukowsky; fig. 5: with the permission of the Trustees of the Imperial War Museum, London; fig. 6: © 1988 Columbia Pictures Industries, Inc. All rights reserved. Courtesy Columbia Pictures; fig. 7: courtesy Alex Panchenko; fig. 8: courtesy Central Institute of Aviation and Cosmonautics; fig. 10: courtesy Landesbildstelle Berlin; fig. 11: courtesy Filmmuseum Potsdam; fig. 12: courtesy Altus Associates; fig. 13: courtesy The Art Institute of Chicago.

Schmidt

figs. 1, 2: Abrams, New York, 1987; fig. 3: by permission of the Houghton Library, Harvard University; fig. 4: Macmillan Co., New York, 1948; figs. 5, 6: The Museum of Modern Art, Film Stills Archive; fig. 7: courtesy Deutsches Filmmuseum, Frankfurt am Main; fig. 8: © Bonestell Space Art; fig. 9: Private collection.

Palmer

figs. 1, 2: Film stills from Yakov Protazanov, *Aelita*, 1923; fig. 3: University of Chicago Press, Chicago, 1991; figs. 4–6: Guggenheim Museum, New York, 1992; fig. 7: courtesy Leonard Hutton Galleries, New York.

Brodherson

fig. 1: London, 1851; fig. 2: courtesy Yerkes Observatory; fig. 3: © 2000, The Art Institute of Chicago. All rights reserved; fig. 4: Buffalo and Erie County Historical Society; figs. 5, 12: Manuscripts Division, The New York Public Library; Astor, Lenox and Tilden Foundations; figs. 6, 8, 9: Architecture Photograph Collection, Ryerson & Burnham Libraries, The Art Institute of Chicago; fig. 7: Chicago Historical Society, ICHi-17542; fig. 10: courtesy City of Dallas Park and Recreation Department; fig. 11: Private collection.

Hales

fig. 1: National Museum of Photography,

Film & Television; figs. 2, 3: © Time Inc.; figs. 4–8: courtesy NASA.

Collins Goodyear

figs. 1–3, 8: courtesy National Air and Space Museum, Smithsonian Institution; fig. 4: *Look* magazine, Apr. 20, 1965; fig. 5: photograph by B. F. Herzog, Milton, Mass., courtesy The Norman Rockwell Museum, Stockbridge, Mass.; fig. 6: courtesy Galleria degli Uffizi, Florence; fig. 7: courtesy Musei Vaticani.

Simpson

figs. 1, 2, 4, 6, 7: courtesy Russian National Scientific and Technical Archive.

Houchin

figs. 1, 3–5: courtesy Boeing; fig. 2: from *USSR*, no. 1 (16), the Embassy of the Soviet Socialist Republics, Washington, D.C.

Rau

fig. 1: courtesy Boeing; fig. 2: courtesy Lockheed Martin NE&SS-Akron; figs. 3–5: courtesy Landor Associates; fig. 6: the Netscape N logo is a registered trademark of Netscape Communications Corporation in the United States and other countries. Used with permission; fig. 7: courtesy Landor Associates; © General Motors Corp.; fig. 8: reproduced with permission from the Langenscheidt Publishing Group.

McCurdy

fig. 1: Paramount Pictures Stock Footage Library; figs. 2, 4, 5, 9: courtesy NASA; fig. 3: Private collection; fig. 6: Frederick I. Ordway III Collection-U.S. Space & Rocket Center; fig. 7: courtesy Lockheed Martin NE&SS-Akron; fig. 8: courtesy Alex Panchenko.

Ordway

figs. 1, 2, 4, 5: © Bonestell Space Art; figs. 3, 6–10: courtesy Frederick I. Ordway III Collection-U.S. Space & Rocket Center.

Dalvesco

figs. 1, 3–7: courtesy NASA.

Hall

fig. 1: Harper & Brothers, New York, 1959; fig. 2: courtesy Theodore W. Hall; figs. 3, 4: Archives and Special Collections Department, Otto G. Richter Library, University of Miami, Coral Gables, Fl.; fig. 5: courtesy NASA; fig. 6: NASA Scientific and Technical Information Office, 1977; fig. 7: © 1979 Danjaq, LLC, and United Artists Corporation. All rights reserved.

Armstrong

fig. 1: Columbia Studios. Wiley Post Collection. Courtesy Archives and Manuscripts Division of the Oklahoma Historical Society; fig. 2: courtesy Boeing; fig. 3: courtesy NASA; fig. 4: courtesy Brand Griffin; fig. 5: photograph by Tony Figallo, courtesy Stelarc; fig. 6: courtesy Wimberly Allison Tong & Goo.

Plates

pls. 20, 26, 29, 32, 48, 80, 82, 86–88: courtesy NASA; pls. 1, 2: courtesy Film Center of The School of the Art Institute of Chicago; pl. 3: courtesy Bundesarchiv-Filmarchiv; pl. 4: photograph by James Steinkamp. © Steinkamp/Ballogg. Courtesy Lohan Associates; pls. 5, 6: © dbox, inc./Polshek Partnership Architects; pl. 7: © Bonestell Space Art; pls. 8, 9: courtesy Michael Böhme; pls. 10–13: courtesy Deutsches Museum; pl. 14: with the permission of the Trustees of the Imperial War Museum, London; pl. 15: courtesy Bundesarchiv-Militaerarchiv; pl. 16: courtesy Deutsches Historisches Museum; pl. 17: Private collection; pl. 18: courtesy Bildarchiv Preussischer Kulturbesitz; pl. 19: photograph by John Zukowsky; pl. 21: photograph from the Lawrence D. Bell Aircraft Museum, Inc., Mentone, Ind.; pls. 22, 27, 28, 30, 31, 41, 81: courtesy Boeing Historical Archives; pl. 23: courtesy Daimler-Chrysler Aerospace (formerly Daimler-Benz Aerospace); pl. 24: courtesy The Art Institute of Chicago; pl. 25: photograph by Julius Shulman, courtesy San Diego Aerospace Museum Archives; pl. 33: courtesy BRC Imagination Arts; pl. 34: courtesy

Kevin Craig; pl. 35: courtesy Holt, Hinshaw, Pfau, Jones; pl. 36: photograph by John Zukowsky; pl. 37: courtesy Hellmuth, Obata and Kassabaum; pl. 38: courtesy Film Center of The School of The Art Institute of Chicago/© 1967 Danjaq, LLC, and United Artists Corporation. All rights reserved; pl. 39: photograph by John W. Darr; pl. 40: Private collection; pl. 42: © Paul Brokering, courtesy Leo A. Daly; pls. 43, 44: © 1997 TriStar Pictures & Touchstone Pictures. All rights reserved; pl. 45: courtesy Film Center of The School of The Art Institute of Chicago/Footage from *Alien* (1979), courtesy Twentieth Century Fox Film Corporation. All rights reserved; pl. 46: courtesy Alex Panchenko; pl. 47: courtesy Film Center of The School of The Art Institute of Chicago/© 1979 Danjaq, LLC, and United Artists Corporation. All rights reserved; pls. 49–51: courtesy Lockheed Martin NE&SS-Akron; pl. 52: Paramount Pictures Stock Footage Library; pls. 53–55: courtesy Arianespace; pls. 56–59, 76: courtesy Boeing; pl. 60: courtesy Landor Associates; pl. 61: courtesy NBBJ Architects; pl. 62: courtesy Carlson Technologies, Inc.; pl. 63: courtesy Garmin Products; pl. 64: courtesy La Cañada Design Group; pl. 65: courtesy Hughes Space and Communications Company; pls. 66, 79, 83–85, 94: courtesy John Frassanito and Associates; pl. 67: Poughkeepsie, N.Y., 1958; pl. 68: courtesy Revell-Monogram; pls. 69, 70: Private collection; pls. 71–73: courtesy Film Center of The School of The Art Institute of Chicago/*2001: A Space Odyssey* © 1968 Turner Entertainment Co. A Time Warner Company. All rights reserved; pl. 74: © Disney Enterprises, Inc.; pl. 75: ™, ® & © 2000 Paramount Pictures. *Star Trek* is a registered trademark of Paramount Pictures. All rights reserved; pl. 77: courtesy Kelly Space & Technology; pl. 78: courtesy Kistler Aerospace Corporation; pls. 89, 90: courtesy Shimizu Corporation; pl. 91: courtesy Kawasaki; pl. 92: courtesy Paramount Pictures. *Star Trek* © 2000 by Paramount Pictures. All rights reserved; pl. 93: *Babylon 5* © Warner Bros. All rights reserved.